# Best Dog Hikes
# Northern California

# Best Dog Hikes
# Northern California

Linda B. Mullally

David S. Mullally

**FALCON**GUIDES

GUILFORD, CONNECTICUT
HELENA, MONTANA
AN IMPRINT OF GLOBE PEQUOT PRESS

Dedicated to Gypsy, who embraced the joys of the trail
from the first day he joined our pack following the loss of his mom, our
friend Karen. Gypsy proves that you can show old dogs new joys.

To buy books in quantity for corporate use
or incentives, call **(800) 962-0973**
or e-mail **premiums@GlobePequot.com.**

# FALCONGUIDES®

FalconGuides is an imprint of Globe Pequot Press.
Falcon, FalconGuides, and Outfit Your Mind are registered trademarks of Morris Book Publishing, LLC.

All interior photographs by David S. Mullally.

Project editor: Lynn Zelem
Layout: Casey Shain
Maps: Hartdale Maps © Morris Book Publishing, LLC

Library of Congress Cataloging-in-Publication data is available.

978-0-7627-9235-1

Printed in the United States of America
10 9 8 7 6 5 4 3 2 1

# Contents

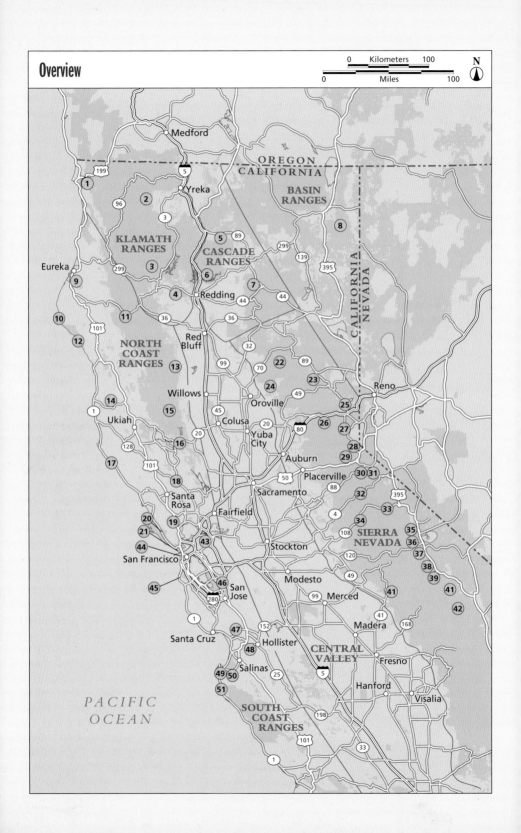

# Overview

0 Kilometers 100
0 Miles 100

**N**

**OREGON**
**CALIFORNIA**

Medford

**BASIN**
**RANGES**

Yreka

**KLAMATH**
**RANGES**

Eureka

**CASCADE**
**RANGES**

Redding

**NORTH**
**COAST**
**RANGES**

Red Bluff

Willows

Oroville

Ukiah

Colusa

Yuba City

Auburn

Reno

Santa Rosa

Sacramento

Placerville

Fairfield

Stockton

**SIERRA**
**NEVADA**

San Francisco

San Jose

Modesto

Merced

Santa Cruz

Hollister

Madera

Salinas

**CENTRAL**
**VALLEY**

Fresno

Hanford

Visalia

*PACIFIC*
*OCEAN*

**SOUTH**
**COAST**
**RANGES**

**CALIFORNIA**
**NEVADA**

*Returning to trailhead at Lands End*

# Legend

| | |
|---|---|
| Interstate Highway | Barbeque |
| US Highway | Bench |
| State Road | Bridge |
| County Road | Boat Ramp |
| Unpaved Road | Campground |
| Railroad | Campground, primitive |
| Selected Route | Gate |
| Trail or Fire Road | Information Panel |
| Paved Trail | Lighthouse |
| Steps/boardwalk | Mountain/Peak |
| Spring | Parking |
| Rapids | Pass/Gap |
| Waterfall | Picnic Area |
| River or Creek | Point of Interest |
| Intermittent Stream | Ranger Station |
| Water Body | Restroom |
| Wetland | Scenic Viewpoint |
| | Tower |
| | Town |
| | Trailhead |
| | Visitor Information Center |
| | Water |

*Returning from Gem Lakes*

# Acknowledgments

Anyone who has ever had a friend or family member write a book on any topic knows how tedious it is to hear them angst about their deadline every time you ask, "How is the book coming along?" So I must express my profound appreciation to friends and family for their support over the course of the nine months it took to deliver this book. I was as bored with myself saying, "I have to work on the book" as much as they dreaded hearing it every time I declined an invitation to distraction. I appreciate that no one rolled their eyes, at least not to our faces when they asked about David's and my most recent trip, given that the answer was predictably, "We were north hiking for the book."

I am grateful to Mike DeGive, editor at the *Monterey Herald* newspaper, as well as the readers of my monthly travel column "Away We Go," for never complaining about the diet of Northern California–only destinations I fed them for almost a year.

This book would not have been half as much fun for us or our dog Gypsy had our friends not trusted us with their four-legged children as companions on many of the hikes and models for the chapters. Chance, the cover husky at Gypsy's side; Atka; Murphy; Tibby; Finnegan; Kramer; Trout; Jake; Rosie; and Harley enhanced the experience.

After almost thirty years as our family veterinarian and friend to all critters, Dr. George Bishop generously continues to be my "go-to" source of veterinary medicine wisdom.

Last but not least, this book could not have been as thorough without the input from park rangers, Forest Service recreation managers, and volunteers in visitor centers and the cooperation of administrative staff in a variety of public land offices. Diane Garcia at the Science Information Services of the US Geological Survey (USGS) graciously shared her expertise so we could provide the most up-to-date information on maps and navigation.

*Unbridled joy on the trail*

# Introduction

There aren't many places on the planet you could travel to and not get a big, long-ing smile at the mention of California. It makes sense that the Golden State would have the wild golden trout as a state fish and the dazzling sunset gold poppy as the state flower. The Grizzly Bear on the state flag, alas, is just a memory. Considered a threat, grizzlies, like wolves, were hunted to extinction. The last grizzly was killed in the Sierra Foothills south of Yosemite in 1922, and the bears' prime habitat in the Central Valley all but disappeared. Different habitat needs and their ability to coexist with humans saved the acorn- and berry-eating black bears.

If California was the promised land of milk and honey to early pioneers, and Hollywood the path to fame and fortune, California's public lands are Shangri-La for hikers and their dogs. The Native American, Mexican, and Spanish legacy—with even a trace of Russian heritage from the colonization of 1812 to 1842 on the North Coast—gives California its unique flavor.

California was under Spanish Rule from 1769 to 1821 when it became the prop-erty of Mexico. Monterey was actually the first capital of what was then Alta California from 1777 to 1846 under both Spanish and Mexican rule. Sacramento, the oldest incor-porated city in California, did not become the official and permanent capital until 1879.

In 1846, settlers who had long been disenchanted with the Mexican government rebelled and formed the Republic of California. In the meantime the United States was at war with Mexico, and Californians supported their American neighbors. The armed combat lasted two years, and in 1848, when the US military stood at the gates of Mexico City, negotiations resulted in the treaty of Guadalupe Hidalgo, which gave the United States much of the southwestern and western territories, including what is now California. Nine days after the signing of the 1848 treaty, gold was discovered in Sutter's Mill, Coloma in the foothills of the Sierra Nevada.

Back then territories needed to have at least 60,000 habitants before they could have statehood status. California's population was sparse, but the news of gold in the area sparked a feverish emigration of 60,000 from around the world just in a few months. There was heated debate between the advocates for California as a "slave state" and those in support of a "free-soil." By 1850, California, rich in natural beauty and resources, became the thirty-first state and free of slavery. It is the third-largest state after Alaska and Texas and the most populous. It encompasses the highest point (Mount Whitney, 14,494) in the contiguous United States and the lowest point (Death Valley, 282 feet below sea level) in North America.

It is a land whose rugged and poetic beauty is born of tumultuous geological events. It sits on the ring of fire where continental plate grinding, volcanoes, and glaciers have sculpted a supernatural landscape between the Pacific Ocean and the Mojave Desert with a centerpiece of mountain ranges. The climate varies from Medi-terranean to subarctic, which makes for diversity in vegetation and hiking ecosystems.

Staying true to my cultural tradition of *"qui prend mari prend pay"* ("she who takes husband takes country"), I relocated to California from Canada thirty years ago. The transition to a new country with my soulmate was made easier by the fact that my outdoor lifestyle found a dog-friendly nature Nirvana in the "sunshine state." My husband David and I initially made the Monterey Peninsula at the south end of Northern California, also referred to as the Central California Coast, our basecamp for our life of trail adventures near and far. It didn't take long for us to be seduced by another Californian outdoor paradise—the Eastern Sierra Nevada (Spanish for "snowy mountain"), which has been our second adventure basecamp for the last twenty-five years. Between the Monterey Peninsula and the Eastern Sierra, we found plenty of room to roam with our first two dogs, Lobo and Shiloh—a pair of coyote/husky pups who came into our lives by happenstance and burrowed a place in our hearts as we met the challenge of their needs for sixteen adventuresome years.

Some people need the ebb and flow of the ocean tides to feel alive, while others only breathe cradled by the majesty of the mountains. California offers the best of both worlds, with the Pacific surf and the Sierra peaks never more than a few hours from anywhere in the state.

Although Northern California's glorious national parks mostly restrict dogs to the parking lots and campgrounds, dogs are welcome in an abundant number of national forests with wilderness areas adjacent to national parks boasting beauty worthy of park status. National recreation areas, some state parks, and national monuments offer limited but precious opportunities for exploring trails with your dog.

Northern California has a sizeable share of Bureau of Land Management open space designated as multiuse including dog-compatible hiking trails. Its many dog-friendly communities boast regional, city and county parks with miles of trails waiting for you and your dog. These communities have creature comforts of restaurants, hotels/motels, cabins, or campgrounds that you and your four-legged companion can enjoy at the end of a satisfying day on the trail.

If you are not already fascinated by the history of the land under your hiking boots, traveling and hiking around Northern California is sure to stir the romantic history buff in you. Native cultures fished, hunted, and thrived on this land. On many trails you will walk in the footsteps of the original inhabitants, subsequent Spanish explorers, and early settlers seeking a better life through farming, cattle ranching, logging, and mining precious metals including gold. California streams, rivers, ocean, and mountain scenery will inspire you in much the same way it did those who first discovered them and those who continue to fight to preserve them.

From the untamed Redwood Empire reaching from the Oregon/California border south to the legendary Big Sur and across High Sierra passes over to the high-desert border of Nevada passing oak studded valleys, gentle grassy rolling hills, and volcanic plateaus, this book will help you discover some of the best hikes for all seasons and why hiking with your dog in Northern California is seductive and addictive.

## Don't Leave Home without Him

Once you've had the companionship of a dog on the trail, you will never be able to imagine hiking without your canine pal. When it comes to hiking, you and your dog share some benefits in common, but your differences are what enhance and compliment your nature experience.

Hiking is an inexpensive opportunity for you and Pooch to stay physically fit and trim while sharing quality time in the absence of all the everyday distractions. The "natural" stimulation of sights, sounds, and smells is a great way for both of you to decompress from the daily urban sensory irritation. You both will be calmer and more relaxed at the end of a day on the trail.

You may be more enthralled than your dog by panoramic vistas, soothed by the gurgling of brooks, excited about the historic significance of the pioneer wagon wheel ruts you see across the trail, or intrigued by the sight of an unusual bird or

*Nosing around on the trail*

# SAMPLE TRAINING REGIMEN

**Weeks 1, 2, and 3**
*Morning and Evening*

15- to 20- minute sniff and stroll (warm-up)

10-minute brisk walk with no pit stops at the fire hydrant (cardiovascular workout)

5-minute sniff and stroll (cooldown)

**Week 4**
*Morning and Evening*

15-minute sniff and stroll (warm-up)

30-minute brisk walk (cardiovascular workout)

10-minute sniff and stroll (cooldown)

By week 4 incorporate some hill or stair work, being sure to stop for rest and water breaks.

**Week 5**
*Morning and Evening*

15-minute sniff and stroll (warm-up)

30-minute brisk walk (cardiovascular workout)

10-minute sniff and stroll (cooldown)

Week 5 a repeat of week 4, but add one additional longer walk at the end of the week (about 1.5 hours including some uphill). This longer walk is about distance not speed.

flowering plant. But the highlight of any dog lover's hike is witnessing the simple euphoric unbridled joy of his or her dog wagging, sniffing, sprinting across a meadow or bounding into a lake. No trail companion is as enthusiastic about snack breaks as your dog. No trail companion will follow you as faithfully, eagerly, and confidently and express as much gratitude as your dog for taking him on an outdoor adventure.

## Getting in Hiking Form

Pups initially receive immunity from their mother's milk, but after they stop nursing they need protection through inoculation. Pups under 4 months old must be protected from infectious disease until they receive all the immunizations recommended by your veterinarian. This is a good time to take your dog outdoors for play and exploring near your home. By 12 weeks and the first of three DHLP-P shots, it should be safe to begin socializing with romps with other pups who have been immunized and are current on rabies boosters. This is the ideal time to sign up for a group puppy class that is as much about practicing good manners and redirecting bad habits as it is about social skills.

Time to start building stamina and confidence in the outside world with daily short (twenty to thirty minutes) but frequent leash walks in a variety of settings. Begin introducing the pup to sights from the trail like backpacks, hiking sticks, tents.

It's never too soon to start getting used to car travel and using a crate will make your pup feel more secure and minimize the risk of sensory overload. Drive the car to nearby parks to build on the positive association of the crate and the car. Crate training if done sensibly and sensitively will produce long-term benefits for both you and your dog.

Four to six months is the ideal time to venture further afield to meadows or local trails on leash, but practice recalls at the end of a long rope with treats. Recalls off leash should be done in the house or in a fenced yard and only when you are certain you have your dog's undivided attention. Beginner group obedience classes with a supportive trainer who practices "positive" reinforcement is the best investment you can make in your relationship with your hiking pal.

Never call your dog to you for a reprimand. Why would you run up to someone who calls you over to berate you and make you feel bad about yourself? You want your dog to associate his name being called with fun, pleasant, or tasty experiences.

Your one-on-one training sessions shouldn't last more than thirty minutes, and two fifteen-minute sessions with a play break in between might get better results if your dog is hyper and has a short attention span.

Do not stress the healthy development of your dog's bones and muscles with over-exertion during the first six months, twelve to eighteen months for large dogs. Stick to flat terrain and take frequent rest and water stops.

Adult dogs also need to condition their muscles and cardiovascular system if they are new to the sport of hiking. Consult your veterinarian regarding the health and age of your dog. Overweight dogs work harder and overheat faster.

Depending on how sedentary or active your dog has been, getting in shape for the trail can take from a couple of weeks to about a month of consistent twice-daily walking. Sprinting to retrieve a ball in the backyard or on the beach is not the same as a sustained walking pace on a trail for an hour or more.

By now you should have a pretty good sense of your dog's fitness. Use week 5 to maintain his fitness level between hikes. Ideally a dog in his prime (2 to 7 years old) should be going outdoors to exercise, socialize, and get mental stimulation two times a day and get at least two hours of physical activity each day. On hot days it is best to exercise early and after sundown. Make sure Pooch has cool fresh water regularly and has access to shade to cool down on hot days.

## A Word of Caution About Food and Exercise

It is best to feed your dog at least a couple of hours before rigorous exercise and perhaps divide his portion into two smaller portions (half two hours prior, the other half thirty minutes after). No one feels good jumping around on a full stomach. Puppies need frequent small feedings throughout the day, and adult dogs should be fed at least two times a day.

Gastric dilatation-volvulus complex (GDV) is commonly known as "bloat," because it causes the stomach to "bloat" and contort. Running and jumping after a large meal can compound the risks of the stomach twisting in the abdomen (especially in large breeds), blocking the flow or absorption of gastric material. GDV can be fatal. Dividing daily portions into smaller, more frequent meals during rest periods on the trail or in camp can help prevent GDV and is a healthier way to fuel your dog's energy during physical activity.

## Pacing and Body Language

Hiking with your dog should not be about forced marches. The whole idea is to get exercise and interact with your dog while your eyes and ears take in your surroundings. This is your best quality bonding time. Savor it. Three miles per hour is a good, steady pace on level terrain at sea level. If you can, time yourself on a local high school track with your dog on leash to get an accurate idea of your pace in ideal conditions. Just remember that on a trail the terrain, weather, and elevation will slow that pace, not to mention your dog's sniff and spray stops, photo ops, and water and snack stops.

Also keep in mind the altitude factor. In the mountains, for every 1,000 feet of elevation gain, you can add an extra mile of walking time. Walking downhill is about three quarters of the time, not the optimistic half of the time most people hope for.

Keep your dog on leash for the first thirty minutes if you are planning to hike more than a couple of miles. Dogs out of the starting gate in a new, natural, stimulating setting can tucker themselves out running in circles. They have no idea about pace.

Watch your dog's body language for tail up and fluid movement to confirm he is feeling strong and happy. Tail down, stiff gait, and lethargy indicate fatigue or injury. When you see this, examine his paws and between the toes for foreign bodies that may be causing discomfort. Stop and rest and offer your dog water and a snack. That might do the trick.

When you head out on the trail, don't forget that you have the distance back to the trailhead to cover, so don't go too far and get stuck having to carry your dog out. If your dog looks drained or demoralized or stops, lays down, or behaves oddly, trust

*The trail is a natural fitness course.*

*Tail up and bounce in step are good signs.*

that something is wrong. Dogs have an innate desire to please, and they will go till they blow. There have been instances of dogs dropping dead from exhaustion on a run with their trusted person. Some dogs just don't have body awareness. Some Labs will drown before they stop swimming out for that ball on the 150th throw. Be sensitive and conservative. Shorten the excursion or abort if necessary. Dogs are not machines. Treat your dog as if he were a child dependent on his parent's loving better judgment.

If your dog is on hyper alert, with ears forward, tail up, or raised hackles (hair standing up on the back or neck), his tension and attention might have been triggered by a sound, smell, or sight that you have yet to notice. Put his leash on, look around, and wait a couple of minutes. Proceed cautiously.

If your dog appears jittery, barks, whines, or howls, he may be sensing a potential threat. Pat him and speak to him reassuringly, but respect his concern. Leash him until you identify the source of his concern, which could be as simple as the odd shape of a boulder ahead, another hiker or dog around the bend, or a small critter darting in the bushes.

You want to share safe, positive experiences that will nurture his and your enthusiasm for hiking. Once you have shared the trail with your dog, any other trail companion will seem uninspiring and a dogless hike will seem humdrum. Hiker dog lovers know that the "high" from hiking begins with having a dog at your side, so prepare wisely and don't leave home without him!

You are solely responsible for your dog's safety and well-being on the trail, as well as his behavior.

There's a hike for every dog (toy, giant, short legged, or fat), but you have to determine the length and pace of your outings by the age, health, physical condition, and breed anatomic characteristics of your dog. While dogs with flatter faces and shorter sinuses—like pugs, for example—are more susceptible to breathing problems exasperated by heat and excessive physical activity, giant breeds like the Bernese mountain dog have bones that grow more slowly, so exercise should be moderate until they reach skeletal maturity around 2 years old. Annual checkups by your veterinarian help establish the status of your dog's health and what exercise regimen is appropriate to start getting fit for the trail.

### Five Building Blocks for Good Trail Dogs

Behind every dog labeled "bad" is usually a naïve, oblivious, or irresponsible person with a dazed, glazed, or insouciant look on his or her face.

*Dogs with short sinuses can overheat more easily.*

Good trail etiquette starts with good manners at home. Here are five tips for building the kind of human/dog partnership on the trail that will make hiking with your dog safe and fun, while promoting good "stewardship of the land" so our public lands can continue to be enjoyed by all:

1. Choose a dog that is compatible with your lifestyle and level of outdoor activity. Some things you need to consider are whether you want a puppy or adult dog and the breed health history, physical characteristics, temperament, and grooming requirements that you want in a dog. Dogs are social pack animals and are not meant to be isolated at home alone for days on end while you work or play without them. They are not meant to sit in a yard by themselves, even if it does look like the gardens of Versailles. Isolation makes dogs bored, depressed, and sometimes destructive. It is nothing short of cruel. Dogs require time and attention, and the tasks associated with having a dog should be a labor of love rather than laborious obligations.

2. Spaying and neutering your canine companion won't make her fat or make him lazy. It reduces risks of mammary gland and prostate cancers. It saves them from being slaves to the hormonal drive to reproduce. He won't be obsessed with roaming, and she won't be scratching her address on fire hydrants. It will make them focus on you and their obedience training homework and make them more congenial with other dogs on the trail.

3. Good manners matter. The only answer to your doubts about your dog's good behavior and responsiveness to your voice commands is a leash. No wildlife should be stressed by a run-a-muck dog, and no one likes to be rushed by an overexuberant dog. Some people fear dogs, and others dislike them—to put it mildly. The easiest solution for park authorities and business owners who receive complaints is to ban dogs from trails, restaurants, and hotels.

   Being off leash is fun, and teaching your dog basic commands like sit, stay, and come is his ticket to the mother of all privileges: off-leash playtime. A well-trained dog is appreciated by fellow hikers and others who share the trail, not to mention that responsiveness to voice commands could someday save your dog's life. Signing up for positive-training obedience classes early on is an investment in your and your dog's relationship that you will never regret. If the only skill your dog learns is to walk at the end of a leash without strangling himself and pulling you off your feet, it will make strolling the neighborhood and the trail a joyful thrill rather than a dreaded exercise in frustration.

4. Socialize your dog around strangers and strange things to prevent "over-reaction" past the "imprint" stage in the tenth to twelfth week of life. Trash cans on the street corner should not be a threat, and neither should boulders on the side of the trail. Pack animals coming up the trail should not unglue

*Safely introduce your dog to the water.*

your dog. Expose your dog to trail sights as early as possible. Pups should have had their series of vaccinations before venturing out, but who says you can't walk around the yard with a backpack and hiking sticks? Get your dog used to objects that move, like bicycles and cars, so he doesn't develop phobias that can trigger neurotic episodes that can endanger him, you, and others on the trail. Introduce your dog to water. Dogs don't have to like dipping in streams and swimming in lakes, but they should learn to walk near and across water without panicking. It requires time and sensitivity on your part.

5. Before hitting the trail, consult your veterinarian about required vaccinations, booster shots (rabies), and the most current preventives for ticks and Lyme disease, mosquitoes, and heartworm. Also ask about the safest flea and tick products.

## Pooch Essentials and Trail Readiness

The following will get your dog started on a safe paw.

### The Essentials

1. Choose a harness. Hands down, harnesses are safer than collars. Dogs don't accidentally choke on harnesses. Harnesses make crossing streams and negotiating passages along precarious stretches of trail much safer. Harnesses allow for a quicker, safer, and solid grab of your dog if necessary. If you don't use a harness, **never** let your dog run around off leash with a choke chain–type collar.

2. Lead your dog with a 6-foot leather or nylon leash. Retractable leashes are an invitation to chaos when passing people with dogs who like to do the ring-around-the-rosy sniff-and-greet dance on the trail. Leather leashes last forever, but colorful nylon leashes can be easily located and dry quickly when wet.

3. Have your dog wear an identification tag. Tattooing and microchipping your dog are a great idea and work better in urban areas. But on the trail, an old-fashioned tag with your dog's name and your cell phone number is much more likely to reunite you with wayward Fido. Always attach a temporary tag with the name of your campground, cabin resort, or whatever lodging you are using as a basecamp on your adventure. Some dog-friendly accommodations include a temporary tag with the business's name and phone number and your room or cabin number.

4. Bring biodegradable dog waste bags for pack-it-in, pack-it-out trails and campground areas.

5. Get your dog used to wearing booties. Hiking dogs should learn to be comfortable wearing booties in the event they are needed on the trail. Fit your dog with booties and let him get used to them in the house and on your neighborhood walks. Always have a set of booties in your or his pack for the unexpected tender tootsies on paw-bruising trails. It's one thing to have to carry a Chihuahua with raw paws out of the backcountry, but the hiker I saw with a husky draped across the top of his backpack and shoulders was not having fun.

6. Pack water and energy-boosting snacks. Never count on finding water on the trail. Instead, carry eight ounces of water for every hour or 2.0 miles of trail. Heat + Altitude + Exertion = Dehydration, which is the most common and preventable hiking hazard for both you and your dog.

7. Trim your dog's nails and cut dewclaws short to prevent snags that can tear the tissue.

8. Groom your long- or curly coated dog for summer hiking for his comfort and your sanity. Choose function over fashion so his coat doesn't sweep up

*Shopping for booties*

and trap burrs, foxtails, and dirt debris and turn your hike into a grooming nightmare.

9. Keep your dog's vaccinations current and carry proof of rabies vaccine in his pack, as you may be asked for this at some park entrances.

10. Carry a basic first-aid kit (see Appendix B).

### Dog Packs

There are several benefits to proper pack training. Some dogs are serious workaholics, and walking along the stream just to smell the wild roses just doesn't cut it. A sense of mission and purpose brings the best out of some of the more hyperactive dogs, while channeling the energies and focus of the smart and free-spirited ones. Carrying some of the load just makes the cut-loose romping time breaks that much more meaningful and ecstatic. Packs should be in proportion to your dog's build and height. It should fit his chest and shoulder contours comfortably without chafing and should be balanced. Dogs should never carry more than one fourth of their own weight.

*Pack fitting*

To get your dog ready to carry a pack, let him get used to the weight of an empty pack. Use treats to reinforce the association of the pack with something pleasant. Let your dog wear the pack on his daily walks. Gradually stuff the pack with paper, face-cloths, treats, kibble, and dog waste bags. Increase the balanced load over a couple of weeks in preparation for trail day. Take frequent snack breaks on the trail and remove the pack.

## What to Expect on the Trail

Knowledge and information can make your excursions more positive and fun experiences for you and your dog, as they help prepare you for wildlife encounters, seasonal nuisances, other trail users, and Mother Nature's changing moods.

### Plan Ahead

Always confirm ahead of time that dogs are welcome on the trail you plan to hike. Policies change, so call the managing agency about any restrictions and abide by the rules.

The managing agency or ranger district office can answer questions about permits, weather (critical information for the high country, where changes can be sudden and extreme even in the summer), road closures, trail damage and changes, campground availability, and special advisories. Budget cuts reduce resources and manpower, which impact trail maintenance and campground operation. Visitor centers often depend on volunteers. National forest headquarters have recreation managers and some national forests have "district" recreation managers, who are typically the most informed. To get the most up-to-date information—especially early in the season—it is important to speak to someone who has recently hiked the trail and traveled the roads to the trailhead.

### Know Where You Are

Carry relevant maps and know how to read a topographic map so you can study the terrain in the area of your hike and anticipate elevation changes, difficulty, shady spots, water sources, and suitability for your dog. It will help you pack and pace yourself (for every 1,000 feet of elevation, add about an extra mile of time).

USGS quad map(s) with a scale of 1:24,000 and a compass are the traditional means of navigation. USGS maps do not show road or trail changes that have occurred since their publication, but the USGS is in the process of updating and digitalizing the "legacy" maps (www.USGS.gov/3DEP). Using a compass with a map requires some study and practice. Consider signing up for a navigation workshop at a local outdoor recreation store like R.E.I. or a local community college.

A good GPS (global positioning system) and maybe even a smartphone with a good app should enable you to determine your approximate location along the trail. Usually, a GPS more accurately shows latitude and longitude, but is less accurate at showing elevation. Electronic devices have their limits. Reception of any electronic device depends on receiving correct signals from satellites or cell towers. Remember to fully charge your devices and carry spare batteries. However, even if you are a techno-savvy hiker, it is wise to also carry a map and compass.

### Other Trail Users and Etiquette

On some hikes you will share the trail with people on horseback going out for a trail ride or on a backcountry trek with pack animals in tow. Mountain bikers may also be on some trails. And you will most definitely meet other hikers with or without dogs on and off leash.

Good trail etiquette breeds goodwill and positive relations with other trail users, especially those who may not be fans of dogs on the trail. Here are some general tips:

1. On or off leash, on the trail or in the campground, your dog must be under control.
2. Friendly exuberance or not, never let your dog charge or bark at other dogs, hikers, or horses. Some people are afraid of dogs. Dogs can also spook horses and jeopardize the safety of the rider. Always step off the trail to the upper side so the horse(s) can see you, keep a tight leash on your dog, and command him to sit until the riders have gone by.
3. Hike only where dogs are permitted and abide by the posted regulations.
4. Stay on the trail, step lightly in pristine wilderness areas, and don't let your dog chase wildlife.

*Yielding to other trail users*

5. Pack out everything you pack in. At the very least bury your dog's scat away from the trail and surface water. Better yet: Carry it out in biodegradable poop-scoop bags. Dog doo on trails is the **number one** complaint by responsible dog owners as well as non–dog owners. It's disgusting and inconsiderate to humans, and it's a territory marker/intruder alert that can stress resident wildlife.

6. Camp in designated campsites in heavily used or developed areas. Never leave your dog unattended in the campground.

## Dogs That Want to Rumble

At one time or another, your dog may be a partner in a dominance dance with another dog. This occurs more frequently between males, especially intact males that reek of testosterone. Dogs well versed in pack hierarchy know to stay out of an alpha dog's face or to assume the subordinate body language that stops the music.

To help avoid problems, neuter your male dog before 1 year of age or as soon as both testicles drop. Overt dominance may not appear until he is 2 years old. Neutering reduces macho and roaming instincts. Be aware that testosterone levels take several months to decrease after neutering. Spay your female. Breeding females can be instinctively more competitive around other females. A female in season should never be on the trail. She will create havoc, and her mating instincts will override her flawless obedience record every time.

A leashed dog can be overly protective. Avoid stress by taking a detour around other hikers with dogs or stepping off the trail with your dog at a sit while the other hiker and dog walk by. Do not panic at the hint of raised hackles and loud talk. Most of it is just posturing. If your dog is off leash, stay calm and keep walking away from the other dog while encouraging your dog to come in your most enthusiastic voice and with the promise of a biscuit. If she complies, reward her with a "good dog" and the promised biscuit for positive reinforcement.

Walking back toward the dogs, screaming, and interfering before they resolve their conflict, can stoke the fires of a more serious brawl. If the squabble escalates into a dogfight, make sure you cover your arms and hands before trying to break it up. Pull the dogs by the tail, lift their hind legs off the ground, or throw water on them to distract them. As a last resort you may have to throw sand or dirt in the eyes of the one with the grip. One hiker, who uses a cane as a hiking stick, reports having broken up a dogfight or two by slipping the crook of his cane under the dog collar or harness to drag the thug away.

To help avoid dogfights, do not give treats to other hikers' dogs. Competition for food and protection of territory are the root of most dogfights.

### Seasonal Nuisances

#### Foxtails

These arrow-like grasses are at their worst in late summer and early fall, when they are dry, sharp, and just waiting to burrow in some dog's fuzzy coat. A dry foxtail can be inhaled by a dog, lodge itself in the ear canal or between the toes, or camouflage itself in the dog's undercoat, puncturing the skin and causing infection. Foxtails have the potential to cause damage to vital organs.

Inspect your dog's ears and toes and run your hands through his coat, inspecting under the belly, legs, and tail. Brush out his coat after excursions where there were even hints of foxtails. Violent sneezing and snorting is an indication he may have inhaled a foxtail. Even if the sneezing or shaking decreases in intensity or frequency, the foxtail can still be tucked where it irritates only occasionally while it travels deeper, causing more serious damage. If this happens, take your dog to a vet as soon as possible. He may have to be anesthetized to remove the foxtail.

#### Poison Oak

Poison oak is a three-leaved, low-growing vine or bush that ranges in color from green to red depending on the season. The plant can cause topical irritations on hairless areas of your dog's body. (You can apply cortisone cream to the affected area.)

Find out if there is poison oak where you plan to hike, and make sure you wash your hands with soap after handling your dog. The resin can rub off your dog onto you, your sleeping bag, your car seat, and your furniture at home. If you are very sensitive to these rashes, bathe your dog after the hike and sponge your arms and legs with diluted chlorine bleach, Tecnu soap, or anti-itch spray. Tecnu soap is an outdoor cleanser that removes plant oil from your skin and also can be used on your laundry.

## Other Poisonous Plants

Unfortunately, your dog may be tempted to taste and chew hazardous plants. This includes plants found in your backyard, like rhubarb. In the wilderness, however, there are similar dangers—plants such as rhododendrons may cause considerable sickness and discomfort for your pet.

If you suspect poisoning, take note of what your dog ate and head back to the car. Once out of the woods, call your vet or an animal poison control center (see Appendix B for phone number).

## Fleas and Ticks

Fleas are uncomfortable for your dog and carry tapeworm eggs, and ticks are one of nature's most painfully potent and tenacious creatures for their size. Some tick bites cause uncomfortable red, swollen irritation to the area of the skin where they attach and can make the area feel like it was pounded by a two-by-four. In some cases, tick bites can inflict temporary paralysis. Other types of ticks found in California can carry Lyme disease, which is reported to be the most common tick-carried disease in the United States.

Ticks thrive on wild hosts (deer are the most common) around lakes, streams, meadows, and some wooded areas. They cling to unsuspecting hikers and dogs. On dogs, they crawl out of the fur and attach to the skin around the neck, face, ears, stomach, or any soft, fleshy cavity. They attach to their hosts by sticking their mouthparts into the skin and then feed on the host's blood and swell up until they dangle from the skin like an ornament.

# REMOVING A TICK

1. **Try not to break off any mouthparts (remaining parts can cause infection), and avoid getting tick fluids on you through crushing or puncturing the tick.**
2. **Grasp the tick as close to the skin as possible with blunt forceps or tweezers or with your fingers in rubber gloves, tissue, or any barrier to shield your skin from possible tick fluids.**
3. **Remove the tick with a steady pull.**
4. **After removing the tick, disinfect the skin with alcohol and wash your hands with soap and water.**

There is an abundance of chemical and natural flea and tick products on the market, including collars, dips, sprays, powders, pills, and oils. Some products have the advantages of being effective on both fleas and ticks, remain effective on wet dogs, and require an easy once-a-month topical application. Consult your veterinarian about a safe and appropriate product.

### Mosquitoes

Avon's Skin So Soft is a less toxic and more pleasant-smelling—though not as effective—mosquito repellent than repellents containing DEET. Mix one cap of the oil with one pint of water in a spray bottle. Spray your dog and run your hands through her coat from head to toe and tail to cover her with a light film of the mixture. Be careful to avoid her eyes and nostrils, but do not miss the outer ear areas. Organic solutions containing eucalyptus can also be used as a mosquito repellent. Besides being annoying, mosquitoes carry heartworm. Consult your veterinarian about preventive medication.

### Bees, Wasps, Hornets, and Yellow Jackets

These insect nests can be in trees or on the ground.

## Moody Mother Nature and Seasonal Hazards

Every season has climatic constants, but Mother Nature can be temperamental, bringing additional unexpected challenges that can affect your safety and the safety of your dog.

### Summer

Heat, albeit "dry" in Northern California valleys and lower elevation foothill regions, can be taxing on your dog. These conditions increase the risks of dehydration and heatstroke. Here are some tips to help avoid heat-related trouble:

- Hike in the early morning or late afternoon.
- Carry at least eight ounces of water per dog for each hour on the trail or 2.0 miles of trail.
- Rest in a shaded area during the intensity of the midday.
- Take frequent rest stops and offer your dog water.
- Let your dog take a plunge in a lake or lie belly down in a stream or mud puddle to cool down.

### Winter

Winter-like conditions can affect your dog's feet, endurance, and body warmth. Crusty snow can chafe and cut your dog's pads, and walking in deep snow is very taxing and can put a short-haired dog at risk of hypothermia. Here are some ways to protect your dog from cold and extra exertion.

- Carry booties for icy conditions and use them on your dog if she is not accustomed to snow and ice. Even dogs accustomed to snow can get abraded paws. Check your pup's feet for chafing and carry a couple extras booties as replacements for any lost in the snow. Keeping your dog on leash while she is in booties makes it easier to know when to adjust them or to retrieve any that slip off.
- Clothing on dogs should be about function, not fashion. Consider a wool or polypropylene sweater for your short-haired dog or down if your dog has no undercoat.
- Encourage your dog to walk behind you in your tracks. It is less strenuous.
- Carry a small sled or snow disk with an insulated foam pad so your dog can rest off the frozen ground.
- Unless your dog is a northern breed that thrives in cold, keep your outings shorter in transition seasons when there is some snow and ice to navigate. Carry snacks like liver or jerky treats and warm drinking water.

Winter in coastal Northern California, unlike in the mountains, is hike friendly, but it can bring heavy rain. Check the weather forecast and be prepared for potential problems to your dog's comfort on the trail.

### Spring
Following the cooler, wetter winter months, spring and sun in coastal Northern California bring fresh crops of wildflowers, but they also offer ideal conditions for ticks, mosquitoes, poison oak, and foxtails to come to life in time to thrive over the summer months.

### Fall
Fall brings shorter daylight hours. Adjust the length of your hikes accordingly. Hunting season in many parts of the backcountry requires extra caution. Check the hunting regulations and dates for the hiking area you have in mind. It is important that you and your dog wear bright colors when hiking anywhere in the fall. Orange hunting vests are available for dogs, and colorful harnesses and bandannas are also a good idea. When in doubt about hunting in forested areas, keep your dog on a leash.

## The High Country
The high country is subject to variable and extreme weather year-round. Check for weather advisories at the ranger station, including thunderstorm warnings and fire danger. Afternoon thunderstorms are common in the afternoon. Rain can quickly turn to hail and snow. Stay below the timberline and off exposed ridges. In spring and fall pay attention to sudden drops in temperature and shifts in wind with system clouds announcing snowfall.

# How to Use This Guide

The book divides Northern California into its six distinct regional mountain range categories: Klamath, Cascade, Basin, North Coast, Sierra Nevada, and South Coast, with an introduction to each geographic region. This is not to say that the hikes chosen were the only hikes suitable to hiking with your dog. On the contrary. In some regions there is such an abundance of fabulous trails that the biggest hurdle was deciding which ones to include. Although there are a few moderately challenging mountain-peak hikes, this book is not about conquering any summits with crampons on your feet and a dog on your back. The goal is to introduce you and your dog to a region on trails of various lengths and difficulty that would showcase the best attributes likely to excite you and your dog and inspire you to explore the region and discover other hikes that could become your and your dog's favorites. The hikes include both new trails and lesser-known trails, as well as some of the most popular superstars and our dogs' own favorites. Park rangers and recreation managers were our best sources for the newest trails. And visitor center volunteers and locals were always eager to share their favorite dog hikes with us.

We agreed to make wilderness areas a priority wherever possible for two reasons:

1. The Wilderness Act of 1964 gave certain portions of federal public lands a special designation to further minimize human impact and allow nature to dominate, making it a privilege for you and your dog to hike these trails on the country's most pristine lands. Nature's timeline rules in these backcountry habitat havens, where mechanized equipment, commercial operations, and permanent human imprint are prohibited. Ideally humans are visitors who should Leave No Trace of their passing through the "backcountry," where they enjoy solitude away from civilization and recreational development of the "front country." The wilderness is a sanctuary for wildlife, native flora, pristine rivers and streams, as well as the guardian of archaeological, geological, and cultural sites. Wilderness areas are under the management of national parks, national forests, and the Bureau of Land Management in cooperation with the US Fish and Wildlife Service in some instances. Wilderness areas are every nature lover's Shangri-La and a dog owner's/hiker's dream come true.

2. With few exceptions, dogs are not allowed on national park trails, let alone in wilderness areas within national parks. But they are allowed in the wilderness areas managed by the US Forest Service and the Bureau of Land Management, which makes hiking with your dog in a wilderness area the crème de la crème of nature experiences.

We chose hikes of various distances and terrain to satisfy both the younger or more eager dog that already has some trail dust under his paws and the older less-ambitious or novice dog on his first foray out of the burbs. It is up to you to build up their fitness with regular consistent exercise and to monitor their body language for signs of discomfort, pain, or fatigue. Don't risk injuring your dog by making him a weekend warrior.

In choosing the fifty-one hikes, we gave preference to trails accessed from paved roads and those with historical highlights, water (lakes or streams), shade, and scenery. Unless there is specific reference to dirt or gravel roads, consider the road access to the trail "paved." We also considered proximity to communities offering services for lodging and food supplies whenever available.

Distances were calculated using USGS, forest, wilderness, and area-specific maps in tandem with a GPS unit for maximum accuracy. Be aware that it is not uncommon for trails to be rerouted from their original USGS mapping as a result of floods, fires, and slides or changes in agency policy.

The Trail Finder section at the beginning of the book allows you to quickly sort hikes by distance, exertion level, leash policy, and suitable overnight trips. Hikes are divided into three categories: easy, moderate, and strenuous. A short hike may be more strenuous than a longer one because of elevation gain. Hikes under 5.0 miles will always mention if there are characteristics that would make the otherwise easy or moderate hike strenuous. The assumption in determining the degree of difficulty is that you and your dog have driven from sea level or low elevation to the trailhead, so hikes with elevations of 5,000 feet and above are labeled moderate at best or strenuous. You must exercise some personal judgment as to the suitability of a hike based on your and your dog's general fitness levels.

The Summary Block below the sketch overview of the hike is an outline to assist you in preparing for the hike. It includes the following features.

Distance is the total round-trip distance of the hike, with a notation on whether the hike is an out and back, loop, or lollipop.

Approximate hiking time is based on a 2.0-mile-per-hour pace, taking into account water and snack breaks, Pooch swim stops, and vista points. Hikers' pace will vary according to individual fitness levels, pack weight, terrain, and elevation range, especially if the hikes begin above 5,000 feet. When hiking uphill, add 1.0 mile or thirty minutes for every 1,000 feet gained in elevation. One way to estimate your average pace per mile on level ground for a baseline is to time yourself walking around a running track.

Difficulty rates hikes as easy, moderate, or strenuous.

Trailhead elevation and Highest point on the hike (use the profiles to evaluate and anticipate the elevation range and terrain) help you prepare for weather and exertion (pick hikes that are suitable to both your and your dog's abilities and fitness levels). Whether you are an enthusiastic newcomer to hiking or introducing your dog to the joys of the trail, it is best to set the bar lower on a first outing and make it a positive, safe experience for both of you. This becomes particularly significant on the Sierra Nevada hikes, which are mostly above 6,000 feet.

Best season to hike a trail is determined by the trail's accessibility during different times of the year, which depends on the regional weather. Too much snow or rain during certain months can make a trail hard to navigate. Spring can last anywhere from early April to late May or mid-June. Summer is typically late June through

August. Fall can begin in early September and last into November. Winter begins to show its teeth in December and lasts through March.

The opening of trails and campgrounds, especially in the Sierra, are subject to the length and intensity of the winter season, and that can vary by several weeks from year to year. Optimally the Sierra season runs from Memorial Day weekend to mid-October, but don't count on it. Trails above 7,000 feet frequently still have snow after Independence Day. Although the trail may be accessible year-round, "Best season" will list the preferable months or seasons for optimal enjoyment and comfort, influenced by temperature, trail traffic, water sources, seasonal highlights like wildflowers and fall foliage, as well as nuisances like excessive mosquitoes and poison oak. Always call the ranger station for trail status.

California has microclimates as well as seasons, which can make some hikes even within just a 20.0-mile radius in the same geographic region more desirable than others. On an August afternoon, for example, a hike along the coast may be a foggy forty degrees cooler than a hike 20.0 miles east in sunny, but sometimes triple-digit inland valleys.

Trail surface indicates what you'll be walking on, which is especially important for dogs' paws. If a trail has a lot of rock or a surface that could be especially abrasive to dogs' paws on extended stretches and booties should be worn, you will see Paw Alert! 🐾 . Other trail users lets you know if you and Pooch will be sharing the trail with horses, which include pack animals, and/or bikes. Those are the two most common trail users and require dogs to be on exemplary behavior, especially if the Canine compatibility is "voice control."

Land status clues you in on the maps you may need as well as the management agency. Different agencies have different policies regarding leashes versus voice control.

Fees and permits applies to parking, day hiking, or overnight camping fees. There is no mention of "campfire" on this line, because it is assumed that campfire permits are required outside of "developed" campgrounds on all trails. In California, "campfire permits" are not restricted to just the building of a campfire. Permits also apply to cooking stoves and anything with a flame. Campfire permits are obtained from ranger stations, and it is essential to check with the managing ranger district as to what the "campfire" policy is along any given trail at any given time, since the policy changes throughout the season on different public lands based on the level of risk of fire. Campfires and the use of anything with a flame are outright prohibited in some wilderness areas and above certain elevations.

Northern California suffered one of its worst forest fires as a result of human negligence and disregard for the campfire rules in effect at the time. The Rim Fire destroyed homes, wildlife habitat, and 400 square miles of national forest and national park wilderness. It also threatened the National Park System's most cherished site—Yosemite Valley—as well as old-growth giant sequoia groves and the Hetch Hetchy Reservoir that serves San Francisco. Most tragic of all was that an unlawful campfire was the spark—a preventable tragedy.

Maps refers you to the appropriate USGS topographical map and/or national forest, wilderness, or additional park or local maps. (Be sure to check the "contour interval" when using USGS maps. Although most are 40 feet, some are 20, 25, or 80 feet, and some are in meters.)

Trail contacts leads you to the best source for information on permits, fees, dog policies, parking, and campgrounds, as well as current information on access to trails, restrictions, and closures. There is no such thing as asking too many questions when it involves your and your dog's safety. Never drive right on past a ranger station and the opportunity to verify your information.

Nearest town lists the largest population center closest to the trail for services such as food and lodging. It is also often the town used as the anchor for Finding the trailhead. Other smaller but more convenient communities may be listed for access to basic supplies and campgrounds or other types of lodging.

Trail tips includes what amenities may be found at the trailhead (toilet, picnic tables, and so on) and other useful information.

Finding the trailhead gives you driving directions to the trailhead from a significant population base or community located along the principal highway route.

The Hike describes the history and other interesting factoids related to the area of the trail, as well as a description of some of the natural or cultural highlights along the trail.

Miles and Directions gets you from the trailhead to the turnaround point with concise directions between way points at trail junctions and significant points of interest.

Creature Comforts lists noteworthy or convenient Fueling Up stops for food (store, takeout, or eat in). It will specify if an establishment has a dog-friendly outdoor dining area. Resting Up is about nearby campgrounds or other dog-friendly lodging, including cabins, inns, motels, or resorts, some with historic significance or "après hike" pampering amenities. Puppy Paws and Golden Years sections are not exclusively for puppies and very senior dogs, but the options focus on providing dogs with added opportunities for physical and mental stimulation that are definitely suitable for that group.

# Trail Finder

## Easy Hikes

5. McCloud Falls
6. Bailey Cove Trail
7. Lake Eiler
9. Elk River Trail
10. Punta Gorda Lighthouse
14. Waterfall Grove Trail
17. Bluff Trail
20. Bolinas Ridge Trail
23. Round Lake/Bear Lakes Loop
25. Sagehen Creek Trail
28. Cascade Falls
31. Hot Springs Falls
33. Sardine Falls
34. Pinecrest Lake Loop
37. Parker Lake
38. McLeod Lake
40. Shadow of the Giants
41. Gem Lakes
43. Mt. Wanda
44. Land's End
47. H. Miller Site Loop
49. Carmel Meadows

## Moderate Hikes

2. Marble Valley
3. Canyon Creek Trail
4. Whiskeytown Falls
12. Black Sands Beach
16. Redbud Trail
21. Wolf Ridge Rodeo Beach Loop
22. Mill Creek
24. Feather Falls
27. Five Lakes Trail
29. Lake Aloha
30. Round Top Lake
32. Duck Lake
35. Frog Lakes
48. Juan Bautista De Anza National
    Historic Trail

## Strenuous Hikes

1. Craig's Creek Trail
8. Pine Creek Trail
11. Pickett Peak
13. Thomes Gorge
15. High Rock
18. Oat Hill Mine Trail
19. Mount Burdell
26. Loch Leven Lakes Trail
36. Gardisky Lake
39. Crystal Lake
42. Lamarck Lakes
45. Montara Mountain
46. Mission Peak Loop
50. Holt Road to Snivleys Ridge
51. Sierra Hill in Brazil Ranch

## Less than 5 Miles

4. Whiskeytown Falls
5. McCloud Falls
6. Bailey Cove Trail
14. Waterfall Grove
20. Bolinas Ridge Trail
23. Round Lake/Bear Lakes Loop
27. Five Lakes Trail
28. Cascade Falls
31. Hot Springs Falls
32. Duck Lake
33. Sardine Falls
34. Pinecrest Lake Loop
35. Frog Lakes
36. Gardisky Lake
37. Parker Lake
38. McLeod Lake
39. Crystal Lake
40. Shadow of the Giants
43. Mt. Wanda
44. Land's End
47. H. Miller Site Loop
49. Carmel Meadows
51. Sierra Hill in Brazil Ranch

## 5 to 10 Miles

1. Craig's Creek Trail
3. Canyon Creek Trail
7. Lake Eiler
9. Elk River
10. Punta Gorda Lighthouse
11. Pickett Peak
12. Black Sands Beach
16. Redbud Trail
17. Bluff Trail
18. Oat Hill Mine Trail
19. Mt. Burdell
21. Wolf Ridge Rodeo Beach Loop
24. Feather Falls
25. Sagehen Creek
26. Loch Leven Lakes Trail
29. Lake Aloha
30. Round Top Lake
41. Gem Lakes
42. Lamarck Lakes
45. Montara Mountain
46. Mission Peak Loop
48. Juan Bautista De Anza National Historic Trail
50. Holt Road to Snivleys Ridge

## More than 10 Miles

2. Marble Valley
8. Pine Creek Trail
13. Thomes Gorge
15. High Rock
22. Mill Creek

## On Leash

3. Canyon Creek Trail
4. Whiskeytown Falls
5. McCloud Falls
6. Bailey Cove Trail
14. Waterfall Grove
17. Bluff Trail
18. Oat Hill Mine Trail
20. Bolinas Ridge Trail
24. Feather Falls
34. Pinecrest Lake Loop
43. Mt. Wanda
44. Land's End

45. Montara Mountain
47. H. Miller Site Loop
49. Carmel Meadows

## Voice Control

1. Craig's Creek Trail
2. Marble Valley
7. Lake Eiler
8. Pine Creek Trail
9. Elk River
10. Punta Gorda Lighthouse
11. Pickett Peak
12. Black Sands Beach
13. Thomes Gorge
15. High Rock
16. Redbud Trail
21. Wolf Ridge Rodeo Beach Loop
22. Mill Creek
23. Round Lake/Bear Lakes Loop
25. Sagehen Creek Trail
26. Loch Leven Lakes Trail
27. Five Lakes Trail
28. Cascade Falls
29. Lake Aloha
32. Duck Lake
33. Sardine Falls
35. Frog Lakes
36. Gardisky Lake
37. Parker Lake
38. McLeod Lake
39. Crystal Lake
40. Shadow of the Giants
41. Gem Lakes
46. Mission Peak Loop
48. Juan Bautista De Anza National Historic Trail
51. Sierra Hill in Brazil Ranch

## Part On Leash/Part Voice Control

19. Mount Burdell
30. Round Top Lake
31. Hot Springs Falls
42. Lamarck Lakes
50. Holt Road to Snivleys Ridge

# Klamath Ranges

The Klamath Ranges are an isolated and rugged series of mountain ranges in the northwest corner of California. They bump up against the Cascades on the east and the North Coast Ranges to the south. The winters are cold and snowfall is heavy. The summers are dry and temperatures are mild. The range includes the Marble Mountains, the North Yolla Bolly Mountains, the Salmon Mountains, the Scott Mountains, the Scott Bar Mountains, the Siskiyou Mountains, the Trinity Mountains, and the Trinity Alps.

Elevations start at about 2,000 feet near the coast and rise to an average of 7,000 feet inland. The highest peaks include Mount Eddy in the Trinity Mountains at 9,025 feet, Thompson Peak in the Trinity Alps Wilderness at 9,003 feet, and China Mountain in the Scott Mountains at 8,551 feet.

The forests are often dense and lush, with redwood, Douglas fir, Jeffrey, ponderosa, sugar pine, cedar, spruce, hemlock, black oak, madrone, and buckeye as well as ferns, dogwood, azalea, and rhododendron. Coastal redwoods are the tallest trees in the world, with the tallest measuring over 370 feet. These cousins of giant sequoia can live to be 2,000 years old. Redwoods were present when dinosaurs had the run of the planet.

Wildlife includes black bears, mountain lions, elk, bobcats, foxes, beavers, and deer. The rivers and streams of the Klamath Ranges are spawning grounds for salmon and trout.

Much of the Klamath Ranges are public land managed by the US Forest Service. National forests include Klamath National Forest, Mendocino National Forest, Shasta-Trinity National Forest, Siskiyou National Forest, and Six Rivers National Forest. The Klamath Ranges boast several wilderness areas, including Marble Mountain Wilderness, Siskiyou Wilderness, Trinity Alps Wilderness, and Yolla Bolly–Middle Eel Wilderness.

The ranges are interlaced with extensive hiking trails, recreation areas, and campgrounds. The population is sparse, and you and your dog may find that you have the trails all to yourselves, even in the middle of summer. Keep an eye out for Bigfoot!

# 1 Craig's Creek Trail

This pleasant, shady, cool, and narrow slope-side trail is a hiker's perspective of the wild and scenic Smith River. The hike encompasses a woodsy experience that overlooks the redwood canopy with the sound of the powerful rush of the Wild Smith below. The trail descends to the bank of Craig's Creek where it pours into the jade pools at the confluence of the South Fork of the Smith River.

**Start:** From the South Fork River access parking lot

**Distance:** 8.0 miles out and back

**Approximate hiking time:** 3.5 hours

**Difficulty:** Strenuous

**Trailhead elevation:** 160 feet

**Highest point:** 573 feet

**Best season:** Late spring to fall

**Trail surface:** Dirt, gravel, slippery rocks, and exposed roots

**Other trail users:** Horses

**Canine compatibility:** Voice control

**Land status:** National Recreation Area

**Fees and permits:** None

**Maps:** USGS Hiouchi; USFS Six Rivers National Forest

**Trail contacts:** Smith River District Ranger Station, 10600 CA 199, Gasquet 95543; (707) 457-3131. Six Rivers National Forest, 1330 Bayshore Way, Eureka 95501; (707) 442-1721.

**Nearest town:** Crescent City

**Trail tips:** The moist coastal climate and shade make for a slippery surface, so be careful when stepping on the rocks and roots along the trail. There are two vault toilets, trash and recycling receptacles, an information board, and a boat ramp in the parking area.

**Finding the Trailhead:** From Crescent City at US 101 and CA 199, drive 7.0 miles on CA 199 North to South Fork Road. Turn right on South Fork Road across the bridge and drive 0.2 mile to the river access parking lot. Walk to the exit sign left of the bathrooms and walk up the exit driveway 500 feet to the road. The Craig's Creek Trailhead is across the road just short of the bridge. **GPS:** N41 47.85' / W124 03.26'

## The Hike

In 1981, a 315-mile stretch of the Smith River was designated "Wild and Scenic," making the Smith River the largest Wild and Scenic river system in the United States. The Smith River is considered the crown jewel. It is in the Six Rivers National Forest and home to redwoods, cedars, and old-growth Douglas firs.

Craig's Creek Trail is in the Smith River National Recreation Area and follows an old pack trail traveled by miners in the 1800s. Be careful crossing the road to the trailhead, as the cars come quickly around the bend. The trail is a narrow slope-side, mostly shady path lined with ferns and lush leafy vegetation above the Smith River. Ignore the temptation to get lured onto the lower overgrown trail closest to the river. Bear left up on the main upper trail. The lower trail may have been the original, now-abandoned trail. The velvety green moss that covers the rocks and roots along the way

*Craig's Creek Trail follows an old miner's pack trail.*

can be very treacherous for both hiker and dog. Step cautiously, especially when you come to some of the seasonal streams and trickles that make the terrain even slicker. The views are mostly of the forested mountains across the river, and although the Smith River does not come into view until about 1.5 miles, you will hear it most of the way, with whitewater stretches being the loudest and also where Craig's Creek pours into the river. At about 0.8 mile, where the uphill stretch finally levels in a clearing before the gradual descent towards the river, you are treated to rhododendron rows, where the trail bursts with pink blossoms in late spring and early summer.

At the T-junction at the 2.8 mile, you turn right for the last mile to the bank of the river at Scott's Creek. Be aware that there is poison oak camouflaged in the vegetation brushing this section of the trail, so you may want to wear long pants to prevent the rashes that result from contact with the plant's resin.

This straightforward out-and-back hike is a real high for your dog, whose nose will unveil the understory of the moist redwood canopy as he wags all the way down to the edge of the Smith River's jade pools at Craig's Creek. There are plenty of rocks on which to sit and soak up the wild beauty of the Smith while you and Pooch enjoy a snack, or you can find a calm pool for a summer dip before heading back to the trailhead.

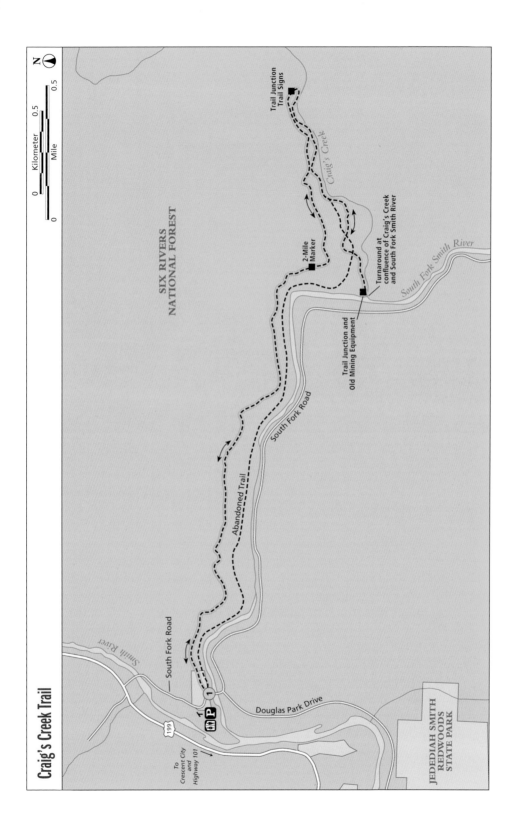

# Craig's Creek Trail

N

0    0.5    Kilometer
0    0.5    Mile

Smith River

To Crescent City and Highway 101

199

South Fork Road

Douglas Park Drive

P

1

SIX RIVERS NATIONAL FOREST

Abandoned Trail

South Fork Road

2-Mile Marker

Craig's Creek

Turnaround at confluence of Craig's Creek and South Fork Smith River

Trail Junction and Old Mining Equipment

Trail Junction Trail Signs

South Fork Smith River

JEDEDIAH SMITH REDWOODS STATE PARK

## Miles and Directions

**0.0** Start at the Craig's Creek trailhead across the road from the river access parking lot.

**2.0** Come to mile marker 2.0 on a tree to the right of the trail.

**2.8** Come to a T-junction with a CRAIG'S CREEK TRAIL sign nailed to a tree on the right. Turn right.

**3.9** Arrive at a T-junction with primitive campsite and rusted abandoned piece of historic machinery. Turn right on the short rugged trail down to the confluence of the Smith River and Craig's Creek.

**4.0** Arrive at Craig's Creek pouring into the Smith River pools. Elevation 235 feet. **GPS:** N41 47.38' / W124 01.54' Enjoy a picnic break on the rocks by the refreshing pools before returning the way you came.

**8.0** Arrive back at the trailhead.

## Creature Comforts

### Resting Up

**Redwoods RV Resort,** 6701 CA 101 North, Crescent City 95531; (707) 487-7404; redwoodsrv.com. This resort offers a campground in a forested setting with spacious full-hookup RV and trailer spaces, tent sites, as well as dog-friendly housekeeping cabins. The resort also has a self-wash pet station.

**Crescent City** has a few dog-friendly motels.

*Craig's Creek flows into South Fork Smith River.*

# 2 Marble Valley

You cannot beat a paved road to the doorstep of a wilderness area. This is a moderate hike on a lightly used trail that rewards hikers and dogs with frequent creeks as it climbs past white blooms of delicate dogwood mingled with cedar, Douglas fir, and hemlock trees. Hikers also enjoy glorious views, and the spring lupine are an extra perk.

**Start:** From the Canyon Creek trailhead to Marble Valley in the hiker parking lot at Lover's Camp

**Distance:** 10.8 miles out and back

**Approximate hiking Time:** 5 hours

**Difficulty:** Moderate, with a steep stretch of about 200 steps of terraced granite

**Trailhead elevation:** 4,190 feet

**Highest point:** 5,741 feet

**Best season:** Early summer to late fall

**Trail surface:** Dirt trail with some rock

**Other trail users:** Horses

**Canine compatibility:** Voice control

**Land status:** National Forest

**Fees and permits:** Campfire permit

**Maps:** USGS Marble Mountain; USFS Klamath National Forest; Marble Mountain Wilderness

**Trail contacts:** Klamath National Forest, Salmon/Scott River Ranger District, 11263 N. CA 3, Fort Jones 96032; (530) 468-5351; www.fs.fed.us/klamath

**Nearest town:** Yreka

**Trail tips:** Lover's Camp is a walk-in campground with a vault toilet at the trailhead. This day hike also makes an excellent overnight trek. In these times of public land budget cuts, hikers will be happy to know that local horseback riders volunteer to help maintain this trail by clearing fallen trees.

**Finding the trailhead:** From Yreka take CA 3 west toward Fort Jones and drive 15.0 miles to Scott River Road. Turn right on Scott River Road and drive 14.0 miles to the Lover's Camp Trailhead sign on your right at the intersection of FR 43N45 on your left. Turn left on FR 43N45 and drive 7.0 miles to Lover's Camp Trailhead. (At 5.3 miles bear left and continue on the paved road). Follow the signs for the Hiker Parking Lot at the end of the road. The Lovers Camp Trailhead is on the left side at the entrance to the hiker parking lot by the information and map kiosk. **GPS:** N41 35.67' / W123 08.55'

## The Hike

Marble Mountain (6,680 feet) earned its name from the light limestone cap that gives it the appearance of marble. Marble Mountain and Boulder Peak (8,229 feet) are the centerpiece peaks in the Marble Mountain Wilderness of Klamath National Forest. As early as 1931 the volcanic- and glacial-sculpted rugged beauty of this region and the diversity of its geology and vegetation were apparent enough to have it designated as the "Marble Mountain Primitive Area," one of California's "oldest formally designated wilderness areas." Thirty-three years later, the Marble Mountain Wilderness's

*Entering the Marble Mountain Wilderness*

almost 250,000 acres of subalpine lakes, lush valleys, and 600 miles of steep paths to maintained trails were protected under the Wilderness Act of 1964.

Due to its isolation from heavily populated urban centers, the "Marbles," as lovers of this wilderness refer to it, are lightly traveled. Black bears, deer, coyotes, mountain lions, wolverines, quail, woodpeckers, rattlesnakes, and trout share this wilderness ecosystem.

The Canyon Creek Trail to Marble Valley offers remarkably easy access into this pristine domain. Drive up the paved road, park at the trailhead, and head up through a display of various green healthy conifers interrupted in late spring and early summer by blooms of blue lupine, mountain violets, and white corn lilies. The elevation is moderate and the climb is gradual for the first 4.0 miles, until you reach the steeper stretch of 200 terraced stone steps.

At 4.5 miles Pooch will welcome the cool cascade tumbling across the trail and you will appreciate the clearing with stunning views of the craggy ridge to the east. Cross the stream at the foot of the cascade and enjoy the last mile leading you to Marble Valley Cabin, built in the 1930s to serve as a staffed ranger station until the 1960s. The Pacific Crest Trail junction just past the cabin is set in a vale boasting views of the marble-like peaks to the northwest. You and your dog have arrived at an idyllic spot that begs for a picnic break and a Kodak moment before going back the way you came.

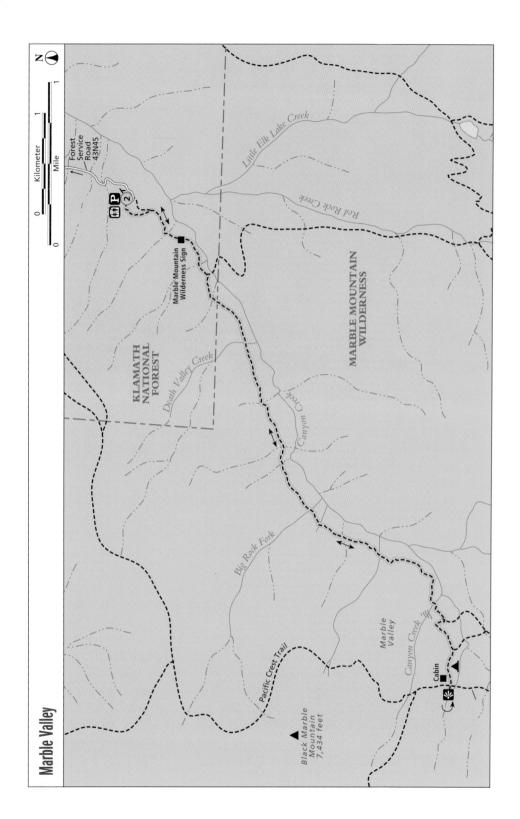

# Marble Valley

N

Forest Service Road 43N45

Little Elk Lake Creek

Red Rock Creek

Marble Mountain Wilderness Sign

KLAMATH NATIONAL FOREST

MARBLE MOUNTAIN WILDERNESS

Death Valley Creek

Canyon Creek

Big Rock Fork

Pacific Crest Trail

Marble Valley

Canyon Creek

Cabin

Black Marble Mountain 7,434 feet

Kilometer

Mile

## Miles and Directions

**0.0** Start at the Lover's Campground trailhead for the Canyon Creek Trail to Marble Valley.

**0.3** The trail crosses FR 43N45A. Continue uphill on the trail, walking in a southerly direction.

**0.7** Enter the Marble Mountain Wilderness.

**1.0** Come to a fork with a trail sign on the ground. Bear right to Marble Valley.

**1.6** Cross Death Valley Creek.

**2.0** Cross a wide stream.

**3.0** Cross a wide stream.

**3.7** Cross a wide stream.

**4.5** Come to cascading Canyon Creek and a waterfall in a clearing with views of Marble Mountain's craggy ridge to the east. Cross the creek below the cascade and above the fall.

**4.7** Come to a fork and bear right toward Marble Valley Cabin.

**5.1** Come to a fork and bear right to Marble Valley.

**5.2** Come to an unmarked fork. The left spur leads to a campsite and fire ring. Bear right to continue to Marble Valley.

**5.4** Arrive at the Marble Valley Cabin and the Pacific Crest Trail junction just beyond the cabin. Elevation 5,741 feet. **GPS:** N41 33.78' / W123 11.92' Linger in this idyllic meadow while feasting on a snack and the views of the Marble Mountains to the northwest. Go back the way you came or enjoy an overnight with your pooch.

**10.8** Arrive back at the trailhead.

*The historic cabin near the Pacific Crest Trail junction*

## Creature Comforts

*Resting Up*

**Baymont Inn and Suites,** 148 Moonlit Oaks Ave., Yreka 96097; (530) 841-1300; bay montinns.com/yreka. There are refrigerators and microwaves in some units.

**Best Western Miner's Inn,** 122 E. Miner St., Yreka, 96097; (530) 842-4355; bestwest ern.com.

**Indian Scotty Forest Service Campground** (www.fs.usda.gov/recarea/klamathnational forest/indianscotty), on the Scott River at the intersection of Scott River Road and FR 44N45. This camp, just 7.0 miles down the road from Lover's Camp trailhead, makes an excellent basecamp if you want to spend more time exploring the Marble Mountain Wilderness trails.

**Yreka RV Park,** 767 Montague Rd., Yreka, 96097; (530) 841-0100; yrekarvpark.com. This park offers RV, trailer, and car camping (no tents) and overlooks the town in an open, quiet setting. Dogs must be on leash, and owners must pick up dog waste. The manager, Lynda Wright, loves dogs, but because of recent bad experiences with irresponsible pet owners, the cabins are unfortunately no longer "pet friendly."

## Puppy Paws and Golden Years

**Greenhorn Park** in Yreka is set around a reservoir by a historic mining encampment. The network of short, mostly level multiuse trails and the picnic area are open to dogs on leash. Pooches can scamper off leash under voice control on the upper trails.

# 3 Canyon Creek Falls

A paved road into a box canyon provides rare convenient access to an otherwise remote albeit grand mountain kingdom. The creek remains within earshot most of the way between glimpses of the falls and dramatic views of craggy peaks as you gradually climb to a clearing that reveals the best view of the falls and surrounding palisades.

**Start:** From Canyon Creek trailhead in the parking lot at the end of Canyon Creek Road
**Distance:** 8.4 miles out and back
**Approximate hiking time:** 4 hours
**Difficulty:** Moderate
**Trailhead elevation:** 3,170 feet
**Highest point:** 4,542 feet
**Best season:** Early spring to late fall
**Trail surface:** Dirt trail and granite rock
**Other trail users:** Horses
**Canine compatibility:** On leash
**Land status:** National Forest; Wilderness

**Fees and permits:** None (no campfires permitted)
**Maps:** USGS Mount Hilton; USFS Shasta-Trinity National Forest; Trinity Alps Wilderness
**Trail contacts:** Shasta-Trinity National Forest, Trinity River Management Unit, 210 Main St., CA 299 Weaverville 96093; (530) 623-2121
**Nearest town:** Junction City
**Trail tips:** If you plan on backpacking for an overnight, no fires are allowed in the Trinity Alps Wilderness.

**Finding the trailhead:** From Redding at the junction of I-5 and CA 299, drive 54.0 miles west on CA 299 to CR 401/Canyon Creek Road. Turn right on CR 401/Canyon Creek Road. Canyon Creek Road is just past the fire station, and the J. C. Deli is on the corner of Canyon Creek Road. Drive 13.0 miles to the end of Canyon Creek Road and into the trailhead parking lot. The trailhead is at the wooden steps at the north end of the parking lot, just past the information board. **GPS:** N40 53.25' / W123 01.46'

## The Hike

The 2-million-acre Shasta-Trinity National Forest, established by President Theodore Roosevelt in 1905, is the largest national forest in California. The Trinity Alps Wilderness bordering Shasta Trinity and two other national forests was known as the Salmon-Trinity Alps Primitive Area until 1984, when Congress designated it a wilderness area. The Wild and Scenic Salmon River is to the north, and the Wild and Scenic Trinity River is to the south of half a million acres of streams, lakes, meadows, and granitic palisades. This is one of California's largest wilderness areas, with over 500 miles of trails, seventeen of which run along the Pacific Crest Trail in the north.

The word "Alp" conjures up romantic images of Europe's legendary peaks that border Switzerland, Austria, Germany, France, and Italy. You won't get any of the civilized amenities associated with the European Alpine huts that serve hot stews, strudel, and hot chocolate with concerts of cowbells in the distance. But you will get

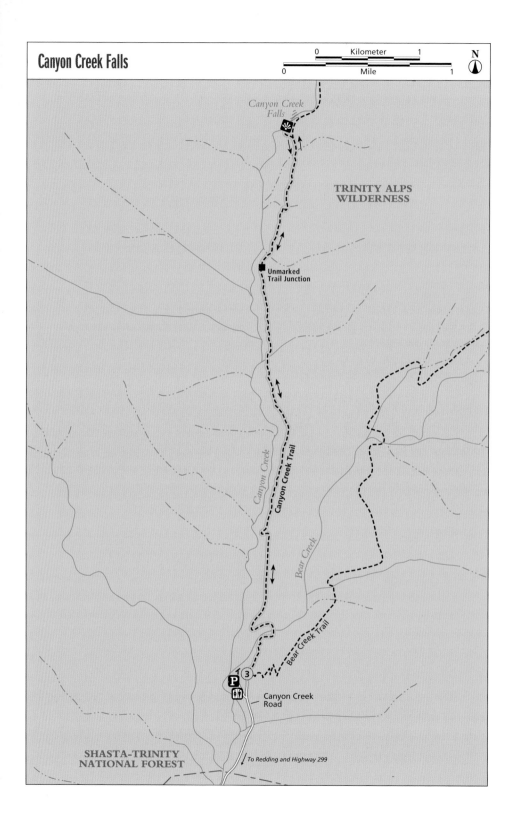

# Canyon Creek Falls

0 Kilometer 1

0 Mile 1

N

Canyon Creek Falls

TRINITY ALPS WILDERNESS

Unmarked Trail Junction

Canyon Creek

Canyon Creek Trail

Bear Creek

Bear Creek Trail

P 3

Canyon Creek Road

SHASTA-TRINITY NATIONAL FOREST

To Redding and Highway 299

*Taking a water break on the way up to Canyon Creek Falls*

a taste of wilderness solitude and the humbling euphoria of getting a glimpse of this remote eye-popping kingdom without having to backpack for days.

The trail begins in the shade of oaks and madrones and becomes scenic with streams lined with dogwood blossoms floating in the clearings dotted with pines and cedar. Blossoms of pink wild roses peek up along the way. At 2.5 miles peaks of the Trinity Alps come into view.

At 3.6 miles you start on the first of three switchbacks that cross the same creek. Hang in there for just over another 0.5 mile and you emerge on a canyon plateau cradled by granite peaks that overlook the lower falls. This setting is a power spot worth a picnic break or pitching a tent for an overnight off the trail.

## Miles and Directions

**0.0** Start at the Canyon Creek Trailhead sign by the wooden steps. Walk 400 feet and turn left on Canyon Creek Trail. Follow the sign for Canyon Creek Trail and enter Trinity Alps Wilderness.

**0.5** Walk across a stream.

**3.1** Come to a fork with a wooden trail sign with an arrow pointing right nailed to a fallen tree. Bear right and walk uphill.

**4.2** Arrive at a granite plateau above Lower Falls that overlooks a cascade above the falls. This is a picturesque spot for a picnic with Pooch before going back to the trailhead the way you came. **GPS:** N40 55.99' / W123 01.30'

**8.4** Arrive back at the trailhead.

*Fueling Up*

**Indian Creek Lodge,** 59741 CA-299, Douglas City, 96024; (530) 623-6294; iclodge .net. Located on the Trinity River about twenty minutes east of Junction City on CA 299 and ten minutes west of Weaverville.

*Resting Up*

**Indian Creek Lodge,** 59741 CA-299, Douglas City, 96024; (530) 623-6294; iclodge .net. The lodge has a few dog-friendly rooms and claims to have upgraded its image with new ownership and management.

**Trinity Canyon Lodge,** 27025 CA-299, Junction City, 96048; (530) 623-6318; trinity canyonlodge.com. The lodge is on the banks of the Trinity River on the way to Canyon Creek Falls trailhead.

**Campground Ripstein** (Forest Service), www.fs.us.gov/shastatrinitynationalforest/ campgroundripstein. This campground, on Canyon Creek Road, is the most con-

venient place to pitch a tent the night before the hike or if you want to take it easy on the way back from the hike. It offers the basic amenities of vault toilets, picnic tables, and fire grills, but no drinking water. Remember to pack out your garbage.

**Redding** has several dog-friendly motels.

## Puppy Paws and Golden Years

Redding's pedestrian Sundial Bridge spans 900 feet across the Sacramento River along the Sacramento National Recreation Trail. The bridge allows bikers and walkers and is a worthwhile attraction. Your pooch may not be wowed by architecture and engineering, but he'll wag at the idea of strolling the banks of the Sacramento River.

◀ *Canyon Creek Falls*

# 4 Whiskeytown Falls

This reasonably shady for summer, peaceful hike along a well-groomed dirt trail follows Mills Creek into a box canyon to the base of the falls. The trail ends at a short, narrow, and steep path of steps carved into the rock with a metal railing to a falls overlook.

**Start:** From the James K. Carr trailhead in the Whiskeytown National Recreation Area
**Distance:** 3.2 miles out and back
**Approximate hiking time:** 1.5 hours
**Difficulty:** Moderate
**Trailhead elevation:** 2,287 feet
**Highest point:** 2,913 feet
**Best season:** Year-round
**Trail surface:** Dirt trail
**Other trail users:** Horses and mountain bikes up to picnic table site only
**Canine compatibility:** On leash
**Land status:** National Recreation Area
**Fees and permits:** Day-use fee at trailhead parking lot $5
**Maps:** USGS French Gulch; Whiskeytown National Recreation Area James K. Carr Trail
**Trail contacts:** Whiskeytown National Recreation Area Visitor Center, 14412 Kennedy Memorial Dr., Whiskeytown 96095; (530) 246-1225; mail: P.O. Box 188, Whiskeytown 96095; www.nps.gov/whis. Sequestration and park closures: Jim Milestone, Park Superintendent, Whiskeytown National Recreation Area, (530) 242-3410
**Nearest town:** Redding
**Trail tips:** The James K. Carr Trail is too recent to be on the USGS map, and as of the 2005 printing of the Whiskeytown Unit map for the Whiskeytown-Shasta-Trinity National Recreation Area, Whiskeytown Falls was not on the map. Information for the James K. Carr Trail to the falls is available at the visitor center and online at www.nps.gov/whis. There is a vault toilet at the trailhead. The steps up to the falls viewpoint are very slippery.

**Finding the trailhead:** From Redding at the junction of I-5 and CA 299, turn west on CA 299 and drive 17.0 miles to Crystal Creek Road. Turn left on Crystal Creek Road, drive 2.0 miles, and bear right at the sign for Whiskeytown Falls. Drive another 1.6 miles and turn left into the trailhead parking lot. The trailhead sign for the James K. Carr Trail to the Whiskeytown Falls is at the east end of the parking lot to the left of the pit toilet. **GPS:** N40 38.30' / W122 40.55'

## The Hike

For thousands of years the Wintu people thrived on these lands once abundant in deer, elk, trout, and salmon, which supplemented acorns as a staple of their diet. The gold fever of 1848 intruded into their lives and upset the delicate balance of their environment and way of life to near extinction. Today Wintu heritage endures through elders who pass on their traditions to the younger generation. Protection of land within the Whiskeytown National Recreation Area helps support the National Park Service's mission to restore the land's abused watershed. The lake has 36.0 miles of shoreline surrounded by 39,000 acres of land with mountain trails and eight year-round creeks.

*Base of Whiskeytown Falls*

No one knows for sure the origin of the name Whiskeytown, but the most colorful of folktales tells of a barrel of whiskey that fell off the back of a miner's mule. It tumbled and spilled into the creek that became known as Whiskey Creek and the gold rush settlement that sprung next to creek in the 1850s called itself Whiskeytown.

Like many communities in the middle of nowhere that blossomed to bustle during the gold-fed boom, Whiskeytown dimmed and died at the turn of the twentieth century, when the glitter left in the hills could no longer support serious prospecting and settlers traveling to Oregon had found other routes.

The end of the Depression brought visions of harnessing Northern California's water resources to boost agriculture in the Central Valley, and Shasta Dam was completed in 1945. The ambitious Central Valley Project also included building a dam at Whiskeytown. The few residents who were left sold their property, and by 1963 the once-prosperous community was submerged; President Kennedy dedicated Whiskeytown Dam on September 28 of that year. The Whiskeytown Post Office and Schoolhouse still stand on the historic site, and the cemetery was relocated below the dam. The drowning of the once-raucous boomtown thus gave birth to a new scenic recreation area that welcomes human and canine visitors.

The Whiskeytown Falls hike is one of many excursions available to you and your pooch. The trail was named after James K. Carr, a Shasta County resident who became the undersecretary of the interior in 1963 under President Kennedy. His dream was for the private logging land in the Whiskeytown Lake area—where the Klamath Range meets the Sacramento Valley—to be set aside as a national park. On November 8, 1963, Congress created what is now the 42,000-acre Whiskeytown National Recreation Area.

Until 1967, with the exception of locals, the only people to know about the "hidden falls" were loggers. Park rangers came into the know in the late 1960s, but the existence of the falls still didn't reach the public's ears until 2004, when a park biologist spotted the falls on an aerial photo and set out to hike and locate them with a park geologist. The best-kept secret was finally out, and a trail to the falls that follows an old logging road was finally built and opened to the public.

The trail starts downhill along an old logging road and across a new bridge that stands over the west fork of Crystal Creek. The shady trail levels off until the junction for Mill Creek Trail and Whiskeytown Falls. Bear right to Whiskeytown Falls, and as you walk up the steep, narrow canyon, just try to imagine this as a roadbed with caravans of logging trucks ferrying loads of Douglas fir, pine, and cedar—it's not easy to do.

At 1.3 miles the Trail Camp area has two picnic tables where you and Pooch can rest for a water break. Horses and bikes are not allowed beyond this point. You cross a bridge just beyond this point and enter the box canyon, where the falls drop into a pool. The air here is cooler and moist, providing a perfect riparian habitat for ferns and mosses beneath the umbrella of big-leaf maples.

Turn left at the base of the falls to climb up the stone steps to two vista points. The first is known as Photographer's Ledge, and the one above is the Artist's Ledge. The moisture from the mist makes the stone steps precarious, so make sure you have one hand on the rail as you go up and down. On a warm day enjoy a snack on the bench at the base of the cool falls before going back the way you came.

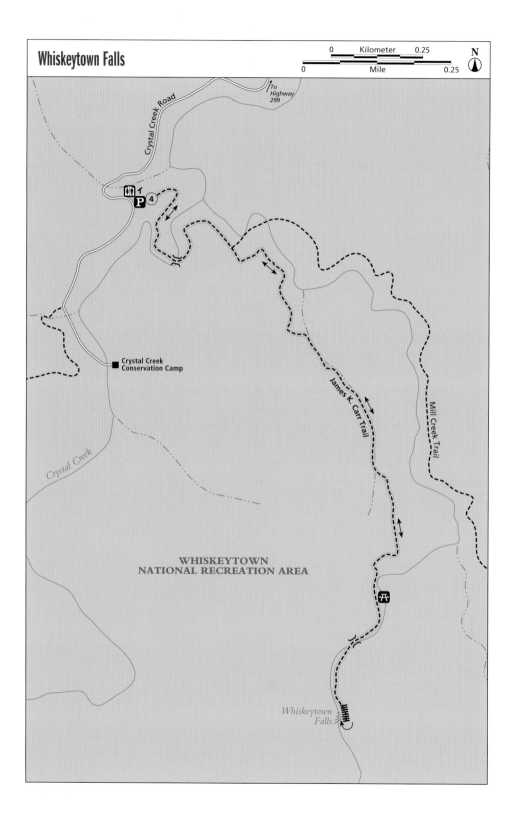

# Whiskeytown Falls

Kilometer
0                           0.25

Mile
0                                    0.25

N

Crystal Creek Road

To Highway 299

P 1 4

Crystal Creek Conservation Camp

James K. Carr Trail

Mill Creek Trail

Crystal Creek

WHISKEYTOWN
NATIONAL RECREATION AREA

Whiskeytown
Falls

## Miles and Directions

**0.0** Start at the James K. Carr trailhead at the east end of the parking lot.

**0.2** Come to a new bridge across the west fork of Crystal Creek.

**0.4** Arrive at a fork with a trail sign for Mill Creek Trail and Whiskeytown Falls. Continue to Whiskeytown Falls.

**1.3** Arrive at a day-use area that has two picnic tables.

**1.4** Cross a bridge over a creek.

**1.5** Arrive in a box canyon and a pool beneath Whiskeytown Falls. Walk up the slippery steps etched in the rock up to a fenced viewpoint to the left of the falls.

**1.6** Arrive at the overlook for a close up of the tiered 200-foot waterfall. Be extra careful coming down the slippery stones. Enjoy a snack and a rest on the bench at the bottom of the falls before turning back to the trailhead. You are at the highest point, elevation 2,913 feet. **GPS:** N40 37.57' / W122 40.13'

**3.2** Arrive back at the trailhead and parking lot.

*Stairway to the top of Whiskeytown Falls*

## Creature Comforts

*Resting Up*

**Oak Bottom Marina and Campground,** 12485 CA-299, Whiskeytown; at the Whiskeytown National Recreation Area off of CA 299; (530) 359-2269; www.nps.gov/whis. There are RV and tent sites.

**Redding** has several dog-friendly motels.

## Puppy Paws and Golden Years

Redding's pedestrian Sundial Bridge spans 900 feet across the Sacramento River along the Sacramento National Recreation Trail. The bridge is open to bikers and walkers and is a worthwhile attraction. Your pooch may not be wowed by architecture and engineering, but he'll wag at the idea of strolling the banks of the Sacramento River.

# Cascade Range

The Cascade Range is a volcanic mountain range, part of the Pacific Ring of Fire. It abuts the eastern edge of the Klamath Ranges along I-5 and extends east to the Basin Ranges and south to the Sierra Nevada. Mount Lassen, at 10,457 feet, at the southern end of the range, last erupted from 1914 to 1921. Mount Shasta, at 14,162 feet, last erupted approximately 200 years ago. Both snowcapped mountains dominate the landscape for many miles around.

The prevailing winds are westerly, and the range receives significant rain and snow. Most of the High Cascades are white with snow year-round. The western slopes are covered with dense forests of Douglas fir, hemlock, and alder, and the drier eastern slopes are covered with forests of Ponderosa Pine.

Shasta-Trinity National Forest, Lassen National Forest, and Thousand Lakes Wilderness are within the Cascade Range.

Wildlife here includes black bears, bobcats, mountain lions, coyotes, and deer.

# 5 McCloud Falls

This short, easy scenic hike on mostly level terrain, except for a couple of switchbacks and a steep stretch of thirty-two steps to Upper Falls, is a nicely developed little gem for hikers and their dogs. The trail passes three waterfalls on the McCloud River and has plenty of trees for shade to keep Pooch cool even on a summer day. There are several interpretive signs along the first mile of the trail that describe the history of Fowl Camp and the McCloud River. Although this hike describes 2.5 miles of trail to the Upper Falls Picnic Area, there are 7.0 miles of trail along the McCloud River for hikers and dogs with time and ambition.

**Start:** From the Shasta-Trinity information board next to the bathroom in the picnic area at the east end of the parking lot
**Distance:** 4.6-mile lollipop
**Approximate Hiking Time:** 2.5 hours
**Difficulty:** Easy
**Trailhead elevation:** 3,260 feet
**Highest point:** 3,538 feet
**Best season:** Year-round (in winter call the McCloud Ranger Station for road and trail conditions and closures)
**Trail surface:** Pavement and dirt
**Other trail users:** None

**Canine compatibility:** On leash
**Land status:** National Forest
**Fees and permits:** None
**Maps:** USGS Lake McCloud; USFS Shasta-Trinity National Forest
**Trail contacts:** Shasta-Trinity National Forest Ranger Station, McCloud Ranger Station, 2019 Forest Rd., McCloud 96057; (530) 964-2184
**Nearest town:** McCloud
**Trail tips:** There are two vault toilets, a faucet, and picnic tables at the trailhead. The trail is narrow, and segments of the trail as it climbs to the Upper Falls are precipitous, so keep your dog safe on leash.

**Finding the trailhead:** From the intersection of I-5 and CA 89 drive east 15.3 miles on CA 89 to Fowlers Camp and Lower Falls. Turn right at the sign for Fowlers Camp and Lower Falls and drive 1.3 miles to the Lower Falls day-use parking lot and picnic area. Walk to the Shasta-Trinity National Forest information board next to the bathroom at the east end of the parking lot and bear left on the paved path pointing upstream to Lower Falls. Walk down the stairs to the right of the picnic table and begin the hike following the paved path and signs for River Trail going to Middle Falls and Upper Falls. The river is on your right. **GPS:** N41 14.44' / W122 01.50'

## The Hike

The Okwanuchu people made the McCloud River home before European explorers and trappers, followed by settlers and lumber companies. One such trapper was a Scotsman named Alexander Roderick McLeod after whom the river was named. McLeod was exploring for the Canadian fur-trading company known as Hudson's Bay Company (HBC), which was originally founded following the successful seventeenth-century explorations of legendary French coureurs des bois Pierre-Esprit Radisson

*Middle Falls*

and Medard DesGroseilliers. By the 1820s the HBC was filtering into Northern California, and McLeod is said to have been hunting and trapping along the McLeod River between 1828 and 1830. At that time it was common for Americans to spell McLeod as "McCloud," and that is one theory on how the river's spelling changed to McCloud.

Land along the Upper McCloud River historically has been claimed by private ownership, at least since the arrival of Europeans. Lumber companies, private fishing camps, and more recently the Nature Conservancy hold large tracts of the land. In 1989 the US Forest Service entered a land-exchange agreement with the Champion International Corporation, a timber company. The exchange finally gave the Forest Service control of 13.0 miles of the Upper McCloud River corridor and 2,600 acres of land. Pretty McCloud Falls is a centerpiece to this rich and scenic outdoor recreational area.

The Upper McCloud River is part of the Southern Cascade Range drainage and the river is also a tributary to the Sacramento River, which feeds the ginormous Shasta Lake created by the dam of the same name downriver.

The national forest's acquisition is a boon for hikers, who now get to enjoy hiking these pretty falls that flow over lava bluffs lined with pine trees.

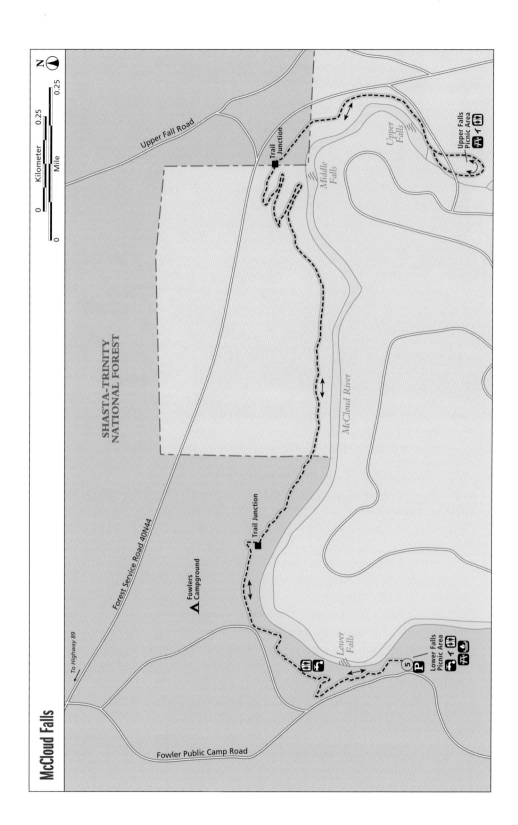

McCloud Falls

N

Kilometer
0   0.25
0   0.25
Mile

To Highway 89

Forest Service Road 40N44

SHASTA-TRINITY
NATIONAL FOREST

Upper Fall Road

Fowlers
Campground

Fowler Public Camp Road

Trail Junction

Trail Junction

Lower Falls

McCloud River

Middle Falls

Upper Falls

Lower Falls
Picnic Area

Upper Falls
Picnic Area

From the information board, the trail is pleasant and easy down the stairs with the river on your right. You enter nicely developed Fowlers Campground. Follow the trail along the river and stop by the interpretive signs that outline the history of the area from the days of the Wintu to the lumber-hyped days of the 1800s and the development of the Fowler Campground built by the Civilian Conservation Corp of Engineers in 1932.

At 0.6 mile you will leave the pavement and turn right toward Middle Falls, 0.5 mile up the trail. This is a popular photo stop with a close-up of the falls above. The trail continues uphill along switchbacks and thirty-two steps toward the Upper Falls.

The trail junction at 1.8 miles leads to a paved path and an overlook on the right. Continue walking along the bluff on River Trail and the Upper Falls Overlook is just 0.5 mile ahead. The falls plummet through a time-carved gorge, which makes this view of the falls the most dramatic. Continue walking to the end of the paved overlook spur along the river. The dirt trail continues southwest along the river. This is a good spot to find a log and sit and contemplate for a few minutes before reaching the Upper Falls picnic area on your left. Enjoy a snack break with your pooch and follow the path from the picnic area back to where it merges into the River Trail at 2.5 miles at the Upper Falls Overlook. Follow the trail back down the way you came and keep your eyes open for glimpses of Mount Shasta to the north.

## Miles and Directions

**0.0** Start at the Shasta-Trinity National Forest information board and McCloud Falls map. Bear left on the paved trail, walk 50 yards north to the right of the picnic table, and walk down the stairs to the river with Lower Falls ahead. Follow the paved path. The river will be on your right.

**0.3** Come to a trail sign that faces the opposite direction for Lower Falls. Enter the Fowler Campground. There is a pit toilet on your left in the campground. Continue walking on the paved path along the river.

**0.6** Come to a trail junction. Turn right on the dirt trail at the MIDDLE FALLS ½ MILE sign.

**1.4** Arrive at Middle Falls. Turn left and walk uphill toward Upper Falls. Walk up thirty-two steps at the top of the switchbacks.

**1.8** Come to a T-junction with a paved path to an overlook on your right. Continue walking along the bluff on the River Trail.

**2.1** Arrive at Upper Falls Overlook. Continue walking on the River Trail.

**2.3** Arrive at the Upper Falls picnic area. This is a lovely place to hang out with Pooch while you have a snack on the riverside. Follow the paved path loop back to the Upper Falls Overlook. Elevation 3,538 feet. **GPS:** N41 14.34' / W122 00.56'

**2.5** Merge back into the River Trail at the Upper Falls Overlook and continue back down to the trailhead the way you came. Keep your eye on the horizon for a glimpse of Mount Shasta through the trees.

**4.6** Arrive back at the trailhead.

*Looking down
at Upper Falls*

## Creature Comforts

*Fueling Up*

**McCloud Market,** 117 Broadway, McCloud 96057; (530) 964-2888.
**McCloud River Mercantile Hotel,** 241 Main St., McCloud 96057; (530) 964-2330; mccloudmercantile.com. You can order your food to go from the restaurant in the Historic McCloud Hotel and munch in the dog-friendly outdoor area with Fido.

*Resting Up*

**Fowler's Camp,** (530) 964-2184; www.fs.usda.gov/rearea/mccloud/fowlercampground. It is on the McCloud River and steps away from the McCloud Falls Trail. This is a nicely developed Forest Service campground with RV (no hookups) and tent sites.
**McCloud River Mercantile Hotel,** 241 Main St., McCloud 96057; (530) 964-2330; mccloudmercantile.com. This hotel has pooch-friendly rooms.

# 6  Bailey Cove

This is a short, easy flat loop in a woodland area with views toward the steep mountainous terrain across the lake. This is a chance for you and Pooch to sample Shasta Lake, California's largest reservoir and the third-largest body of water after Lake Tahoe and the Salton Sea.

**Start:** From the Bailey Cove day-use parking area
**Distance:** 2.8-mile loop
**Approximate hiking time:** 1.5 hours
**Difficulty:** Easy
**Trailhead elevation:** 1,130 feet
**Highest point:** 1,160 feet
**Best season:** Year-round
**Trail surface:** Dirt
**Other trail users:** None
**Canine compatibility:** On leash
**Land status:** National Forest

**Fees and permits:** Day-use pay station, $6
**Maps:** USGS O'Brien; USFS Shasta-Trinity National Forest
**Trail contacts:** Shasta-Trinity National Forest, Shasta Lake Ranger Station, 14225 Holiday Rd., Redding 96003; (530) 275-1587
**Nearest Town:** Redding
**Trail Tips:** Bailey Cove is the closest campground, and Holiday Harbor, just down the road, has a general store for supplies. There is a vault toilet, picnic tables, and a boat ramp at Bailey Cove.

**Finding the trailhead:** From Redding drive 18.0 miles north on I-5 and take the O'Brien and Shasta Cavern exit (exit 695). Drive 0.5 mile on Shasta Cave Road to the Bailey Cove National Recreation Site sign on your right. Turn right on Bailey Cove and drive 0.7 mile to the trailhead parking lot. The trailhead is to the left of the parking lot, just past the vault toilet. **GPS:** N40 47.96' / W122 18.94'

## The Hike

Shasta Dam on the Sacramento River is the second-largest dam in the United States. It took ten years to build (1935–1945), and Shasta Lake was formed in 1948.

Although the dam was built to provide electricity, irrigation, and flood control, Shasta Lake, one of four lakes that make up the Shasta-Trinity National Recreation Area, is best known for water sports and marinas with houseboat rentals.

Bailey Cove, on the McCloud arm of the lake at the southern end off of I-5, features the less than 3.0-mile-long Bailey Cove Trail. This trail is just a speck of Shasta-Trinity National Forest land on 35.0-mile-long Shasta Lake. The full reservoir boasts 365 miles of shoreline.

Some of the best and most scenic hikes here are accessed by boat only. Fortunately Bailey Cove is conveniently and easily accessed from I-5, and this flat, easy trail is a perfect Shasta Lake sampler. The I-5 drone on the west side of the cove can be distracting, but the granite peak views across the McCloud arm on the first half of the

# Bailey Cove Trail

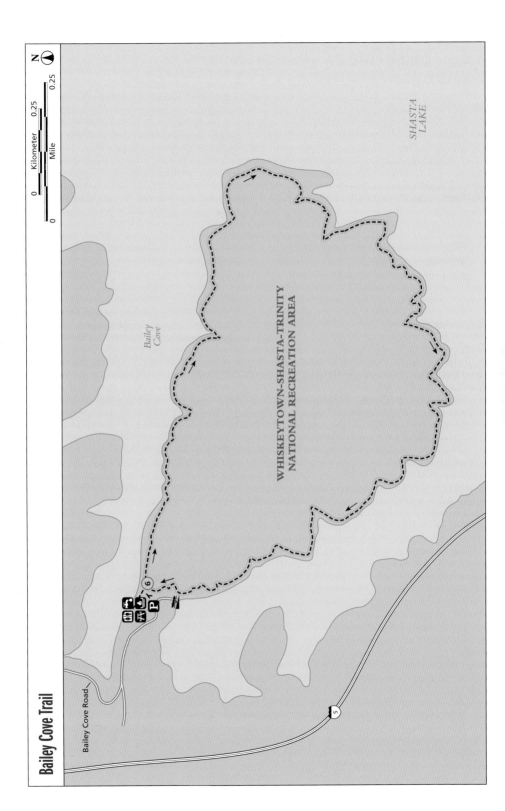

*View of granite peaks in Shasta-Trinity National Forest*

hike before rounding the cove make you feel like you are deep in the wilderness, even with houseboats bobbing offshore.

The lake is fed by the dammed Sacramento River and its tributaries, which depend on rain and winter snowpack. Shasta Lake can be as supernaturally scenic as it can be starkly soulless during a dry spell. When the lake is low, unnatural and steeply terraced dirt shores are exposed. Fortunately the forested slopes and limestone peaks across McCloud Arm seen through a filter of golden sunsets from the Bailey Cove Trail can make you forgive some of the unattractiveness unveiled in drought years.

The hike itself is straightforward to and from the parking area. The tree-shaded picnic tables make a pleasant spot for you and Pooch to snack and rehydrate after the hike.

## Miles and Directions

**0.0** Start at the Bailey Cove trailhead east of the parking lot across from the picnic area and follow the loop trail as it traces the shoreline 50 feet above the water around this shady woodland that rises up almost like an island.

**2.8** Arrive back at the trailhead.

*The water level of Shasta Lake drops during summer.*

## Creature Comforts

*Fueling Up and Resting Up*

**Holiday Harbor Resort,** 20061 Shasta Cavern Rd., O'Brien, 96070; (800) 776-2628; lakeshasta.com. This resort has a tent and RV campground, a restaurant, a general store, and houseboat rentals.

# 7 Lake Eiler

The dirt road to Tamarack trailhead is bumpy in sections but accessible by average vehicles. The relatively flat trail begins in a moonscape volcanic setting before transitioning to forest. It's an easy hike past a few unnamed shallow lakes, and Eiler Lake at the end of the trail is a pleasant surprise perfect for a picnic lunch and dog paddle.

**Start:** From Tamarack trailhead parking lot in the Thousand Lakes Wilderness (trailhead sign may be missing, but there are trailhead posts and a fire permit sign)
**Distance:** 5.4 miles out and back
**Approximate hiking time:** 2.5 hours
**Difficulty:** Easy
**Trailhead elevation:** 5,914 feet
**Highest point:** 6,455 feet
**Best season:** Early summer to late fall
**Trail surface:** Dirt trail with lava gravel and lava rock. Booties are advisable over the lava stretches.
**Other trail users:** Horses
**Canine compatibility:** Voice control
**Land status:** National Forest; Wilderness

**Fees and permits:** Campfire permit
**Maps:** USGS Thousand Lakes Valley; USFS Lassen National Forest; Thousand Lakes Wilderness
**Trail contacts:** Lassen National Forest Hat Creek Ranger District, 43225 E. CA 299, Fall River Mills 96028; (530) 336-5521; www.fs.usda.gov/lassen. There is another ranger station at the intersection of CA 89 and CA 44 in Old Station, but all calls are fielded through the Hat Creek Ranger District.
**Nearest town:** Old Station
**Trail tips:** The last stretch of the road going into the parking lot and trailhead have been relocated and is different than what is shown on the USGS map.

**Finding the trailhead:** From Old Station on CA 89, drive 7.5 miles north and turn left on an unmarked gravel road just past Wilcox Road on your right. This road can be bumpy with some rocky potholes. There is a sign for Thousand Lakes Wilderness and Tamarack trailhead just off the highway. Drive 9.0 miles to the Tamarack trailhead parking lot following the signs for Thousand Lakes Wilderness and Tamarack trailhead. The Tamarack trailhead parking lot sits in a volcanic rock bowl. **GPS:** N40 42.63' / W121 31.98'

## The Hike

The 16,000-acre Thousand Lakes Wilderness was established in 1964 through the Wilderness Act and is within Lassen National Forest. This wilderness area sits in the southern portion of the Cascade Range. The topography of the wilderness, like much of northeastern California, is a result of volcanic and glacial activity. Crater Peak (8,677 feet) is the highest point in the Lassen National Forest, and the base of the volcano is the lowest point in the wilderness (5,546 feet). The small lakes and ponds scattered in the area were created by erosion of the original Thousand Lakes Volcano. Thousand Lakes is an overstatement of the number of lakes, but Lake Eiler, named after Lu Eiler who discovered the Thousand Lakes Valley, is the largest of the seven major lakes in the wilderness.

Trout thrive in all the lakes, and the wilderness is also home to deer, black bears, pikas, and spotted owls, among other species of wildlife.

The proximity to Mount Lassen Volcanic National Park, where dogs are not allowed on trails, makes the Lake Eiler Trail in the Thousand Lakes Wilderness a unique opportunity for hikers with dogs to experience hiking on volcanic terrain.

If you had any doubt about the geology of the region, the volcanic rock surrounding the trailhead parking lot will convince you otherwise. There are no signs at the trailhead, just a couple of posts that have been stripped of the signs. It not unusual to encounter a crew of Forest Service fire fighters doing trail maintenance in the area as part of their "legacy" trail work when not called on forest fire duty.

The trail begins on a narrow barren stretch of volcanic rubble lined with shrubs, pale pink manzanita blooms, and yellow mule ear. The

*Trail to Lake Eiler marked by orange blaze*

landscape soon transitions to stands of pine, cedar, and fir. At 2.0 miles, early in the season, you can catch views of snowy crests. The waters of Lake Eiler ripple less than 1.0 mile ahead, where you can stroll along the shoreline before turning back to the trailhead the way you came.

## Miles and Directions

**0.0** Start at the Tamarack trailhead, which may be unmarked except for posts and a fire permit sign.

**2.2** Come to a fork on the trail for Barret Lake and Lake Eiler. Bear right to Lake Eiler, going west.

**2.7** Arrive at Lake Eiler and a T junction. Elevation 6,455 feet. **GPS**: N40 43.53' / W121 34.02' The trail continues along the lake for a short distance on the right and continues along the shore to the left, with the possibility of a loop route back to the trailhead via Barret Lake if the trail has been cleared of fallen trees beyond Lake Eiler. There is a clearing with a couple of perfect logs to sit on and have a picnic while Pooch enjoys a paddle if he is not mesmerized by the frequent jumping of trout in the lake. Go back to the trailhead the way you came.

**5.4** Arrive back at the trailhead.

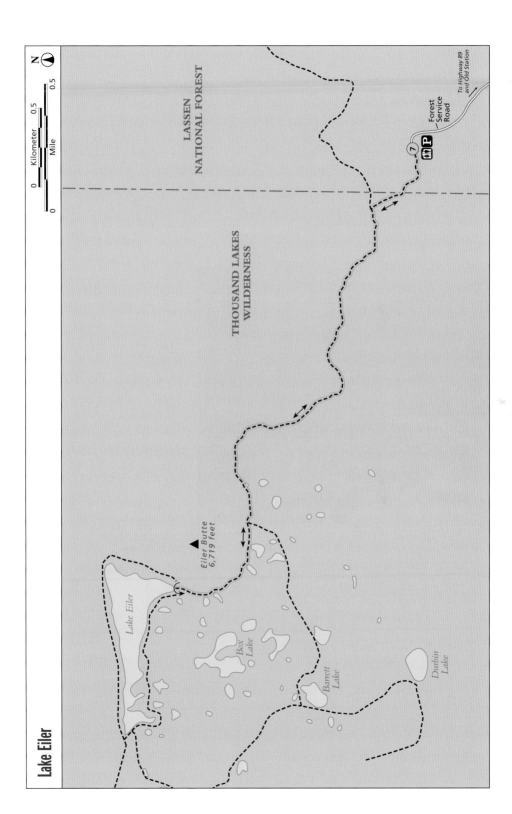

# Lake Eiler

N

| 0 | Kilometer | 0.5 |
| 0 | Mile | 0.5 |

LASSEN
NATIONAL FOREST

THOUSAND LAKES
WILDERNESS

Eiler Butte
6,719 feet

Lake Eiler

Box
Lake

Barrett
Lake

Durbin
Lake

Forest
Service
Road

To Highway 89
and Old Station

*Fueling Up and Resting Up*

**Rancheria RV Park,** 15565 Black Angus Lane, Hat Creek 96040, off CA 89 in the Hat Creek Valley on the way to Thousand Lakes Wilderness; (530) 335-7418; rancheria rvpark.com. This RV park is convenient and attractively set in the Lassen National Forest with its own fishing pond where Pooch can watch fish jump and ducks paddle. There are tent and RV sites as well as dog-friendly cabins. Showers, laundry, and Wi-Fi will remind you of the creature comforts you left at home. The general store has supplies, and you can get take-out orders to sit and eat with Pooch at the picnic table.

**Hat Creek Resort and RV Park,** 12533 CA-44, Old Station 96071; (530) 335-7121; hatcreekresortrv.com. This park has dog-friendly hotel rooms, cabins, and yurts, as

well as a campground. If you've suffered from "connection" deprivation, the resort has Wi-Fi and cable TV. The store and snack bar are convenient, and the location on the forested banks of Hat Creek in the Lassen National Forest begs for you and Pooch to enjoy morning and evening strolls between hikes. There is a segment of the Pacific Crest Trail that runs along the campground that offers a rare chance to walk or bike a segment of the Pacific Crest Trail at lower elevation with your dog.

*Soaking up the view across Lake Eiler*

## Puppy Paws and Golden Years

The creek-side trail in **Hat Creek RV Resort** is a level, narrow, rambling trail that gives dogs with limited stamina a gentle nature experience.

# Basin Ranges

The Basin Ranges occupy the eastern portion of California, separated into two sections, north and south, by the Sierra Nevada at Lake Tahoe. The primary mountain range in the northern section is the Warner Range. It is a volcanic base 60.0 miles long and 20.0 miles wide, with rugged landscape that rises at 25 degrees from west to east and drops off sharply on the eastern side. Within the range is the relatively small South Warner Wilderness, a primitive area of spectacular beauty consisting of pine forests, grassy meadows, and meandering streams. Elevations climb from 4,800 feet to 9,892 feet at Eagle Peak.

Pine, juniper, fir, and aspen alternate with sagebrush and meandering streams and meadows.

Mountain lions, deer, bobcats, coyotes, and beaver populate the area. With no large urban population in the surrounding area, the Warner Range remains lightly trampled and under the radar of most hikers.

# 8 Pine Creek Trail

This is a lightly trampled trail in a small accessible wilderness area in an isolated corner of the state. The canyon trail passes through the forest alongside creeks and shallow unnamed lakes and emerges in a basin laced with ribbons of water that nourishes corn lilies and wild tulips before heading up a steep slope of volcanic rubble. Once through the aspen grove, the trail takes you to the intersection with Summit Trail for unexpected panoramic views, including the white-draped Mount Lassen and Mount Shasta. The beauty of this hike is that the lakes or the basin itself make excellent and rewarding shorter, easier destinations that both you and your dog will relish.

**Start:** From the Pine Creek trailhead parking lot in the South Warner Mountains

**Distance:** 10.3 miles out and back

**Approximate hiking time:** 6 hours

**Difficulty:** Strenuous because of altitude, if you choose to hike all the way to the Summit Trail junction

**Trailhead elevation:** 6,800 feet

**Highest point:** 8,965 feet

**Best season:** Summer to early fall

**Trail surface:** Dirt trail and volcanic rubble

**Other trail users:** Horses

**Canine compatibility:** Voice control

**Land status:** National Forest; Wilderness

**Fees and permits:** Campfire permit

**Maps:** USGS Eagle Peak and Soup Creek; USFS Modoc National Forest; South Warner Wilderness

**Trail contacts:** Modoc National Forest, Warner Mountain Ranger District, 710 Townsend St., Cedarville 96104; (530) 279-6116; www.fs.usda.gov/modoc

**Nearest town:** Alturas

**Trail tips:** Access to the trail is subject to winter snow levels. The basin will be accessible earlier, but you may have to cross snow patches and snow fields to the Summit Trail junction, which can make this last steep stretch of the hike unreasonably arduous for your dog. Take frequent water breaks, as the dry air and altitude will dehydrate you quickly. Take rest stops and offer your dog water.

**Finding the trailhead:** From US 395 in Likely, 19.0 miles south of Alturas, drive 9.3 miles east on Jess Valley Road to a sign for Mill Creek Falls. Bear left toward Mill Creek Falls and drive 2.5 miles to the end of the paved road and start on the gravel road. Drive 6.5 miles on the gravel road and turn right at the sign for Pine Creek trailhead. Drive 1.5 miles to the parking lot at the end of the road. The trailhead is at the far end of the parking lot, next to the information board and metal registration box. **GPS:** N41 21.51' / W120 17.05'

## The Hike

The South Warner Wilderness is at the south end of the Warner Mountains in the north easternmost corner of California in Modoc County, the most sparsely populated county in California. Alturas, with a population of under 3,000 people, is the county seat and only 12.0 miles from the South Warner Wilderness. It's the region's

*Pine Creek Meadow and Warner Mountains in the distance*

remoteness—not the lack of natural beauty and outdoor recreation opportunities—
that makes this wilderness area one of the most lightly visited.

The area was designated a primitive area in 1931 and upgraded to a wilderness
in 1964. California's Wilderness Act of 1984 later added more acreage, which makes
the South Warner Wilderness a 70,000-acre oasis of towering cliffs, stream-fed swales
with forested slopes to the west in contrast to the steeper volcanic escarpments to the
east. The Warner Wilderness is laced with 80 miles of trails, with five trailheads and
five campgrounds surrounding the area.

Hikers share this wilderness with deer, mountain lions, beaver, and coyotes. Bird-
ers will be excited to realize that the wilderness is on the Pacific Flyway, while those
with a strong interest in wild canids and wolf-population recovery will be happy to
know that there have been reports of wolf sightings in the Warners.

This hike makes for a lovely day jaunt. It begins along the south fork of Pine
Creek and heads up the forested slopes of pine and fir past a couple of small lakes
before the opening up to the scenic Pine Creek Basin at 3.0 miles. The meadow will
enchant you with its backdrop of cliffs and crests and delight your dog with a clearing
that invites her to run circles and leap across the streams. The lake on the left below
the basin is another splendid destination if you want to skip the next 2.0 miles of huff
and puff coming up.

# Pine Creek Trail

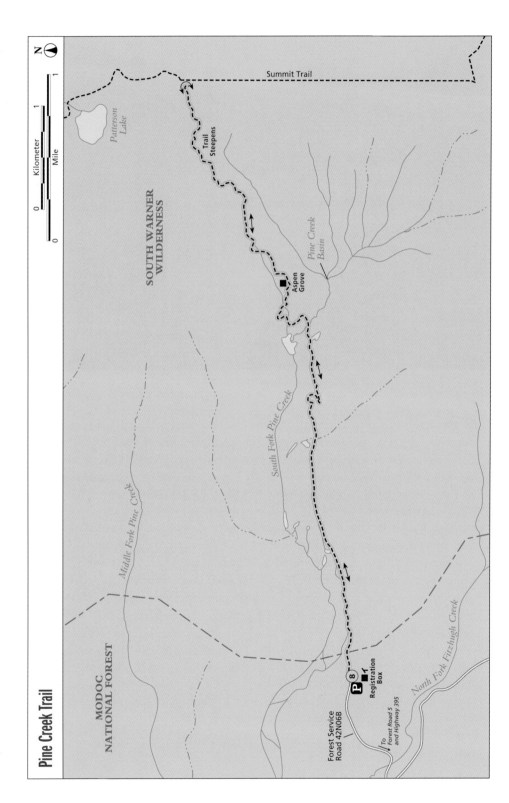

MODOC
NATIONAL FOREST

SOUTH WARNER
WILDERNESS

Patterson
Lake

Summit Trail

Trail
Steepens

Aspen
Grove

Pine Creek
Basin

Middle Fork Pine Creek

South Fork Pine Creek

Forest Service
Road 42N06B

P 8

Registration
Box

To
Forest Road 5
and Highway 395

North Fork Fitzhugh Creek

Kilometer

Mile

N

Up ahead, an aspen grove separates the basin's lushness of mountain tulips and corn lilies from the steep pine-dotted alley between the volcanic escarpment and the rock fall. The purple flowers that peer up unusually from below their leaves are woolen breeches.

At 5.0 miles your efforts are rewarded with the Summit Trail junction and the expansive panorama east over Surprise Valley and the Great Basin and south to Eagle Peak (9,892 feet). Standing on the ridge looking eastward, it is as if a curtain has been lifted to reveal a different world. The contrast between the lusher western slopes of the South Warner Wilderness and the high desert plains below the eastern escarpment is dramatic and spectacular.

After resting, drinking, snacking, and snapping a few photos, go back the way you came and prepare to be astonished by the views of Mounts Lassen and Shasta to the west as you come down to the basin.

## Miles and Directions

**0.0**  Start at the Pine Creek Trail trailhead.

**0.4**  Enter the South Warner Wilderness.

**0.9**  Come to a pond and meadow as you begin your climb out of the bowl.

**1.5**  Come to a lake below the trail on the left. Views toward the mountains open up above the forest canopy.

**2.5**  Come to an unnamed lake on the right. The trail skirts the lake on the left.

**3.0**  Arrive at Pine Creek Basin and the meadow laced with ribbons of water. Keep your eyes open for a low pile of rocks on both sides of South Fork Pine Creek that mark the area where you cross the creek to continue on the narrow faint trail on the other side. This is an excellent scenic destination for you and a tail-wagging playground for your dog.

**3.2**  You see a lake below the trail on the left. This is another alternate destination to the Summit Trail junction or side trip on the return down, depending on available time and your and your dog's energy.

**3.5**  Come to an aspen grove. The trail can be moist and muddy from runoff.

**4.5**  The trail steepens significantly as it climbs up the forested slope between a volcanic escarpment on the left and a boulder fall on the right.

**5.15** Come to the trail junction for the Pine Creek Trail Basin and Summit Trail. Elevation 8,965 feet. **GPS:** N41 22.42' / W120 12.96' Take time to catch your breath and rest your dog while you enjoy the views from this unique perch. Feed your dog a protein snack to boost his energy for the return trip. The sight of Mount Lassen southwest and Shasta northwest towering in the distance is worth the haul to the Summit Trail junction. Head back to the trailhead the way you came.

**10.3** Arrive back at the trailhead.

## Creature Comforts

*Fueling Up*

**Munch Box,** US 395 North, Alturas 96101; (530) 233-2426. Open for lunch and dinner with outdoor tables to dine with Fido.

*Junction of Pine Creek Trail and Summit Trail*

## Resting Up

**Best Western Trailside Inn,** 343 N. Main St., Alturas 96101 (530) 233-4111.

**Likely Place Golf and RV Resort,** 1255 Likely Place, Alturas 96101; on Jess Valley Road off US 395; (530) 233-4466; likelyplace.com. An RV and golf resort seems like an "unlikely" place for hikers with dogs to park themselves. But if you are car camping or traveling in any kind of recreational vehicle, this RV park is one of the most bucolic settings for camping we came across in Northern California. It is a convenient dust-free basecamp for South Warner Wilderness wanderings. The golf course cafe is a bonus.

**Soup Spring Campground** (Forest Service), off Jess Valley Road. The campground has vault toilets, water, picnic tables, and fire rings. **Mill Creek Campground** (Forest Service), off Jess Valley Road. This campground has vault toilets, water, picnic tables, and fire rings. Visit www.fs.usda.gov/recarea/south warner wilderness.

# North Coast Ranges

The North Coast Ranges overlap the southern end of the Klamath Ranges and extend southward along the western edge of California, paralleling the Pacific Coast down to San Francisco Bay. The Central Valley traces the eastern slopes.

The North Coast Ranges include the King Range, Mayacamas Mountains, South Fork Mountains, and South Yolla Bolly Mountains. The mountains rise sharply on the west side, from sea level to 4,000 to 6,000 feet, to over 8,000 feet in the South Yolla Bolly Mountains. Unlike the Sierra Nevada, these ranges taper off more gently on their eastern slopes.

These ranges showcase several national forests and wilderness areas, including the Six Rivers and Mendocino National Forests, Snow Mountain, and Cache Creek Wilderness.

The highest peak, South Yolla Bolly Mountain, is 8,092 feet. Other peaks include Black Butte at 7,448 feet, Snow Mountain at 7,056 feet, and Mount Sanhedrin at 6,175 feet.

The peaks step down, and annual rainfall decreases from 40 to 80 inches as the ranges trail off southward toward the Golden Gate National Recreation Area and San Francisco Bay.

Carpets of fern and lichen crawl under the canopy of coastal redwoods, the tallest trees on Earth. A few miles inland, the dryer climate supports Douglas fir, oak, madrone, and laurel trees.

The North Coast Ranges are great habitat for mule deer and ground squirrels.

# 9 Elk River Trail

This lush, green, and gentle educational trail with historical and cultural interpretive signs along a narrow peaceful stretch of the Elk River is accessible to disabled visitors along the first paved mile and transitions to dirt for the last 2.0 miles. The voice control option is a boon for hikers with responsive dogs.

**Start:** From the Headwaters Forest Reserve trailhead in the parking lot off of Elk River Road
**Distance:** 6.7 miles out and back
**Approximate hiking time:** 2.5 hours
**Difficulty:** Easy
**Trailhead elevation:** 70 feet
**Highest point:** 286 feet
**Best season:** Year-round
**Trail surface:** Dirt and redwood needles
**Other trail users:** Mountain bikes
**Canine compatibility:** Voice control
**Land status:** BLM
**Fees and permits:** None
**Maps:** USGS McWhinney Creek; BLM Headwaters Reserve Map
**Trail contacts:** Bureau of Land Management Arcata Field Office, 1695 Heindon Rd., Arcata

95521; (707) 825-2300; www.blm.gov/ca/arcarta. California Department of Fish and Wildlife, 619 Second St., Eureka, 95501; (707) 445-6493; www.fws.gov/arcata.
**Nearest town:** Eureka
**Trail tips:** Although obedient dogs can be off leash, dogs are not permitted in the river, as it is a spawning ground for fish. The first mile of the trail is paved and ADA accessible. There is a vault toilet, trash and recycling containers, an information kiosk with maps, and a picnic table at the trailhead. There is also a dog waste bag dispenser close to the beginning of the trail and benches along the first ADA-accessible mile.

**Finding the trailhead:** From the intersection of US 101 and Elk River Road in Eureka, take the Elk River Road exit and follow the signs to Headwaters Forest Reserve going east. Turn right at the sign for Elk River Road and Headwaters Forest Reserve. Drive 1.5 miles and turn right on Elk River Road. This is an enchanting country road with a bucolic landscape, complete with a couple of covered bridges on the right and wildflower meadows surrounded by dense forest. Drive 3.2 miles and turn right across a one-lane bridge. Drive 0.08 mile to the end of the road and into the Headwaters Forest Reserve parking lot. **GPS:** N40 41.52'/W124 08.44'

## The Hike

The Headwaters Forest Reserve is over 7,000 acres previously under private ownership. In 1999 Humboldt County acquired the land, and the Bureau of Land Management (BLM) manages it for public access. A Resource Management Plan was completed in 2004 to "conserve and study the land, fish, wildlife and forests . . . while providing public recreation opportunities and other management needs." The reserve protects old-growth redwood and Douglas firs while providing layers of habitat, including safe havens for endangered species such as the northern spotted owl and the marbled murrelet, a seabird that thrives in dense canopied forests. Chinook and

*Dense vegetation along a historic trail*

coho salmon and steelhead trout are protected in the streams, and there is no fishing in the reserve.

The old mill town of Falk, founded in 1884 by Noah Falk, once bustled along the Elk River. By 1937 it was abandoned, but the Elk River Trail passes by the ghost town site. You can get a glimpse of what was with the help of the Quest paper map that is sometimes available at the trailhead. The map identifies ten stops over the first mile that blend ecological and cultural education with clues of the past visible to the observant hiker.

Trail use is restricted to hikers and cyclists, but dogs and bikes are allowed on the first 3.0 miles of the 5.5-mile trail.

The trail begins by the information boards in the parking lot and is a straightforward journey to the bridge and the gate that marks the end of the dog-friendly stretch.

At 0.4 mile you see a dirt spur on the right. This is a short side trip option to a few reminders of the abandoned mill town. The spur rejoins the main trail in about 0.2 mile. You can take this short shady spur on the way back for variety. Most of the buildings were bulldozed in the 1970s, but the old locomotive house was moved along the Elk River Trail in 2008, and the train barn is now the Headwaters Education Center, which you see on your left at 0.6 mile.

# Elk River Trail

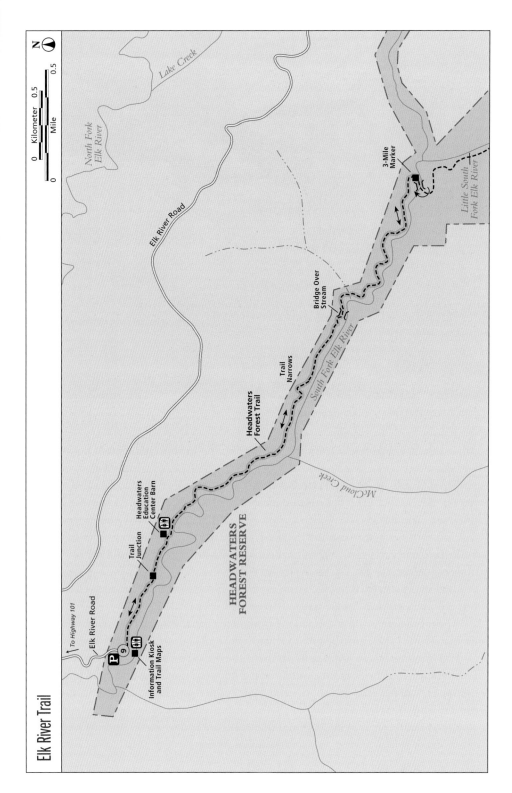

The trail narrows and bears left at 1.8 miles, where it runs above the river gulch. You cross a bridge at 2.4 miles and come to a trail mile marker for 3.0 miles, where you will hear the water. The trail bends and goes down to another bridge. The end of your trail is just across the bridge at the No Dogs and No Bikes sign. Although there are still a couple more miles of trail on the south shore of the Elk River, this is as far as Pooch is allowed to go.

## Miles and Directions

**0.0**   Start at the trailhead in the Headwaters Forest Reserve.

**0.4**   Come to a fork with a spur trail going right. Continue on the paved trail, or you may follow this 200-yard-long path past a river overlook before it rejoins the paved trail.

**0.6**   Arrive at the Headwaters Education Center and a bathroom.

**1.8**   Trail narrows and bears left above the river gulch.

**2.4**   Cross a bridge.

**3.3**   Arrive at mile marker 3.0. Continue downhill on the trail.

**3.35** Arrive at the bridge with the No Bicycles and No Dogs sign on the other side of the bridge. Turn around and go back the way you came. Elevation 223 feet. **GPS:** N40 40.41' / W124 05.99'

**6.7**   Arrive back at the trailhead

# PROTECTING THE REDWOOD EMPIRE

The Redwoods National and State Park partnership, formed in 1994, protects the narrow 450-mile stretch of redwood coastland from Southern Oregon to south of Big Sur. The agencies' alliance also protects 40 miles of coastline north of Eureka to Crescent City and 45 percent of the remaining coastal redwood forests, the tallest tree species on Earth, along with numerous prehistoric sites. The Redwoods National Park System was designated a World Heritage Site in 1980 and a Biosphere Reserve in 1983. Although this is not the most dog-compatible park system, it is nevertheless an ecological and cultural treasure. The Kuchel Visitor Center, north of Eureka at Orick on US 101, is a fabulous visitor center with a pet-friendly picnic area. Dogs are allowed on the Cal-Barrel Road Trail off the B. Drury Scenic Parkway (parallels US 101 and shows off old-growth groves), north of the Kuchel Visitor Center. Crescent Beach, just south of Crescent City, is also a friend to dogs on leash. For more information on dog-friendly trails within the Redwood National Park Biosphere Reserve, go to www.nps.gov/redw/planyourvisit/pets.htm.

*The bridge at the turnaround point*

## Creature Comforts

*Fueling Up*

**North Coast Co-op,** 25 Fourth St., Eureka 95501; (707) 443-6027. Buy food supplies from a Whole Foods–style market that supports locally grown and sustainable food products.

*Resting Up*

**Carter House Inns,** 301 L St., Eureka 95501; (707) 444-8062; carterhouse.com. This is a luxury B&B in a historic mansion.

# 10 Punta Gorda Lighthouse

This hike meanders along sand dunes and on a beach to a decommissioned lighthouse. This is the north end of the Lost Coast Trail and King Range.

**Start:** From the Mattole Campground
**Distance:** 6.7 miles out and back
**Approximate hiking time:** 4 hours
**Difficulty:** Easy
**Trailhead elevation:** 10 feet
**Highest point:** 68 feet
**Best season:** Year-round, but seasonal creeks can be full following heavy winter rainfall
**Trail surface:** Soft and hard-packed sand
**Other trail users:** Horses
**Canine compatibility:** Voice control
**Land status:** BLM
**Fees and permits:** Free permits for one or more overnights on the Lost Coast Trail and backcountry; permit also serves as a California campfire permit
**Maps:** USGS Petrolia and Cooskie Creek; BLM King Range
**Trail contacts:** BLM King Range Project Office, 768 Shelter Cove Rd., Whitehorn 95589; (707) 986-5400; www.ca.blm.gov/arcata
**Nearest town:** Ferndale
**Trail tips:** There is a vault toilet at the trailhead and water in the campground. This stretch of coast can whip up some strong winds from the north in the afternoon, and the fine sand can sting hikers' bare legs. Carry a pair of wind pants in your pack.

**Finding the trailhead:** From Garberville on Hwy 101 north, drive 25.0 miles and take exit 663 to South Fork and Honeydew. Make a left at the T intersection and drive under the freeway. In 0.2 mile make a sharp left and follow the signs for Honeydew (this road is Mattole Road). Drive 22.0 miles and cross a bridge over the Mattole River. Make a right turn at the T intersection toward Mattole River Mouth. Drive 13.4 miles and make a left onto Lighthouse Road. Drive 0.5 mile to the Mattole Campground. The trailhead to the lighthouse is at the southwest end of the parking lot, just past campsite number 15. (If you are coming from the north, drive 34.0 miles south on Mattole Road to Lighthouse Road and turn right to the trailhead.) **GPS:** N40 17.34' / W124 21.36'

## The Hike

Punta Gorda was first operated as a fog station in 1888. The lighthouse was built in 1911 and lit in 1912. The remote and challenging location of the two-story concrete Punta Gorda Lighthouse earned it the nickname "Alcatraz of Lighthouses." Assignment to Punta Gorda was considered more banishment and punishment than promotion or reward. The original compound consisted of three dwellings and several support outbuildings on 22 acres. The Coast Guard took charge of the lighthouse during World War II, and it was decommissioned in 1951, when a more cost-effective lighted buoy was placed offshore. The property was transferred to the Bureau of Land Management in 1963. By the late 1960s, at the height of "flower power," unauthorized occupants of the buildings were evicted by local law enforcement and the BLM

*Historic Punta Gorda Lighthouse at the turnaround point*

burned all the buildings except for the lighthouse and oil house. Punta Gorda was placed on the National Register of Historic Places in 1976. The Fresnel lens and flagstaff pole can be seen in Eureka's Humboldt Bay Maritime Museum.

Today the isolated lighthouse is a scenic hike at the northern end of the wild and untamed King Range National Conservation Area across the windswept beach and grassy slopes south of the Mattole River mouth.

This hike is a straightforward trek that begins on the beach at the end of the Mattole Campground and parallels the surf. You walk south along the beach and/ or weave up and down along the grassy bluff a few feet above the beach. You cross at least four seasonal streams along the way. The stream at 1.3 miles has created a lush corridor of vegetation that bursts with colorful blooms in the spring.

A little over 1.0 mile farther along the trail you come to a couple of weather-lashed wooden cabins and a robust Fourmile Creek, which requires some ankle

*Spring wildflowers along trail*

wading at best in the summer and fall but may be impassible during a stormy winter or in early spring. If the creek is low enough to wade but fast, play it safe and leash your dog.

The lighthouse awaits less than 1.0 mile up the beach. There is a certain romance to lighthouses, and Punta Gorda's rugged isolation is no exception. Take time to soak up the vibes of history and enjoy a snack in the solitude of Northern California's Pacific Coast before going back the way you came.

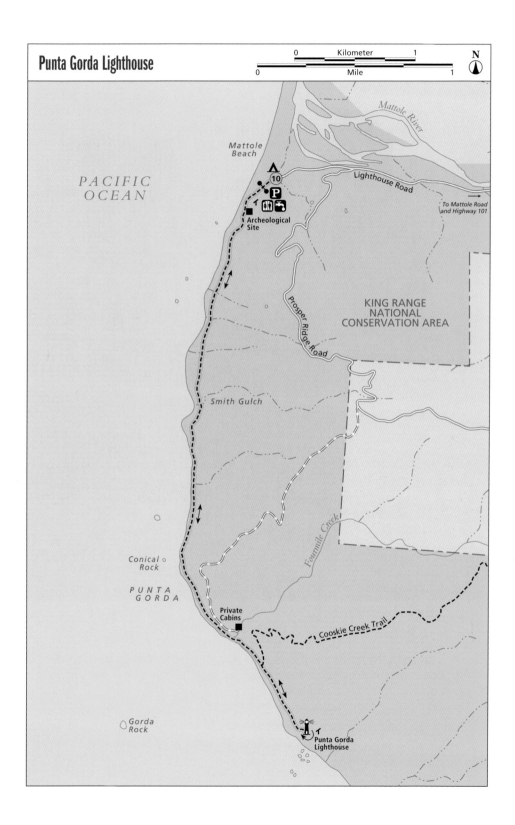

# Punta Gorda Lighthouse

PACIFIC
OCEAN

Mattole River

Mattole
Beach

Lighthouse Road

To Mattole Road
and Highway 101

Archeological
Site

Prosper Ridge Road

KING RANGE
NATIONAL
CONSERVATION AREA

Smith Gulch

Fourmile Creek

Conical
Rock

PUNTA
GORDA

Private
Cabins

Cooskie Creek Trail

Gorda
Rock

Punta Gorda
Lighthouse

N

0 — Kilometer — 1
0 — Mile — 1

## Miles and Directions

**0.0** Start at the southwest end of the Mattole Campground by the information kiosk and walk around the gate. Bear left on the beach path and follow the fence line on your left.

**0.2** Come to a fenced archaeological area with a faded interpretive sign about Mattole Indians and a midden of seashells. You can walk on the beach the entire stretch or alternate between the beach and sections of a parallel bluff trail just a few feet above the beach.

**0.7** Cross a seasonal stream.

**0.8** Cross another seasonal stream.

**1.0** Cross a third seasonal stream.

**1.3** Come to a seasonal stream feeding a lush corridor at the base of the hill.

**2.6** Arrive at two weathered cabins on private property and Fourmile Creek. You may need to wade across Fourmile Creek to continue along the beach depending on the time of year and rainfall. This is a great spot for your dog to splash in the fresh water and safer than the surf, which can be very rough along this coast.

**3.0** Cooskie Creek Trail goes up the slope on your left.

**3.35** Arrive at the Punta Gorda Lighthouse, oil storage house, and interpretive sign about the history of the lighthouse and what life was like for the Punta Gorda's light keeper. Enjoy a snack and water break before retracing your steps back to the trailhead. **GPS:** N40 14.96' / W124 21.01'

**6.7** Arrive back at trailhead.

## Creature Comforts

### Resting Up

**Mattole Campground,** www.blm.gov/ca/st/en/fo/arcata/kingrange/campground.html. The RV (no hookups) and tent sites managed by the Bureau of Land Management are minimally developed but conveniently located at the trailhead for the Punta Gorda Lighthouse.

**The Shaw House Inn,** 703 Main St., Ferndale 95536; (707) 786-9958; shawhouse.com.

### Puppy Paws and Golden Years

**Ferndale** is a California Historical Landmark. Strolling the streets of this Victorian village can be a pleasant excursion to share with Pooch on the way to or from your hike.

# 11  Pickett Peak Trail

This hike follows a lightly used trail up to a forested summit in the Six Rivers National Forest system and climbs 2,500 feet in 3.0 miles. Although there are no spectacular summit views as a prize for the exertion, the first mile offers views of pretty Ruth Lake through the trees. There are three things that make this uphill trail worth your and your dog's time: It is easily accessible from a paved road, it starts across from an attractive Forest Service lakeshore campground, and it has historic significance. As an extra perk, you get to hike a trail that is so new in the trail system you will feel like an explorer yourself.

**Start:** From the Forest Service trailhead across the road from Bailey Canyon Campground
**Distance:** 6.0 miles out and back
**Approximate hiking time:** 3 hours
**Difficulty:** Strenuous because of the steady uphill
**Trailhead elevation:** 2,806 feet
**Highest point:** 5,455 feet
**Best season:** Year-round; spring is loveliest, summer is hot; check on snow elevations in winter
**Trail surface:** Dirt trail with pine needles and dried foliage
**Other trail users:** Horses
**Canine compatibility:** Voice control

**Land status:** National Forest
**Fees and permits:** None
**Maps:** USGS Ruth Lake; Six Rivers National Forest
**Trail contacts:** Six Rivers National Forest, Mad River Ranger Station, 741 CA 36, Bridgeville, 95526; (707) 574-6233
**Nearest town:** Fortuna
**Trail tips:** This lightly used trail is more difficult to follow on the way down because of the stretches that are camouflaged by fallen oak leaves. It would be helpful for you to make mental notes of bends or oddly shaped trees to keep your sights on the trail on the way down.

**Finding the trailhead:** From Mad River on CA 36, turn south on Lower Mad River Road toward Ruth Lake. Drive 11.0 miles along Lower Mad River Road to the Bailey Canyon Campground. Park on the wide shoulder just short of the campground entrance. The trailhead is across the road from the campground entrance. **GPS:** N40 20.47' / W123 23.85'

## The Hike

This region of the Six Rivers National Forest is located near the headwaters of the Mad River and west of the Yolla Bolly Wilderness. One of the first stories Ranger Steve Pollard was told when he came to the Six Rivers Forest Service Ranger Station over thirty years ago was that Pickett Peak was named after an escaped convict named Pickett who hid out on this mountain. His daughter apparently hiked up the mountain to bring him supplies.

*Bridge at beginning of trail*

In the 1990s the rangers from the Six Rivers National Forest discovered evidence of an old mountain trail, now known as the Pickett Peak Trail. Blazes on some of the trees confirmed there had once been a trail on this slope, and this or a section of it was probably the trail traveled by Pickett's daughter on her way to deliver supplies to her father.

It is believed that the trail was first constructed at the turn of the twentieth century to facilitate access to a fire lookout. The trail, considered historic, was restored and added to the Six Rivers National Forest system. Even if your dog has less than no interest in "history," he will be happy to hear that he can get his uphill workout and woodsy smell fix on this stitch of natural history off leash.

"Pickett Peak Trail," as it is known—although the Pickett Peak Trail hike officially ends 1.0 mile short of the "peak"—is now one of the newest trails in the Six Rivers National Forest system. The Six Rivers National Forest is almost 1 million acres and was established in 1947 by President Truman. Parts of the Siskiyou, Klamath, and Trinity National Forests make up the Six Rivers National Forest, with the Eel, Duzen, Mad, Trinity, Klamath, and Smith Rivers running through it.

# Pickett Peak Trail

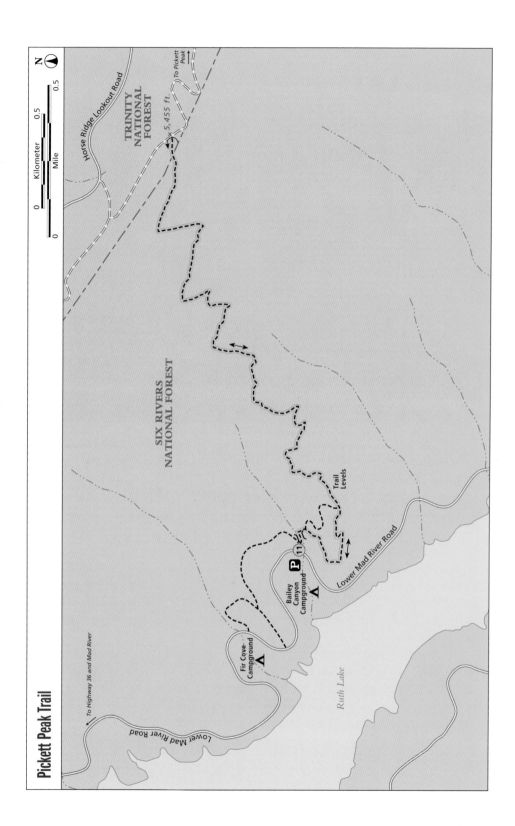

A section of the Pickett Peak Trail once crossed private property, but it was reconfigured to begin across from Bailey Canyon Campground on US Forest Service land and connect with the original trail farther up the mountain.

As you begin the climb, look back for views of Ruth Lake through the trees. Although Ruth Lake was created by damming the waters of the Mad River, it is surprisingly natural looking. The lake was named after Ruth McKnight, the daughter of a settler.

Spring boasts pink shooting stars and yellow mule's ears basking in the sunlight before the trail enters oak and Douglas fir woodland. The flatter saddle at about 0.5 mile is your best bet for a catching your breath before continuing up to the upper section clearing, where you see some old-growth black oak. Keep your eye out for some of the old blazes carved into the trees.

The clearing on the upper section where you will turn around is a good place to let Pooch spin and indulge his nosy senses before heading back down the way you came.

## Miles and Directions

**0.0**  Start at the Forest Service trailhead marker on the east side of the Lower Mad River Road across from the Bailey Canyon Campground. Walk 200 feet to the trail junction for Forest Service Trails #7E29 and #7E33. Turn right on #7E33 and cross the bridge over the creek. Follow the trail uphill, with views of the lake through the trees for the first mile.

**0.6**  The trail reaches a saddle. Enjoy the brief flatter section for a rest and water break.

**3.0**  Arrive at a clearing and dirt road. This summit is your destination. Elevation 5,455 feet. **GPS:** N40 20.90' / W123 22.32' Although there are no views from here, take time for a snack and listen to the wind strum the tops of the pine and fir trees. This is a good place for Pooch to romp and sniff around if the uphill hasn't tuckered him out. When you both get your second wind, follow the trail back down the way you came to the trailhead.

**6.0**  Arrive back at the trailhead.

## Creature Comforts

### Resting Up

**Fir Cove Campground** and **Bailey Canyon Campground** (www.usda.gov/ca/ruthlake) are the two most convenient Forest Service campgrounds in the area. They are within 1.0 mile of each other and across the road from the Pickett Peak Trail trailhead. The facilities are basic, with vault toilets and drinking water. Fir Cove has nineteen campsites; Bailey Canyon has twenty-five. **Ruth Lake Recreation Campground** (12200 Mad River Rd., Mad River 95552; 707-574-6196 or 707-574-6332; ruthlakecsd.org) accommodates tents and RVs. There is a store for supplies, flush toilets, showers, and boat rentals.

# 12  Black Sands Beach

Black Sands Beach with its coarse charcoal sand is not just another beach. This is a unique portal into the remote world of the Lost Coast at the foot of the King Range. This 8.4-mile out-and-back hike makes for a pleasant day and gives you a good sense of the isolated beauty of this stretch of coastline. Your pooch will enjoy the safe roaming space off leash, with a couple of opportunities to splash around in the seasonal creeks that run out of the canyons to the ocean.

**Start:** From Black Sands Beach trailhead to the left of the bathroom in the parking lot
**Distance:** 8.4 miles out and back
**Approximate hiking time:** 5 hours
**Difficulty:** Moderate (although it is flat along the beach, the distance along sand and rock with some sloping is more demanding)
**Trailhead elevation:** 114 feet
**Highest point:** 114 feet
**Best season:** Year-round; spring and fall have the least amount of fog; expect heavy rain in winter, but clear days between storms; can be windy year-round

**Trail surface:** Paved sidewalk before you reach black coarse sand and some rocky beach stretches. Booties are highly recommended to protect your dog's paws.

**Other trail users:** Horses
**Canine compatibility:** Voice control
**Land status:** BLM
**Fees and permits:** Free permits for one or more overnights on the Lost Coast Trail and backcountry; permit also serves as a California campfire permit
**Maps:** USGS Shelter Cove; King Range National Conservation Area
**Trail contacts:** BLM King Range Project Office, 768 Shelter Cove Rd., Whitehorn 95589; (707) 986-5400; www.ca.blm.gov/arcata
**Nearest town:** Shelter Cove has food and lodging; Garberville is a larger town with more services, including gas

**Trail tips:** The Black Sand Beach is very coarse and rocky. Booties are highly recommended to protect your dog's paws. Although this stretch of the Lost Coast is wide, it is a good idea to check the tide chart and coordinate your plans with the tide. Two flush toilets, a drinking fountain, and an information kiosk are available at the trailhead. Rattlesnakes like to slumber under driftwood logs, so be alert when you look for a rest spot.

**Finding the trailhead:** From Garberville on US 101, take exit 639 B to Shelter Cove. Drive 2.8 miles west on Redwood Drive and turn left onto Briceland Thorn Road toward Shelter Cove and the Kings Range Conservation Area. Drive 12.2 miles and bear left following signs for Shelter Cove. Briceland Thorn Road becomes Shelter Cove Road. The road is steep with paper clip turns as it wends down to Shelter Cove. Drive 8.0 miles and turn right onto Beach Road (Refuse Disposal Site sign). Drive 0.9 mile to the trailhead parking lot. Turn right on Beach Road. **GPS:** N40 02.72' / W124 04.63'

*View of Black Sands Beach from near the trailhead*

## The Hike

The challengingly sinewy road with a steep grade from US 101 to Shelter Cove gives you a taste of the isolation ahead. This remote realm was populated by Sinkyone and Mattole Native North American tribes until the nineteenth century, when European settlers discovered the wealth of resources for commercial logging, fishing, ranching, and tanning.

The King Range National Conservation Area was created in 1976 and 42,585 of the 68,000 wild and rugged acres were designated King Range Wilderness in 2006. The rocks and islands offshore were designated as a National Monument in 2000 under President Clinton. The King Range is excellent habitat for a variety of mammals, including black bears, deer, and elk. The old-growth forests are home to owls, bald eagles, and coopers hawks. Offshore seals, sea lions, and marine birds share the tide pools, rocky monuments, and kelp beds, while California grey whales swim by on their migration route in winter and spring.

The highest of the Douglas fir peaks is King Peak, 3.0 miles inland from the coast, at 4,088 feet. The King Range is at the edge of the North American Plate, one of three tectonic plates (Pacific, North American and Juan de Fuca) continuously

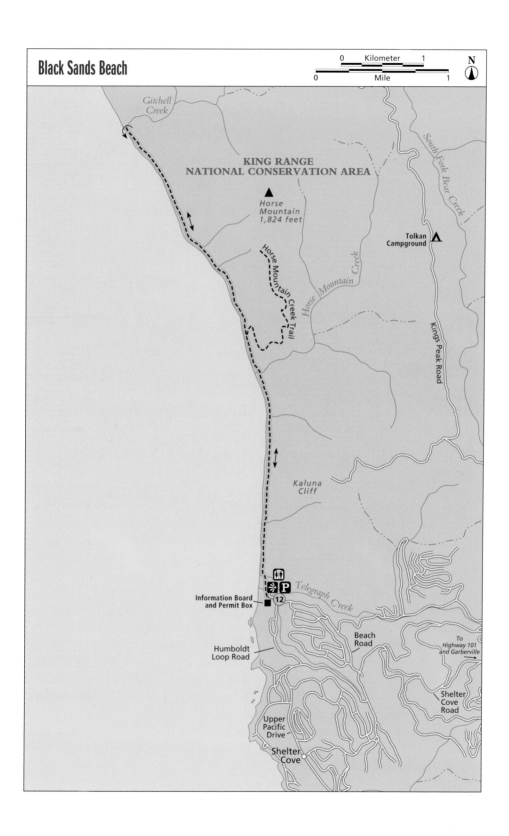

# Black Sands Beach

0 Kilometer 1

0 Mile 1

N

*Gitchell Creek*

**KING RANGE NATIONAL CONSERVATION AREA**

▲
*Horse Mountain 1,824 feet*

*South Fork Bear Creek*

Tolkan Campground ⊼

*Horse Mountain Creek Trail*

*Horse Mountain Creek*

Kings Peak Road

*Kaluna Cliff*

🚻

🚶 🅿
12

*Telegraph Creek*

Information Board and Permit Box ■

Beach Road

To Highway 101 and Garberville

Humboldt Loop Road

Shelter Cove Road

Upper Pacific Drive

Shelter Cove

bumping and grinding offshore, which has caused the mountains to rise 66 feet in the last 6,000 years. It is no wonder that CA 1 and US 101 were routed so far inland. The dark sands of Black Sands Beach come from the palisades' dark gray crumbly sandstone known as greywacke, rather than from volcanic particles.

The Lost Coast is the "longest undeveloped stretch of coast in California," with a 25-mile-long beach hike between Shelter Cove at the south end of Black Sands Beach to the Mattole River Campground at the north end.

The 8.4-mile out-and-back hike is flat, and it can be tempting to extend your outbound trek, especially on a magically sunny day, but remember that you must still hike the distance back and walking on sand and rock can be surprisingly exerting, not to mention wearing on your dog's paws.

Also be aware that at least 4.5 miles of beach beyond the turnaround point in this hike is "tide" sensitive and impassable at high tide. It is best to make a leisurely day of this hike, letting your dog enjoy frolicking in the seasonal streams along the way and savoring the views over a picnic lunch once you reach Gitchell Creek at 4.2 miles.

Sunscreen and a hat are imperative to protect yourself from the burning combination of rays intensified by water reflection and wind even on a foggy day. If you want to hike the entire length of the Lost Coast Trail, the backpacking trek is typically done over three days and two nights from north to south.

## Miles and Directions

**0.0** Start at the trailhead left of the toilets at the south end of the Black Sands Beach parking lot and walk approximately 500 feet down along the sidewalk to Black Sands Beach.

**0.4** Walk across seasonal Telegraph Creek.

**0.8** Walk across another seasonal creek.

**1.5** Come to another seasonal stream and walk across it.

**2.0** Come to Horse Mountain Creek and continue on the beach across the creek. The coarse sand beach becomes rockier.

**2.4** Come to Horse Mountain Creek trailhead heading up into the forest above the beach on the right. Continue walking on the beach. Notice clumps of California poppies, Indian paintbrush, and morning glories happily growing against the grassy banks and at the base of the slopes where the beach bumps up abruptly.

**4.2** Come to seasonal Gitchell Creek, which is your turnaround point. Elevation 2 feet. **GPS: N40 05.62' / W124 06.13'** This creek flows wider and heavier across the beach later in the season than the previous seasonal creeks and may require you to remove your hiking boots if you want to walk across. This is usually a great freshwater splash zone for Pooch, and the large driftwood logs (check that there are no rattlesnakes napping under the log) make a comfortable and scenic oceanfront picnic site. Be aware that if you are tempted to walk farther, at high tide the beach trail beyond Gitchell Creek becomes impassable for the next 4.5 miles. Take time to absorb the beauty and solitude of this unique hike before retracing your steps back to the trailhead.

**8.4** Arrive back at the trailhead.

*A backpacking surfer and his dog hike north to south.*

## Creature Comforts

### Fueling Up

**Delgada Pizza and Bakery** (707-986-7521) at the Inn of the Lost Coast (see the resting up section) has outdoor tables to accommodate pooches. The deli at the **Shelter Cove RV Park/Campground/Store/Deli** (707-986-7474) serves succulent fish-and-chips on the dog-friendly patio.

### Resting Up

**Inn of the Lost Coast,** 205 Wave St., Shelter Cove 95589; (707) 986-7521; innofthe lostcoast.com.

**Shelter Cove RV Park/Campground/Store/Deli,** 492 Machi Rd., Shelter Cove; (707) 986-7474. The campground overlooks the Pacific and the relocated Cape Mendocino lighthouse.

**Campgrounds in the King Range,** Visit www.blm.gov/ca/st/en/fo/arcata/kingrange/ campground.html.

## Puppy Paws and Golden Years

**MalCoombs** grassy park, with the historic Mendocino Lighthouse overlooking tide pools just across from the Shelter Cove Campground, invites pooches to romp.

# 13 Thomes Gorge

This is a long, exposed hike that begins as an easy, undistinguished jaunt in California chaparral country, not the terrain you expect in a national forest. Having said that, any time you get the opportunity to be in wilder open space with your dog off leash within easy access from busy highways and urban areas, it is a treat. Except for the burned-out area from the Whiskey Fire of 2008, the trail to the top of the gorge is relatively pleasant; you pass a couple of seasonal streams and spring blooms of Indian paintbrush and white fiddleneck while catching distant views of Mounts Lassen and Shasta. The last steep mile, dropping down into the wide gorge to Thomes Creek, is the scenic payoff, and the boulder-strewn rushing waters are an amazing contrast to the dry landscape above.

**Start:** From Thomes Gorge trailhead
**Distance:** 11.2 miles out and back
**Approximate hiking time:** 6 hours
**Difficulty:** Strenuous because of the distance, the mile-long descent to Thomes Creek, and some overgrown vegetation
**Trailhead elevation:** 2,060 feet
**Highest point:** 2,060 feet
**Best season:** Year-round; spring is ablaze with Indian paintbrush and other wildflowers; summers are very hot
**Trail surface:** Dirt trail with rock and patches of fallen limbs in the burned-out areas
**Other trail users:** Horses, mountain bikes
**Canine compatibility:** Voice control
**Land status:** National Forest
**Fees and permits:** None
**Maps:** USGS Hall Ridge; Mendocino National Forest
**Trail contacts:** Mendocino National Forest Supervisor's Office, 825 Humboldt Ave., Willows 95988; (530) 934-3316; www.fs.usda .gov/mendocino
**Nearest town:** Orland
**Trail tips:** There are a picnic table, campsite, and helicopter landing spot at trailhead. On a recent visit, the trail was in excellent condition for the first 2.5 miles, but the burned-out area still had limbs obscuring parts of the trail. You should call the Mendocino National Forest Station to inquire about current trail conditions. There was a lot of poison oak where the vegetation was overgrown, so if you are subject to severe reactions to poison oak, this trail is not for you and your dog. Others should wear or carry long pants and a long-sleeved top to minimize poison oak contact with the skin. Your dog will more than likely come in contact with some poison oak on the narrow overgrown stretches of the trail, so a bath or good rinse is advisable when you get home or to your campground.

**Finding the trailhead:** From Orland on I-5 take exit 619/Newville Road. Drive 27.0 miles to Round Valley Road/FR M4 and turn left on Round Valley Road. Drive 10.5 miles to the Thomes Gorge Trailhead sign on the right. Turn right and drive 0.1 mile to the trailhead parking lot. **GPS:** N39 49.17' / W122 38.88'

*On descent into Thomas Gorge*

## The Hike

In the spring the drive from I-5 across the green grass and purple vetch pasture-land before entering the national forest boundary will probably be the most visually enchanting part of your excursion until you reach the Thomes Gorge, named for local indigenous people. Although the hike is located within the Mendocino National Forest, at this lower elevation the rolling landscape is arid California chaparral.

The trailhead opens to views of the Sacramento Valley and snowy Mount Lassen to the east. The first 2.5 miles treat you to three seasonal small stream crossings, with the third being a cascade offering the coolest and shadiest rest stop under an oak canopy. Notice the red balls on some of the oak trees along the way. These are called "galls"—tissue produced by the oak tree to wrap around insect eggs such as wasps.

At 2.8 miles the trail wends its way through residual debris from the 7,783-acre Whiskey Fire of 2008 for about 0.5 mile before it rises. Views of snow-topped volcanic Mounts Lassen and Shasta on the northeastern horizon will lift your spirits. In another 0.5 mile the trail bends and overlooks a meadow sitting above the gorge.

It's a gentle descent to Dead Rabbit Pond, which may look more like a marsh than a pond depending on how wet or not the winter may have been. The last mile down to Thomes Creek at the bottom of the gorge is steep, narrow, and bordered by as much poison oak as California fuchsia. Although the strength of flow depends on the winter's precipitation, a picnic sitting on a boulder with feet and paws soaking in the invigorating clear cool waters as you look across to the gorge's palisade is a splendid reward and re-energizing break before the uphill hoof back out of the gorge and hike back to the trailhead.

## Miles and Directions

**0.0**  Start at the Thomes Gorge and Thomes Creek # 7W10 trailhead at the north end of the campsite and parking area.

**0.6**  Walk across a culvert for seasonal Bennett Creek.

*View down Thomes Gorge*

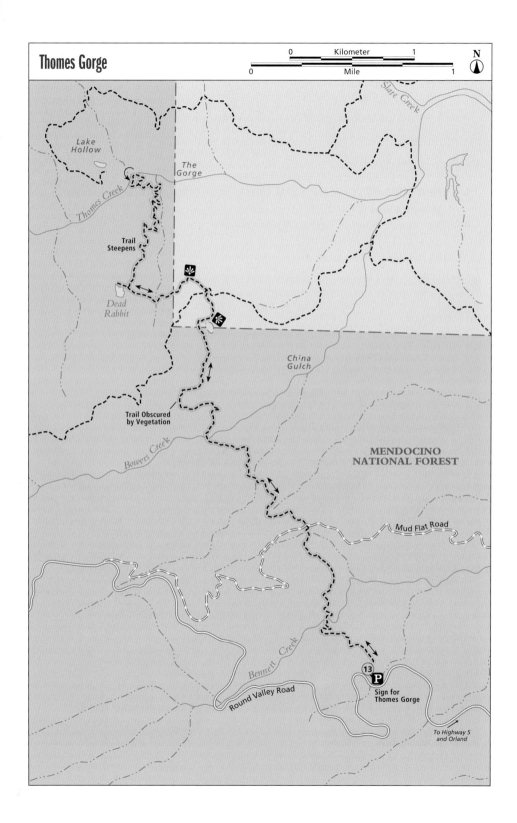

**1.3** Cross another seasonal stream.

**1.4** Come to an intersection of the trail and Mud Flat Road. Continue walking straight across the road and walk between the fence posts to continue on the trail.

**2.4** Come to shaded seasonal Bowers Creek and a small cascade. This is a good place to take a break and give your dog water before crossing the creek.

**2.8** Come to the beginning of the burned-out area, where patches of the trail are obscured by tree limbs and some overgrown vegetation.

**3.4** Arrive at a seasonal pond on your right.

**3.5** The trail opens up and rises, revealing views of Mount Lassen and Mount Shasta to the northeast.

**3.7** Come to an unmarked trail junction. Bear left and walk in a northwestern direction.

*Soothing tired feet in Thomes Creek*

**3.8** The trail bends left, offering a panoramic view of the meadow below and the gorge.

**4.2** Come to Dead Rabbit seasonal pond, which can look more like a marsh than a pond. Bear right with the pond on your left as you continue walking along the faint trail in a northeasterly direction. The pond will be behind you.

**4.6** The trail begins a steeper descent into the gorge.

**5.6** Arrive at Thomes Creek in Thomes Gorge, elevation 1,140 feet. **GPS:** N39 51.22' / W122 40.29' If the water is not too high or fast, enjoy this spectacular cool wet payoff by finding a warm rock to sit and soak your feet while your dog explores the vernal pools. This is an idyllic picnic site, and the gorge can make a pleasant overnight stay. Since the last few yards of the trail that drop down to the water are overgrown, it is likely that you may not leave the bank at the exact same spot. Go back up the bank and follow the trail back to the trailhead.

**11.2** Arrive back at the trailhead.

## Creature Comforts

*Resting Up*

There are dog-friendly lodgings in Corning, north of Orland, and Willows, south of Orland.

**Orland Inn,** 1052 South St., Orland 95963; (530) 865-7632; orlandinn.com.

**Parkway RV Resort and Campground,** 6330 CR 200 (Newville Rd.), Orland 95963; (530) 865-9188; theparkwayrv.com. This smaller RV and campground off of busy I-5 is surprisingly quiet, with pleasant grassy areas and leafy trees for shade.

**Black Butte Lake Campground,** Buckhorn Recreation Area, 19225 Newville Rd., Orland 95963-8901; (530) 865-4781. Ninety-three campsites are available here. Visit reserveamerica.com.

# 14 Waterfall Grove Trail

This an easy loop in the Jackson Demonstration State Forest that begins by going down to a seasonal waterfall with a rare glimpse into an old-growth redwood canyon before coming back up a trail that merges with a forest road back to the trailhead.

**Start:** From Chamberlain Creek Waterfall trailhead off FR 200
**Distance:** 1.6-mile loop
**Approximate hiking time:** 1 hour
**Difficulty:** Easy, because it is short and the steep descent at the trailhead is down a thirty-six-step wooden staircase with handrails
**Trailhead elevation:** 1,063 feet
**Highest point:** 1,245 feet
**Best season:** Spring, summer, fall (roads are impassable in wet winters)
**Trail surface:** Dirt
**Other trail users:** Hikers only

**Canine compatibility:** On leash
**Land status:** State
**Fees and permits:** None
**Maps:** USGS Northspur; Jackson Demonstration State Forest
**Trail contacts:** Department of Forestry and Fire Protection, Jackson Demonstration State Forest, 802 N. Main St. (CA 1) Fort Bragg; (707) 964-5674
**Nearest town:** Fort Bragg
**Trail tips:** There are no bathrooms or water at this trailhead, which is in an undeveloped area of the forest.

**Finding the trailhead:** From Fort Bragg at the intersection of northbound CA 1 and CA 20, turn right (east toward Willits) on CA 20. Drive 17.1 miles and turn left on the well-maintained gravel Road 200 just past the Chamberlain Creek Bridge. Bear left and follow the signs for Road 200. Drive 4.5 miles on Road 200. You will see a wooden staircase going down on the left, with a hiker and trailhead sign on the railing. Park on the shoulder next to the trailhead. **GPS:** N39 24.04' / W123 34.60'

## The Hike

The Jackson Demonstration State Forest is California's largest state forest (almost 50,000 acres) and operates as a "working" forest for research and sustainable forest management for balancing healthy ecosystems with timber harvesting. The land once owned by the Caspar Lumber Company is open for recreation and guided educational tours and is managed by the California Department of Forestry and Fire Protection. The forest is rich in biodiversity, from rich plant communities including redwood, fir, pine, tanoak, and madrone trees; ceanothus, Manzanita, and poison oak shrubs; as well as iris, columbine, and redwood violet flowers. You may not have the privilege of sighting bears, deer, or mountain lions, but they share the forest with other smaller mammals, salmon and steelhead trout, as well as several birds of prey including hawks and owls.

*Trail descent to Waterfall Grove*

The centerpiece of the Waterfall Grove Trail is the reserve of virgin old-growth redwood. This short but memorable hike begins with a steep descent into the grove down thirty-six steps and follows a narrow trail with a few gentle switchbacks to the canyon floor, where you enter the reserve of old-growth redwood. Ferns make their home in the moist shadow of these spectacular trees. The velvety moss-covered fallen trees almost look like an artful mosaic, and those that lay across the trail have been integrated by notching out steps to make getting over the trees easier without having to disturb the natural landscape. In only 0.2 mile you come to the waterfall where it drapes a 25-foot rock face. Water-magnet dogs will love to splash around in the shallow pool at the base of the waterfall. The trail continues to the left of the waterfall, and at 0.3 mile you pass another grove of redwoods on your left before climbing up the slope on your right along a series of gradual switchbacks. You will find occasional benches on which to sit and absorb the quietude and marvel at one of nature's masterpieces. The trail contours a canyon and at 0.8 mile you cross the stream that feeds the fall where the trail makes a sharp turn to the right. Walk for another 0.3 mile to a clearing at the intersection of Roads 1000 and 200. Turn right on Road 200 and walk 0.5 mile down the road back to the trailhead.

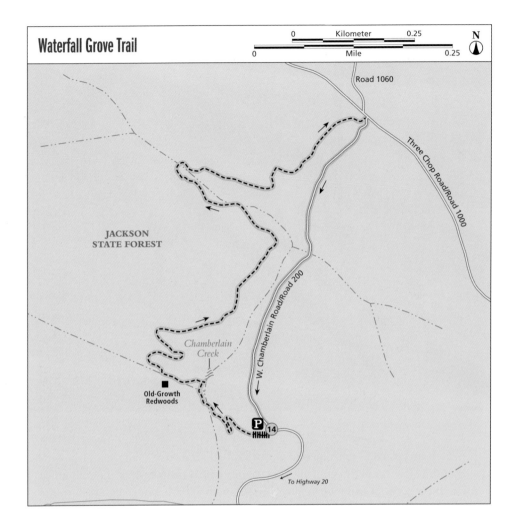

## Waterfall Grove Trail

Road 1060

Three Chop Road/Road 1000

JACKSON
STATE FOREST

W. Chamberlain Road/Road 200

Chamberlain
Creek

Old-Growth
Redwoods

P 14

To Highway 20

0  Kilometer  0.25

0  Mile  0.25

N

## Miles and Directions

**0.0**  Start at the Chamberlain Creek Waterfall trailhead at the top of the wooden staircase and walk down thirty-six steps.

**0.2**  Arrive at the base of the waterfall.

**0.3**  Come to a grove of old-growth redwood trees and continue on the trail going up the slope on the right.

**0.8**  Come to an arrow on a tree indicating a sharp right turn on the trail. You will cross the stream that feeds the waterfall.

**1.1**  The trail emerges in a clearing where it meets the intersection of Roads 1000 and 200 at the highest point. **GPS:** N39 24.38' / W123 34.50' Elevation 1245 feet. Turn right and walk down Road 200.

**1.6**  Arrive back at the trailhead.

## Creature Comforts

The picturesque headland **village of Mendocino** is a good basecamp for hiking in the Jackson Demonstration State Forest just 10.0 miles north. There are several restaurants and cozy country inns waiting to welcome you and your dog.

*Resting Up*

**Stanford Inn by the Sea,** 44850 Comptche-Ukiah Rd., Mendocino 95460; (707) 937-5615; stanfordinn.com. This inn was our dogs Lobo and Shiloh's favorite getaway. Ocean air, organic garden herbs, and earthy farm smells will be like an aromatherapy spa experience for your dog.

**Nicholson House Inn,** 951 Ukiah St., Mendocino 94560; (707) 937-0934; nicholson house.com. Great central location to walk the historic village.

*Waterfall*

# 15 High Rock

This is a hard-core 12.8-mile out and back or overnight into the little-traveled Snow Mountain Wilderness of the Mendocino National Forest. The hike begins with a 1.0-mile gradual descent to a lovely fast-moving creek and up 3,000 feet through pine and oak forests, eventually revealing panoramic views of the Sacramento Valley and the forested mountains. Only the fittest dog and his human should hike the entire 12.0 miles as a day hike or the 6.0 miles to High Rock for an overnight. Having said that, there are three sites along the way that can make for a shorter but satisfying outing with Pooch.

**Start:** From Deafy Glade trailhead on FR M10
**Distance:** 12.8-mile out and back
**Approximate Hiking Time:** 7 hours
**Difficulty:** Strenuous
**Trailhead elevation:** 3,280 feet
**Highest point:** 6,305 feet
**Best season:** Year-round; spring is magnificent, and late fall is pleasantly cool. Although the trailhead is open year-round, the rapid elevation gain once you cross the gorge and start uphill is subject to snow in the winter. Unless you are planning to limit your hike to a 2.0-mile out and back down to the creek, the summer heat on the dry slopes makes this hike unpleasant and puts your dog at risk of heatstroke.

**Trail surface:** Dirt and scree
**Canine compatibility:** Voice control
**Land status:** National Forest and Wilderness
**Fees and permits:** None
**Maps:** USGS Fouts Springs, Potato Hill; Mendocino National Forest; Snow Mountain Wilderness
**Trail contacts:** Stonyford Work Center, 5171 Stonyford-Elk Creek Rd. (P.O. Box 160), Stonyford 95979; (530) 963-3128; www.fs.fed.us
**Nearest town:** Willows

 **Trail tips:** This hike in its entirety is for *superfit* dog/hiker teams. Carry booties for your dog in the event of tender tootsies on the way back.

**Finding the trailhead:** From Willows on I-5 take exit 603 for CA 162 and Elk Creek. Drive 20.5 miles toward Elk Creek and turn left onto Road 306 toward Elk Creek. Drive 18.5 miles to Fout Springs Road (some road maps will incorrectly name it Fout Spruce Road). The Stonyford Work Center US Forest Service Mendocino is on the northwest corner of Fout Springs Road. Turn right on Fout Springs Road (M10/43A) and drive 12.6 miles along the wending paved road to the Deafy Glade trailhead on the right side of the road at the end of the paved road, 0.6 mile past the Dixie Glade Campground. Park in the turnout at the trailhead. The Deafy Glade sign is missing on the national forest information board at the trailhead. Be sure to add your information to the sign-in sheet in the metal box at the trailhead. **GPS:** N39 20.01' / W122 42.67'

*Panoramic views at High Rock turnaround point*

## The Hike

Just the fact that you can access a little-known wilderness area on paved roads is a boon. The approach to the trailhead begins with the excitement of seeing the white ridge of snow on the top of Snow Mountain as far away as from I-5 and as late as May in many years. In spring, even the first 40.0 miles of the drive from I-5 is worth the trip. You would never guess that there is such a bucolic unspoiled landscape of green and purple just off this major transportation artery. Then you cross the national forest boundary and witness a shocking contrast, where the Mill fire scorched over 29,000 acres of the Mendocino National Forest in the summer of 2012. Fortunately, once you drop over the ridge, you trade the devastation for the nourishing green of the forest that will surround your hike.

The Mendocino National Forest covers over 900,000 acres, of which 37,000 acres were designated as the Snow Mountain Wilderness in 1984, with an additional almost 24,000 acres in 2006 through the Northern California Coastal Wild Heritage Wilderness Act. The Wilderness straddles the North Coast Range within three counties, with East Snow Mountain Peak being the highest point at 7,056 feet and Snow Mountain being the southernmost peak in the North Coast Range.

The hike takes you to various ecozones of vegetation as you climb through black oak and conifers and past meadows and seasonal streams up to the crest's firs, Jeffrey pines, and some cedar. In the lush spring season expect displays of bush lupine, Indian warrior, and hound's tongue, named for the leaf's resemblance to a panting dog's tongue. What was once home to native tribes and grizzly bears is now habitat for mountain lions and black bears.

The hike begins with a 1.0-mile gradual descent into the gorge to the cool waters of South Fork Stony Creek, which is a pleasant destination in and of itself and the last reliable water source. From here the hike is an uphill climb to High Rock, except for the last 0.4 mile. At 3.4 miles the trail transitions to narrower and steeper stretches of scree. It is a good idea to attach your dog's leash to his harness along these stretches.

Black oak and pines provide comfortable shade for the first 4.5 miles, at which point you reach an exposed ridge and the Summit Spring Trail. Deafy Glade's meadow at 1.4 miles is another lovely destination for hikers and dogs who aren't up to the exhausting haul to High Rock. Summit Spring junction at 4.6 miles on the ridge is your next best bet for a satisfying hike rewarded by grand views. With almost 2.0 more miles on a mostly exposed slope of scree to High Rock, this is an excellent spot to evaluate your dog's condition and your water supply before committing to the full 6.4-mile outbound route.

At 6.0 miles you will reach the last trail junction, where you make a right turn to High Rock. The incense cedars and pines are a welcome sight and smell as you follow the trail to High Rock on your right. At this higher elevation you will hear the waves of wind rolling through the treetops. The exposed flats by the rock outcrop make a great vista point and picnic area while you and Pooch enjoy a well-deserved rest. If you came up for the night, there are a couple of fire rings and scenic sites to set up camp. When you are ready, go back the way you came for the downhill trip to the trailhead.

## Miles and Directions

**0.0**  Start at Deafy Glade trailhead #8W26 on the right side of the road. Walk down the trail to South Fork Stony Creek.

**0.2**  Cross a seasonal creek.

**0.4**  Come to a trail junction where an unmarked trail comes into your trail from the right.

**1.1**  Arrive at South Fork Stony Creek. Depending on the flow, expect to wade across the creek in at least ankle-deep water. Leash your dog to cross the creek as a safety measure. Begin the uphill climb.

**1.4**  The trail opens up to a grassy clearing known as Deafy Glade above Deafy Rock.

**1.7**  Come to a wooden trail marker nailed to a tree for Fout Springs with an arrow pointing right and Summit Spring with an arrow pointing straight. Continue walking 50 feet to a trail junction for Bathhouse going right downhill. Continue walking on Deafy Glade Trail left, going west uphill.

**3.8**  Come to a seasonal stream and the unmarked entry into the Snow Mountain Wilderness.

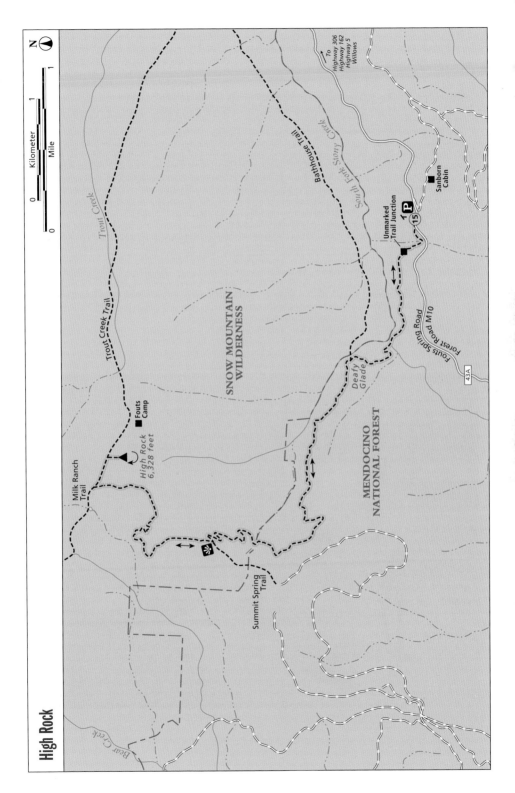

# High Rock

**N**

Kilometer

Mile

Trout Creek

Trout Creek Trail

Milk Ranch Trail

Fouts Camp

High Rock 6,328 feet

Summit Spring Trail

SNOW MOUNTAIN WILDERNESS

Deafy Glade

Bathhouse Trail

South Fork Stony Creek

MENDOCINO NATIONAL FOREST

Unmarked Trail Junction

Fouts Spring Road

Forest Road M10

43A

P

15

Sanborn Cabin

To Highway 306 Highway 162 Highway 5 Willows

Bear Creek

**4.6** Come to a T junction for unmarked Summit Spring Trail on an exposed ridge with views east, west, and south. Deafy Glade Trail ends here. The T junction has a signpost for Deafy Glade and South Fork Stony Creek, with an arrow pointing down the trail you came up. Turn right and walk up the trail in a northerly direction.

**6.0** Come to a trail junction in a pine tree hollow with a wooden sign on a tree for Snow Mountain Summit going straight and High Rock, Trout Creek, Dark Hollow, and Foutch Camp to the right. Turn right to High Rock.

**6.4** Arrive at High Rock on your right, elevation 6,305 feet. **GPS:** N39 21.57' / W122 44.36' Walk into the clearing and reward yourself and Pooch with snacks, water, and a rest while feasting on the views south and west. The High Rock ridge area is a good spot for an overnight. Otherwise go back to the trailhead the way you came.

**12.8** Arrive back at the trailhead.

## Creature Comforts

*Resting Up*

**Dixie Glade Campground** has seven RV or tent sites with tables and grills, two vault toilets, and no water. It is 0.6 mile before the Deafy Glade trailhead. There are a few dog-friendly motels in Willows. Visit www.fs.fed.us.

*Descending from High Rock*

# 16 Redbud Trail

This moderately strenuous hike will be an unexpected treat if you are accustomed to the frequently remote and barren public lands typically associated with the Bureau of Land Management territories. The Redbud Trail is within a thirty-minute drive of Clear Lake and the town of Clearlake for lodging and services. The 5.4-mile out and back crosses a meadow before the gradual climb to a saddle with views of steep forested slopes and eroded palisades before descending to Cache Creek along a series of long switchbacks.

**Start:** From the Redbud Trail trailhead
**Distance:** 5.4 miles out and back
**Approximate hiking time:** 3 hours
**Difficulty:** Moderate
**Trailhead elevation:** 980 feet
**Highest point:** 1,465 feet
**Best season:** Year-round; spring brings wildflowers and it is hot in summer
**Trail surface:** Dirt trail
**Other trail users:** Horses and seasonal hunters
**Canine compatibility:** Voice control
**Land Status:** Bureau of Land Management
**Fees and permits:** None
**Maps:** USGS Lower Lake
**Trail contacts:** Bureau of Land Management, 2550 N. State St., Ukiah 95482; (707)

468-4000; www.blm.gov. Department of Fish and Wildlife North Central Area; (916) 358-2900; www.dfg.ca.gov
**Nearest town:** Clearlake
**Trail tips:** If you want to hike past Cache Creek, be aware that forging the creek is dependent on the flow, which varies based on seasonal rainfall as well as water release from the dam above. You should contact Yolo County Flood Control (530-662-0266 or www.YCFCWCD.org) for flow conditions and schedule. There is a vault toilet at the trailhead, but all garbage must be packed out. Baton Flat at Cache Creek makes an excellent overnight for beginner backpackers.

**Finding the trailhead:** From Clearlake at the intersection of CA 53 and Lakeshore Drive, drive 4.5 miles on CA 53 to CA 20. Turn right onto CA 20 toward Williams. Drive 5.3 miles and turn right at the Cache Creek Management sign just before the bridge. Continue 0.1 mile to the trailhead parking lot. **GPS:** N38 59.22' / W122 32.36'

## The Hike

French trappers with the Hudson Bay Company who hid their pelts in this area originally named this creek Riviere Cache (*cacher* means "to hide"). Cache Creek in the east-flowing Coast Range drainage is an 87.0-mile-long tributary to the Sacramento River, but it only reaches the river in very wet years. Nevertheless, because the dam above Clear Lake stores water that is released in the summer to irrigate the farmland downstream, forging Cache Creek to the other side can be impossible at certain times of the year. Clear Lake (19.0 miles long and 8.0 miles at the widest point) is the largest natural lake entirely in California. Cache Creek is the only outlet to the lake.

*Leashes are optional on the trail.*

The Bureau of Land Management (BLM) and the California Department of Fish and Wildlife (formerly called the California Department of Fish and Game) cooperatively manage the Cache Creek Natural Area's 70,000 acres. Two decades ago the area was considered extremely remote, until the BLM and California Department of Fish and Wildlife joined forces to acquire public lands that allowed trail access from CA 20. In 2006, with the Northern California Coastal Wild Heritage Wilderness Act, Congress designated almost 30,000 acres as Cache Creek Wilderness, making Cache Creek one of the newest protected wild areas. Over 30.0 miles of the Cache Creek are designated a California Wild and Scenic River. Tule elk and bald eagles are two of the most thrilling wildlife sightings you might encounter.

The Redbud Trail begins left of the information kiosk, and there is a metal box with maps at the trailhead. You will walk past a picnic table on your right and walk across an open meadow. There are two forks of Cache Creek to nourish the land.

At 0.2 mile the narrow trail crosses the service road, and you leave the flat meadow for a gradual climb into an oak and pine woodland with some manzanita. In the spring the trail bursts with green grass and is splashed with pink shooting stars, shocking pink redbud, and Indian warrior's burgundy bloom. The burgundy Indian warrior flowers with fernlike leaves look especially exotic against the oak shrub land.

If your dog is responsive to voice commands, this is an excellent place to let her gallivant off leash and sniff to her nose's content. The trail steepens after the first mile, and views open up to a stadium of forested mountains up to 3,000 feet high. At 1.5 miles you come to a saddle and a T junction for the Redbud Trail (left) and Perkins Creek Trail (right). The southeast view across the canyon is especially dramatic at this point. Turn left to continue on Redbud Trail toward Baton Flat and take pleasure in the surrounding views as the trail begins to descend gently east. Don't miss the trail junction for Inspire Point. This is a stunning viewpoint overlooking Cache Creek and worth the short stroll down and back up. If you have limited time, this would be the absolute perfect spot to end your hike with a picnic lunch with Pooch. If you plan on hiking the rest of way down to the creek, take a moment for a snack and water break. Walk back up to the trail and continue down a series of sweeping switchbacks to the valley floor.

You see a sign for the Wilderness Boundary at 2.6 miles and a wooden footbridge over a seasonal stream just before the trail junction for Baton Flat coming in from the left. Cross the stream. Cache Creek is straight ahead. When you reach the shores of Cache Creek you see a trail marker for WILSON VALLEY TRAIL 3.0 MILES. If the creek is low enough to forge, and you have time and spare energy, you can cross and hike farther.

Wilson Valley is the official end to the Redbud Trail for a total out and back of 12.0 miles. It is important to contact the flow department for the schedule of water release in the creek, even in the summer, which can change the creek from an easy forge on the way to impassable on your return. Otherwise, let your dog enjoy a cool paw soak in the creek and refuel with some snacks before the return trek back the way you came.

## Miles and Directions

**0.0** Start at the Redbud Trail trailhead by the information kiosk.

**0.2** You will come to the service road. Walk across the service road and follow the sign for the Redbud Trail on the right.

**0.8** The trail steepens.

**1.5** Arrive at a saddle and a trail junction for Redbud Trail going left and Perkins Creek Trail going right. Turn left and continue on the Redbud Trail along the grassy saddle east downhill. Elevation 1,465 feet. **GPS:** N38 58.49' / W122 31.75' You have reached the highest point of the hike.

**1.6** Come to a trail junction for Inspire Point. Walk down to Inspire Point on your right for a dramatic view of Cache Creek in the canyon below. This is a great spot for a midway snack and water break or a shorter hike ending on a high note. Walk back up the trail to continue the hike and turn right at the junction to begin the sweeping switchbacks down to the flats.

**2.6** Come to a wilderness boundary marker and the sloping meadow.

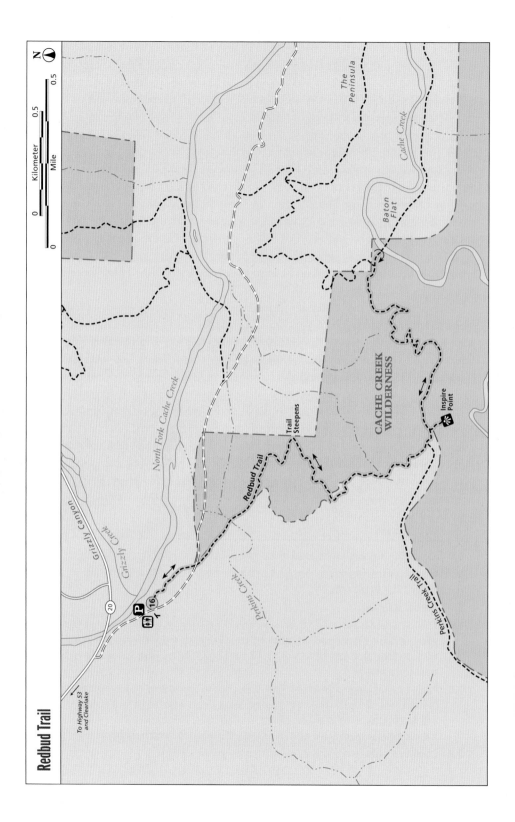

# Redbud Trail

To Highway 53
and Clearlake

20

P

16

Grizzly Canyon

Grizzly Creek

North Fork Cache Creek

Redbud Trail

Perkins Creek

Trail
Steepens

CACHE CREEK
WILDERNESS

Inspire
Point

Perkins Creek Trail

Baton
Flat

The
Peninsula

Cache Creek

N

Kilometer
0        0.5

Mile
0        0.5

**2.7** Walk across a wooden footbridge over a seasonal stream and come to a trail junction for Baton Flat coming in from the left. Continue straight to Cache Creek ahead and the trail marker for Wilson Valley Trail 3.0 Miles. Enjoy a picnic lunch by the creek while your dog cools her paws, then go back the way you came or set up camp if you got a campfire permit and backpacked in for an overnight. Elevation 1,000 feet. **GPS:** N38 58.64' / W122 31.16'

**5.4** Arrive back at the trailhead.

## Creature Comforts

*Resting Up*

**Clear Lake Marina and Cottages,** 13885 Lakeshore Dr., Clearlake 95422; (707) 995-5253; clearlakecottagesandmarina.com.

**Cache Creek Regional Park Campground,** 1475 CA 16, Rumsey 95679; (530) 406-4880; yolocounty.org.

*Indian warrior flowers along trail*

# 17 Bluff Trail

In a spectacular remote region with open space dominated by state parks that restrict dogs to the parking lot or campground, it is a treat to find a hike that serves rugged Pacific Coast panoramas with a trail suitable for all levels of human and canine energy. Bluff Trail's flat meadow terrain with patches of coastal forest is exposed to sun, wind, and fog depending on Mother Nature's mood. The short ADA-accessible loop within the park is a perk that allows physically disabled visitors with dogs to connect with nature on the invigorating Pacific Coast. The trail begins at the visitor center in Gualala Point Regional Park and traces Sea Ranch's private community bluffs for 3.0 miles along a public-access trail.

**Start:** From the interpretive sign behind the Gualala Point Regional Park Visitor Center
**Distance:** 7.4-mile lollipop
**Approximate hiking time:** 3.5 hours
**Difficulty:** Easy, because it's flat
**Trailhead elevation:** 87 feet
**Highest point:** 87 feet
**Best season:** Year-round; December to March brings wetter weather for a spring bloom of wildflowers; expect bluer skies from October to May and foggier summer days
**Trail surface:** Pavement, grass, dirt, and gravel
**Other trail users:** Hikers only
**Canine compatibility:** On leash
**Land status:** Regional Park
**Fees and permits:** Parking fee, $7

**Maps:** USGS Gualala, Stewarts Point; Gualala Point Regional Park
**Trail contacts:** Gualala Point Regional Park, 42401 CA 1, Gualala; Ranger Station: (707) 785-2377. Sonoma County Regional Parks, 2300 County Center Dr., #120A, Santa Rosa 95403; (707) 565-2041; parks.sonomacounty .ca.gov
**Nearest town:** Gualala
**Trail tips:** There are flush toilets, water, and picnic tables at the visitor center. There are benches for soaking up the views along the trail. The trail is exposed to wind, sun, or fog, depending on the day. The adjacent campground has nineteen sites plus a few walk-ins, water, showers, and a dump station.

**Finding the trailhead:** From Geyserville on US 101 take the Canyon Road exit heading west for 2.0 miles. Turn right onto Dry Creek Road and drive 3.2 miles. Turn left onto Stewarts Point-Skaggs Springs Road and drive 15.4 miles. Bear left and continue on Stewarts Point-Skaggs Springs Road for another 21.0 miles to CA 1. Turn right and drive 10.4 miles to Gualala Point Regional Park. Turn left into the parking lot and walk down to the visitor center. The trailhead is to the left of the interpretive sign behind the visitor center. **GPS:** N38 45.55' / W123 31.40'

## The Hike

Gualala Point Regional Park overlooks the picturesque Gualala River estuary and is lucky to have the private residential community of Sea Ranch as a neighbor. The park's and its residential neighbor's land both share the same history, beginning with

*Leaving Whale Watch Point*

the Pomo Indians, whose seasonal migration to the shores and lifestyle were gentle on the environment. In the early 1800s the Russians' endeavors of hunting sea otters and logging redwoods left a much less kind imprint. Other Europeans soon followed. The gold rush and the 1906 earthquake fueled the growing San Francisco's insatiable appetite for lumber and made Captain Bihler's settlement prosper at Bihler's Landing, where Sea Ranch Lodge now stands. By the time the frenzy abated in the early 1900s, it had taken its toll on the Pomo Indians and the land. Prohibition gave this northern coast a brief jolt of economic stimulation, when smugglers came to drop off the illegal firewater from Mexico and Canada to quench San Francisco's thirst.

By 1941 the abused landscape had returned to its pastoral condition, and Rancho Del Mar's 5,200 acres were acquired by Ed Ohlsen. The rancher's sheep grazed the coastal meadows for twenty years before architect and planner Al Boeke was seduced enough by the location's beauty to seek investors who would get on board with his plans for an environmentally sensitive second-home community. No lawns, no fences, and salt-washed wooden structures in visual and physical harmony with the natural setting became the "Sea Ranch" (translated from the Spanish *Rancho Del Mar*) trademark, winning it several architectural and environmental awards. The original 5,200 acres became 2,310 individual building sites on 3,500 acres. The rest was dedicated as common open space and forest reserve with 200 acres set aside for the Gualala Point County Park and Campgrounds.

Sea Ranch stretches along 8.0 miles of rugged coastline. There are six public coastal-access trails across Sea Ranch from CA 1 to the beaches. Only two of these access trails are open to the public as part of an easement agreement with the Gualala Point Regional Park. They connect the north end of the park to Walk-On Beach parking lot at the south end of CA 1.

The coastal-access parking lots, including Walk-On Beach, have a few parking spots, one bathroom, and no water. For the same parking fee of $7, Gualala Point Regional Park has the advantage of a visitor center, flush toilets, and water. Your

*Giving trail right-of-way to local residents*

hike begins left of the interpretive sign on the paved path behind the visitor center and makes a right turn off the paved path onto the grassy trail by the dog waste bag dispenser.

This lollipop hike is a scenic feast every step of the trail, from beginning to end. The Gualala estuary opens up on your right with Gualala village perched across the river as you skirt the meadow's grasses with bush lupine and cypress groves laced with California blackberry.

At 0.4 mile the path going right will take you down to the beach. Depending on how much time you have, you can either take a quick jaunt to the beach now or save the beach for later.

At 0.5 mile you come to a picnic table, toilets, and a water fountain. Turn right onto the grassy trail with the bluff on your right and the meadow on your left.

At 0.7 mile take the unmarked trail on the right and loop around the bluff to Whale Watch Point. At the T junction bear right along the bluff fence. You will see the beach below on the right. Tall people beware as you walk through a tunnel of low cypress limbs before merging back with the Bluff Trail. Notice how the surf washes over the cliff's sediment layers so neatly and vividly stacked.

At certain times of the year, the coast is bobbing with kelp heads that may appear to be sea otters. Keep your eyes out for the occasional otter floating in the kelp beds. At 1.1 miles you see a sign for the bluff top and public-access trail to the Salal Beach Trail and Walk-On Beach Trail, along with a sign indicating you are entering private property with coastal access.

Continue straight into the Sea Ranch development laced with private trails identified by their horned logo representing a ram's head in homage to its sheep-ranching history. Stay on the Bluff Trail that will continue for another 3.0 miles into the Sea Ranch community, with gloriously rugged coastal views highlighted by coast iris and calla lilies as you cross narrow gullies over wooden bridges above seasonal streams occasionally weaving through cypress groves. Your pooch will love the smells trailing behind herds of grazing deer and the herons patrolling the bluffs. Don't forget to offer your dog water along the way.

The sea-bleached wooden homes and their distinctive architecture add an interesting dimension to this hike. At 4.1 miles you will come to the end of the public access and a sign for the "closed" Walk-On Beach. Go back the way you came until 7.2 miles, back at the Gualala Point Park boundary. Turn right on the trail that parallels the fence until the trail merges with the paved path. Bear right and stay on the paved path to the visitor center at 7.4 miles.

## Miles and Directions

**0.0** Start at the interpretive sign behind the Gualala Point Regional Park Visitor Center. **GPS:** N38 45.54' / W123 31.40' This is the highest point, elevation 87 feet. From the trailhead walk approximately 170 feet along the paved path to the dog waste bag dispenser and turn right onto the grassy trail past the bench on the left.

**0.1** Come to an unmarked trail junction with a trail heading right. Continue walking straight past the junction.

**0.2** Come to another unmarked trail junction with a trail heading left. Continue walking straight past the junction. Notice the cypress grove on your left and the Gualala River estuary on your right.

**0.3** Bear right at the fork.

**0.4** The trail merges with the paved path. Turn right on the path and turn immediately left at the bench. (A path going right just past the left turn is the path going down to beach.)

**0.5** Arrive at a picnic table, flush toilets, water fountain, and a trail junction with a grass trail going right. Turn right along the trail that traces the bluff. The sound of the surf will replace the road noise from CA 1.

**0.7** Come to a trail junction going right. Turn right and loop to Whale Watch Point.

**0.75** Come to a T junction at a fence. Turn right. The beach will be below on your right. Bear right through the short tunnel of cypress limbs and merge back with Bluff Trail.

**1.1** Arrive at trail junction with a sign for public access to the Salal Beach Trail and Walk-On Beach Trail and a sign notifying you that you are entering private property with coastal access. Continue straight into the Sea Ranch private development and stay on the trail.

**1.5** Come to a fork. The trail to the right is an unmarked viewpoint with a driftwood bench. Enjoy the view and take advantage of this stop to give Pooch a lap of water and a treat. Get back on the trail.

**2.1** Arrive at a trail junction and a wooden bridge over a seasonal stream. The left trail is the Salal Trail back to Gualala Point Regional Park, and the trail to the right leads to the Walk-On Beach Trail parking lot and end of the public access trail. Turn right.

**2.5** Walk across a wooden bridge over a seasonal stream.

**3.4** Walk across a wooden bridge over a seasonal stream.

**3.7** Walk across a wooden bridge over a seasonal stream.

**4.1** Arrive at the end of public access and a sign for "closed" Walk-On Beach. Elevation 28 feet. **GPS:** N38 44.21' / W123 29.58' Take the trail back the way you came, until you reach the Gualala Point Regional Park and Sea Ranch boundary.

**7.2** Exit Sea Ranch community and enter Gualala Point Regional Park. Turn right at the trail junction and continue on the trail paralleling the fence on the right. There is a golf course on the other side of the fence.

**7.3** Your trail merges into the paved trail. Bear right onto the paved trail.

**7.4** Arrive back at the trailhead and visitor center.

## Creature Comforts

### *Resting Up*

**Sea Ranch Lodge,** 60 Sea Walk Dr., The Sea Ranch, 95497; (800) 732-7262; sea ranchlodge.com.

**Gualala Country Inn,** 47975 Center St., Gualala, 95445; (800) 564-4466; gualalacountry inn.com.

**Gualala Point Regional Park Campground,** (707) 565-2267; parks.sonomacounty.ca .gov.

# Bluff Trail

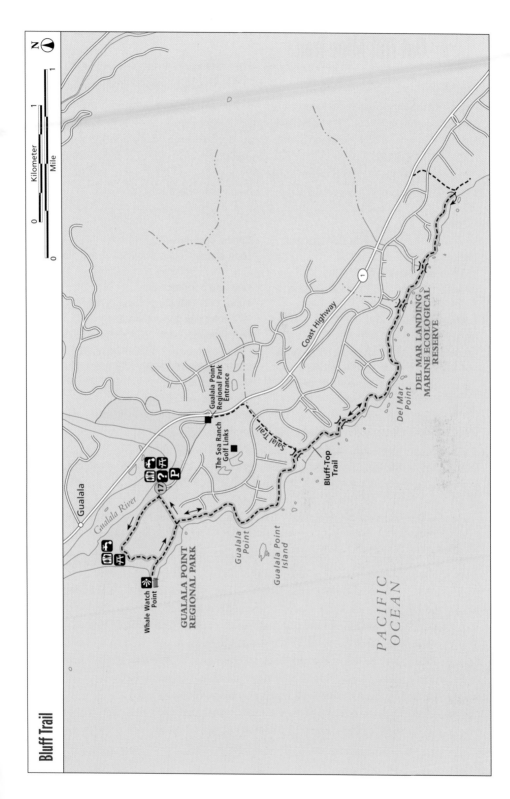

# 18 Oat Hill Mine Trail

Oat Hill Mine Trail follows the original route connecting Calistoga to the quicksilver mines north. This historic road, built from 1873 to 1893, is now a recreational trail for hikers, mountain bikers, and horseback riders. The 4.7-mile stretch to Karl Gustov Holm's homestead is a sustained uphill climb over a rough rocky and often eroded surface. The wide trail begins in an oak woodland mixed with gray pine and wends up to open grasslands dotted with wildflowers in the spring. The views over the Napa Valley vineyards and across to the rugged palisades are worth the effort.

**Start:** From the Oat Hill Mine Trail trailhead
**Distance:** 9.3 miles out and back
**Approximate hiking time:** 5 hours
**Difficulty:** Strenuous, because of sustained uphill and distance
**Trailhead elevation:** 407 feet
**Highest point:** 2,336 feet
**Best season:** Year-round; spring brings green and wildflowers; summers can be hot.
**Trail surface:** Dirt trail with some rock. Booties are needed for the rough rocky stretches.
**Other trail users:** Horses and mountain bikes

**Canine compatibility:** On leash
**Land status:** County Open Space and State Park
**Fees and permits:** None
**Maps:** USGS Calistoga; Napa County Regional Park and Open Space District
**Trail contacts:** Napa County Regional Park and Open Space District, 1195 Third St. #10, Napa 94559; District Secretary (707) 259-5933; napaoutdoors.org
**Nearest town:** Calistoga
**Trail tips:** Make sure you bring plenty of water for your pooch.

**Finding the trailhead:** From Calistoga at the intersection of CA 29 and the Silverado Trail, the trailhead parking lot is at the intersection on the east side of CA 29. **GPS:** N38 35.36' / W122 34.64'

## The Hike

Napa County had several mines in the 1800s, and the Oat Hill Mine was the third-largest quicksilver mine in the nation from 1872 to the late 1960s. Cinnabar deposits were mined to produce quicksilver (mercury). The construction of the Oat Hill Mine Road to connect the mines and Calistoga took twenty years, from 1873 to 1893. The Oat Hill Mine Trail covers 8.3 miles from Calistoga to the western end of Aetna Springs Road in Pope Valley, but this hike takes you to the midway point, 4.65 miles to the ruins of Karl Gustov Holm's homestead cabin, originally built in 1893. You will see part of his barn's stone wall when you reach Holm's Place.

This historic route is now part of a recreational trail used by hikers, mountain bikers, and horseback riders. The trail passes through land administered by the county

*Foundation of Holm's Place at the turnaround point*

regional park and the state parks, as well as a section of private property. Remarkably dogs are allowed on this trail, even though part of the trail passes through Robert Louis Stevenson State Park. The hike is along a wide but rough trail. The first couple of miles pass through shady oak woodland laced with some gray pine and poison oak vines. The latter is a good reason to keep Fido on leash. The valley's vineyards dominate the views until the trail transitions to open grassy slopes laced with purple vetch and trailside bush lupine.

At about 3.0 miles you begin to see the ruts in the rock left by heavy wagons. The manicured landscape of vineyards is replaced by a backdrop of rugged mountains with volcanic buttes and palisades. Make sure you check your dog's feet for tender spots along the way if he isn't already wearing his booties. Make frequent stops to offer him water, especially once you leave the shaded protection of the woodland. At 4.6 miles you come to the only trail junction on this hike, and you will turn left to

*Descent with buttes behind*

the Palisades Trail. In 0.5 mile you see the sign for Holm's Place and the remains of the homestead's stone walls. This protected little hollow is a splendid location to share a snack with your dog and drink up before heading back down to the trailhead the way you came.

## Miles and Directions

- **0.0** Start at the Oat Hill Mine Trail trailhead.
- **0.5** Come to a bench overlooking Calistoga and the Napa Valley vineyards to the southeast.
- **2.1** Views open to a crown of volcanic palisades to the north.

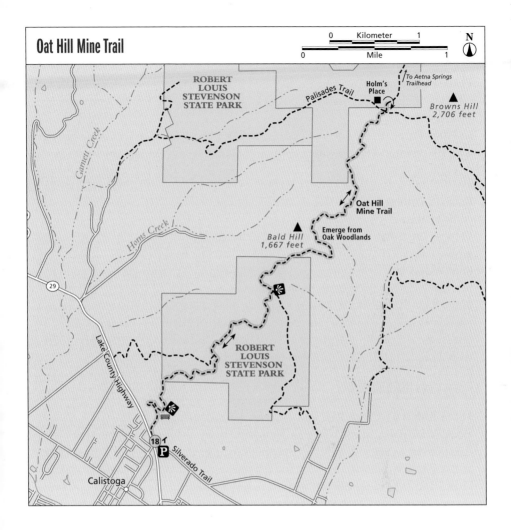

**Oat Hill Mine Trail**

ROBERT LOUIS STEVENSON STATE PARK

Garnett Creek

Holm's Place

To Aetna Springs Trailhead

▲ Browns Hill 2,706 feet

Palisades Trail

Oat Hill Mine Trail

Horns Creek

▲ Bald Hill 1,667 feet

Emerge from Oak Woodlands

29

Lake County Highway

ROBERT LOUIS STEVENSON STATE PARK

18 **P** Silverado Trail

Calistoga

**3.2** Come out of the oak and manzanita woodland onto open grassy slopes and the trail wends around the base of the palisades.

**4.6** Arrive at a trail junction. Aetna Springs trailhead straight and Palisades Trail to the left. Turn left onto the Palisades Trail.

**4.65** Arrive at the HOLM'S PLACE sign. Elevation 2,336 feet. **GPS:** N38 37.33' / W122 32.93' This is the highest point of the hike. Let your dog rest, drink, and snack. Go back to the trailhead the way you came.

**9.3** Arrive back at the trailhead.

# Creature Comforts

## Fueling Up

**Pizzeria Tra Vigne,** 1016 Main St., St. Helena, 94574; (707) 967-9999; travignerestaurant.com. Enjoy Italian flavors with Pooch on the patio in the wine country's sophisticated setting.

**La Prima Pizza,** 1923 Lake St., Calistoga, 94515; (707) 942-8070; Laprimapizza.com. This restaurant is across the street from the trailhead. Pooch can join you on the deck.

## Resting Up

**Brannan Cottage Inn,** 109 Wapoo Ave., Calistoga, 94515; (707) 942-4200; brannancottageinn.com.

**Cottage Grove Inn,** 1711 Lincoln Ave., Calistoga 94515; (800) 799-2284; cottagegrove.com.

**Napa Winery Inn,** 1998 Trower Ave., Napa; (707) 257-7232; napawineryinn.com. The best value for dog-friendly accommodations in Napa.

**Bothe-Napa State Park,** St. Helena Highway; (800) 444-7275; napaoutdoors.org. Just 4.0 miles south of Calistoga (between Calistoga and Napa), this park has a unique and outstanding location in the heart of wine country. In addition it offers flush toilets, coin showers, picnic tables, grills, and tent and RV sites.

# Puppy Paws and Golden Years

**Alston Park,** Dry Creek Road off Redwood Road, Napa; (707) 257-9529; naparec.com. Your pooch doesn't have to be a wine connoisseur or care about pinots or chardonnays to enjoy Napa Valley's premier dog-friendly park. Alston Park has acres of flat and hilly vineyard-view romping open space and loops for walkers, runners, hikers, and horseback riders. Bikers are only allowed on the paved trails. Canine Commons in Alston Park is a 3-acre fenced dog park for pooches who need to cut loose with boundaries.

**Pawsport Napa Valley,** napahumane.org/Pawsport/NV. This annual dog-friendly wine-tasting fundraiser event for Napa Humane Society takes place in the spring. The "Pawsport" ticket price offers includes pooch and person shuttle service to participating wineries between Napa and Calistoga to enjoy complimentary wine tasting, treats, souvenirs, discounts, and a variety of perks.

# 19 Mount Burdell

The hike up to Mount Burdell is typical of the San Francisco Bay area's open space landscape and vegetation. The trail wanders through an oak woodland at the base of the more than 1,500-foot-high mountain and quickly transitions to oak-dotted grasslands with grazing cattle as it traverses the slopes and wends to the top, revealing expansive views toward the bay. The fact that dogs can be off leash on the fire roads that cross the leash-only single-track trails is a real perk for Pooch.

**Start:** From Dwarf Oak Trail trailhead off of Novato Boulevard
**Distance:** 8.3 miles out and back with a loop
**Approximate hiking time:** 4.5 hours
**Difficulty:** Strenuous, because of distance
**Trailhead elevation:** 126 feet
**Highest point:** 1,558 feet
**Best season:** Year-round; spring is green and dappled with buttercups; summers are hot and dry
**Trail surface:** Dirt and some rocky sections
**Other trail users:** Mountain bikes on the fire roads, horses

**Canine compatibility:** On leash on the single-track trails; off leash on the fire roads
**Land status:** County
**Fees and permits:** None
**Maps:** USGS Novato, Petaluma; Marin County Parks and Open Space
**Trail contacts:** Marin County Civic Center, 3501 Civic Center #260, San Rafael 94903; (415) 473-6387; www.marincountyparks .org/depts/pk/divisions/open-space/ mount-burdell
**Nearest town:** Novato
**Trail Tips:** Leash your dog if cattle are present.

**Finding the trailhead:** From Novato at Highway 101 and San Marin Drive, head west on San Marin Drive for 2.7 miles. Turn right on Novato Boulevard and drive 0.2 mile. Park between the two No Parking Anytime signs, just before the Horse Crossing sign. The Dwarf Oaks Trail trailhead is on the right just before the Horse Crossing sign. **GPS:** N38 07.17' / W122 36.83'

## The Hike

Although the trailhead for this hike is clearly in a suburban neighborhood, the road noise and excited screams of kids on the San Marin High School playing field will vanish within a mile. This is a minor tradeoff for the miles of hiking trails within Marin County's open space preserves for outdoor recreation. Marin County Open Space District (MCOSD) and local residents purchased Mount Burdell Preserve in 1977 to protect the 1,627 acres for the public's enjoyment. Mount Burdell prides itself in being home to some of Marin County's "finest and oldest" specimens of oak and bay trees, as well as species of birds less abundant elsewhere in Marin. Listen for lazuli buntings and lark sparrows as you watch for the butterfly residents.

The Dwarf Oak Trail begins as a narrow public-access trail between a residential neighborhood and the San Marin High School. In about 300 feet the trail crosses

*Dwarf oak trees along trail*

seasonal Sandy Creek and shortly thereafter crosses a paved service road with a PUB-
LIC TRAIL sign and a trail marker for the Bay Area Ridge Trail straight ahead. At 0.4
mile you come to the trail marker for the Dwarf Oak Trail to the left. The narrow trail
going straight is a switchback cutoff. Ignore it.

Turn left as the arrow indicates and follow the trail bearing right up the switchback that merges with the trail cutoff you saw at the trail marker. The Dwarf Oak Trail
traverses the slope, and the high school's athletic fields will be below you. At 0.9 mile
you come to a junction for the Dwarf Oak Trail and the Myrtle Place Trail. Continue
walking straight on the Dwarf Oak Trail going northeast, and the bay and Mount
Diablo across the bay will come into view. Another 0.3 mile and the trail leaves the
hum of suburbia for the shade and quiet of an oak woodland. Be aware there is poison
oak along the trail—but luckily Fido is on leash and not romping and rolling himself
silly in the green leaves mimicking harmless ivy and vines. At 1.5 miles you come to
a wide fork with an unmarked narrow trail on the right. Bear left and you will soon
see a fenced-in water tank on your right. Spring brings Douglas iris, miner's lettuce,
and shooting stars to brighten the trail.

Just beyond is the trail junction for Dwarf Oak Trail and Little Tank Fire Road. You will continue straight on the Dwarf Oak Trail until you reach the gate and a sign for the Marin County Open Space District in another 0.5 mile. Walk through the gate and make sure you latch the gate behind you. You and your dog will be sharing the open space on fire roads with cattle between here and the top of Mount Burdell. Although your dog can be off leash on the fire roads, for his own safety, be sure he's on his best behavior around the cattle. The fire roads are mostly exposed with occasional oak canopies. On a sunny day make sure you take advantage of every spot of shade to give your dog a cool-off break and a drink of water while you enjoy the hilly views.

The next 2.5 miles of the hike to the top of Mount Burdell traverse the grassy slopes linking with several different fire roads, some of which are part of the Bay Area Ridge Trail. At 3.7 miles you leave Deer Camp Fire Road for the Cobblestone Fire Road for the last mile to the summit. This is a rough and rocky road, as the name suggests. This is a good time to pull out the booties if your dog is not used to this paw-pounding surface. At 4.4 miles you leave Cobblestone Fire Road for a 0.1-mile jaunt up a single-track trail to the summit, elevation 1,558 feet, where your efforts are rewarded with expansive views northeast toward the Napa Valley. Notice the stone wall tracing the perimeter of the summit. Your return route will continue along Cobblestone Fire Road and onto Middle Burdell Fire Road past Hidden Lake, a seasonal pond teeming with frogs and salamanders in the wet season. This sensitive wildlife and rare plant area is off-limits to dogs. Where Middle Burdell Fire Road becomes San Andreas Fire Road, remember to turn right and walk back through the gate onto Dwarf Oak Trail to return to the trailhead.

## Miles and Directions

**0.0** Start at the Dwarf Oak Trail trailhead.

**0.2** Walk across seasonal creek.

**0.3** Come to an intersection with a paved service road and continue straight across the road to the Public Trail sign and Bay Area Ridge Trail marker.

**0.4** Cross the creek bed on a footbridge and come to a trail marker for the Dwarf Oak Trail to the left. Turn left (northwest) and proceed along the dirt trail switchback that traces the slope.

**0.6** Come to an unmarked trail junction with a post on the left and a narrow trail going up the hill. Continue walking east, traversing the slope with the high school athletic fields below you.

**0.9** Come to a trail junction for the Dwarf Oak Trail and Myrtle Place Trail. Continue straight on Dwarf Oak Trail (with northeast views of San Francisco Bay and Mount Diablo).

**1.2** Enter an oak woodland as the trail heads northwest.

**1.5** Arrive at a fork. Bear left on the wider trail.

**1.6** Pass a water tank on your right.

**1.65** Come to the trail junction for Dwarf Oak Trail and Little Tank Fire Road. Continue straight on Dwarf Oak Trail.

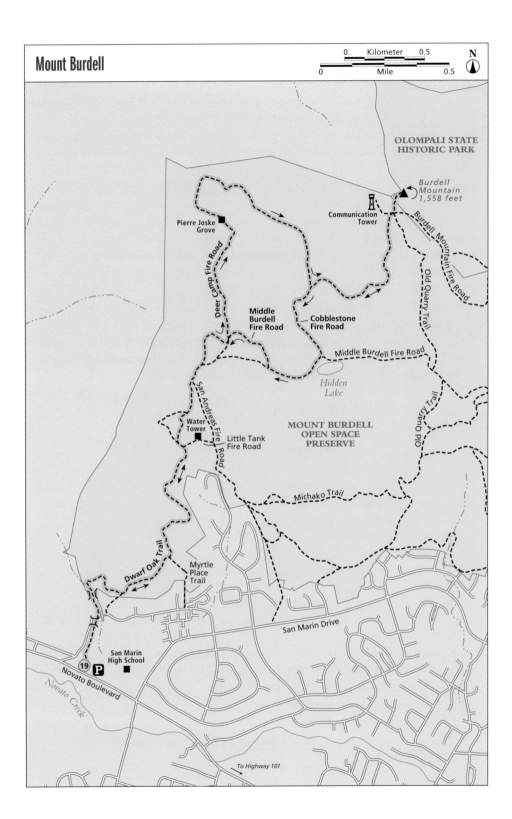

# Mount Burdell

Kilometer
0        0.5

Mile
0        0.5

N

OLOMPALI STATE
HISTORIC PARK

Burdell
Mountain
1,558 feet

Communication
Tower

Pierre Joske
Grove

Deer Camp Fire Road

Middle
Burdell
Fire Road

Cobblestone
Fire Road

Burdell Mountain Fire Road

Old Quarry Trail

Middle Burdell Fire Road

Hidden
Lake

San Andreas Fire Road

Water
Tower

Little Tank
Fire Road

MOUNT BURDELL
OPEN SPACE
PRESERVE

Old Quarry Trail

Michako Trail

Dwarf Oak Trail

Myrtle
Place
Trail

San Marin Drive

19
P

San Marin
High School

Novato Boulevard

Novato Creek

To Highway 101

*The trail shares open range with cattle.*

**1.9** Arrive at a gate for the Marin County Open Space District. Walk through the gate and latch it. Trail merges with San Andreas Fire Road. Walk uphill.

**2.0** Come to a trail marker post. San Andreas Fire Road becomes Middle Burdell Fire Road. Continue straight up.

**2.2** Come to a fork for Middle Burdell Fire Road and Deer Camp Fire Road. Turn left on Deer Camp Fire Road/ Bay Area Ridge Trail.

**2.8** Pierre Joske Grove on the left.

**3.7** Come to a trail junction for Deer Camp Fire Road and Cobblestone Fire Road. Turn left on Cobblestone Fire Road and Bay Area Ridge Trail. Cobblestone Fire Road is rough and rocky.

**4.4** Come to Burdell Mountain Ridge Fire Road and Old Quarry Trail. Walk across Burdell Mountain Ridge Fire Road. Walk north up the single track.

**4.5** Arrive at a summit of Burdell Mountain, elevation 1,558 feet. **GPS:** N38 08.77' / W122 35.49' Go down the single track and go back the way you came on Cobblestone Fire Road and stay on Cobblestone Fire Road until the junction with Deer Camp Fire Road.

**5.4** Arrive at a trail junction for Cobblestone Fire Road and Deer Camp Fire Road. Turn left and continue down Cobblestone Fire Road.

**5.7** Arrive at a T junction. Cobblestone Fire Road ends. Turn right on Middle Burdell Fire Road, going southwest. There is a seasonal pond and sensitive wildlife area.

**6.3** Come to a trail junction for Middle Burdell Fire Road and Deer Camp Fire Road. Continue walking down Middle Burdell Fire Road.

**6.6** Come to the gate into Dwarf Oak Trail ahead. Walk through gate and retrace your steps back to the trailhead.

**8.3** Arrive back at the trailhead.

## Creature Comforts

### Fueling Up

**Rickey's Restaurant at Inn Marin** (250 Entrada Dr., Novato 94949; 415-883-9477; rickeysrestaurant.com) has a lawn area next to the pool area. Pooch can be on the lawn area while you dine on the adjacent patio.

### Resting Up

**Inn Marin,** 250 Entrada Dr., Novato 94949; (415) 883-5952.

# 20 Bolinas Ridge Trail

This hike takes you up gently rolling open terrain along a dirt ranch road where cattle graze unfazed by dogs or bikes. Seeing the endless undulation of rich green pastures interrupted by oak groves surrounded by pristine views, you'll quickly understand why California cows are called "happy cows." This is an easily accessed trail in a geologically remarkable region of coastal Northern California.

**Start:** From the Bolinas Ridge Trail trailhead on Sir Francis Drake Boulevard

**Distance:** 4.8 miles out and back

**Approximate hiking time:** 2.5 hours

**Difficulty:** Easy

**Trailhead elevation:** 349 feet

**Highest point:** 780 feet

**Best season:** Year-round

**Trail surface:** Dirt ranch road through cattle grazing land

**Other trail users:** Mountain bikes

**Canine compatibility:** On leash

**Land status:** National Recreation Area

**Fees and permits:** None

**Maps:** USGS Inverness, San Geronimo; National Park Service Point Reyes National Seashore

**Trail contacts:** Golden Gate National Recreation Area, Fort Mason, Bldg. 201, San Francisco, 94123; (415) 561-4700; www.nps .gov/goga

**Nearest town:** Olema and Point Reyes Station

**Trail tips:** Although dogs are not allowed inside the nearby Point Reyes National Seashore Visitor Centers, the Bear Valley Visitor Center and its educational exhibits are well worth a stop for an up-close and personal encounter with the famed San Andreas Fault. You may want to check out one or all three of Seashore's leashed dog-friendly beaches if you have time. There are no toilets or water on the trail.

**Finding the trailhead:** From San Francisco on the north side of the Golden Gate Bridge, drive 4.0 miles north on US 101/CA 1 (Redwood Highway). The picturesque Sausalito Harbor will be on your right and Mount Tamalpais (elevation 2,574 feet) will rise up ahead. Take the Mill Valley/Stinson Beach/CA 1 exit on the right. Follow the green signs for CA 1. Drive 0.8 mile and turn left at the signal and the sign for Stinson Beach/Mount Tamalpais/Muir Woods onto Shoreline Highway, which is also CA 1. Be prepared for a scenic wending journey. Drive slowly and smoothly to spare your pooch and other passengers the discomfort of motion sickness. Drive 2.5 miles and bear left to follow the signs for CA 1/Stinson Beach. Continue another 2.5 miles to the next CA 1/Stinson Beach sign. Drive 5.8 miles and bear left through the town of Stinson Beach on CA 1. Continue driving 5.0 miles past a sign for Dog Town (population 30). Weaverville became known as Dog Town for the large number of hunting dogs living here. Another 0.5 mile past Dog Town, you will see a sign on the left indicating you are entering Point Reyes National Seashore. Drive 8.0 miles to a stop sign, a sign for the Samuel Taylor State Park on your right, and the intersection of Sir Francis Drake Boulevard (the street sign will be on your left) and CA 1. Turn right, drive 1.0 mile, and park on the shoulder at the Bolinas Ridge Trail trailhead on your right. **GPS:** N38 02.77' / W122 46.23'

*Point Reyes National Seashore in the distance*

## The Hike

This Point Reyes region of the California coast is one of those places you never tire of. In addition to being visually seductive, especially in the spring, it has a significant place in the history books as a landing spot for Sir Francis Drake in 1579.

The North American and Pacific tectonic plates that grind along the San Andreas Fault zone in the Olema Valley make this a veritable living geological classroom. Be baffled and astounded by the fact that rocks along this rugged Northern California coastline match those of the Tehachapi Mountains of Southern California. One plate travels northwestward and the other westward, but at different rates. When the pressure builds up from the rough and uneven rub of other small faults within the San Andreas Fault zone, rocks eventually shake loose and the surface occasionally takes a jump significant enough to result in earthquakes like the devastating one that shook San Francisco in 1906. In that case, the Point Reyes Peninsula, which rides atop the Pacific Plate, leaped 20 feet northwestward.

The Miwok made this region their home, hunting, harvesting, and fishing the land for 5,000 years before European explorers set foot here in the 1500s. It was Don Sebastian Vizcaino who gave Point Reyes its name in 1603 on his way north from Monterey. He passed the rocky headlands on January 6, the day of the Feast of the Three Kings, and was inspired to call it La Punta de Los Tres Reyes. The Spanish rule ended with the Mexican revolt in 1821, during which time it was common for large swaths of California land to be divided and held under "land grants." Point Reyes was divided into three land grants until the Mexican-American War, when Americans conquered California in 1848. The senior partners of a San Francisco law firm acquired the land and divided it into several dairy ranches. That was the beginning of the dairy and cattle legacy you see on the green meadows of Point Reyes.

Point Reyes National Seashore was created in 1962 and allowed existing ranches and dairies to operate under the land and resource stewardship of the park. Point Reyes encompasses 71,000 acres, of which 45 percent is designated as wilderness. The park shares boundaries with the Gulf of the Farallones National Marine Sanctuary, California Coastal National Monument, Samuel Taylor and Tomales Bay State Parks, and the Golden Gate National Recreation Area, of which the Bolinas Ridge is a part. In 1988 the United Nations' Man and the Biosphere Program included Point Reyes in the Central California Coast Biosphere, recognizing its global importance. In 2001 Point Reyes was added to the list of one hundred "Globally Important Bird Areas."

With the exception of three beaches, dogs are not allowed on the trails in the Point Reyes National Seashore. Fortunately the Golden Gate National Recreation Area has a remote finger of land called the Bolinas Ridge that reaches north to the Olema Valley and parallels the forested ridge of the Point Reyes National Seashore where you and your dog can enjoy a romp in this unique and accessible pocket of Northern California.

The complete stretch of the Bolinas Ridge Trail is 11.0 miles one way, but the outbound 2.4 miles that make up this hike treats you to an easy ramble across a meadow landscape dotted with rock outcroppings, swales of oak groves, ribbons of redwood canyons, and patches of California buttercups. With only two trail junctions, this is a very straightforward out and back.

The first junction is unmarked at 1.2 miles; you turn right and go through the gate at the wooden walk-in stall. The second junction on the Bolinas Ridge Trail (part of the Bay Area Ridge Trail system) is at 1.4 miles, where you come to signs for Jewell Trail straight and Randall Trail right. (Disregard the arrow for Jewell Trail going straight. That is incorrect). You will turn right, heading south uphill toward Randall Trail. This last mile heading south along the ridge transitions to more chamise on the left and California blackberry lacing the fence on the right as you walk parallel to Point Reyes National Seashore's forested ridgeline above the San Andreas Fault zone across the Olema Valley to the west.

At 2.4 miles the picnic table on the left invites you and your dog to have a snack and water break. Rover will be in such sniff overdrive that he would never realize the earth was moving under his paws. As you scan north to the Tomales Bay, soak up the mind-bending fact that you are standing at the edge of the North American Plate and looking across the fault zone where it bumps and grinds against the Pacific Plate. Rocks from this rugged coastline matching rocks from the Tehachapi Mountains 300 miles south is evidence of a land in motion.

Take time for a few photos before going back to the trailhead the way you came for a 4.8-mile hike. If you decide to extend your hike farther along the ridge before turning back, make sure your dog still has enough energy to make it back to the trailhead and that you have enough water to go the extra distance and the return.

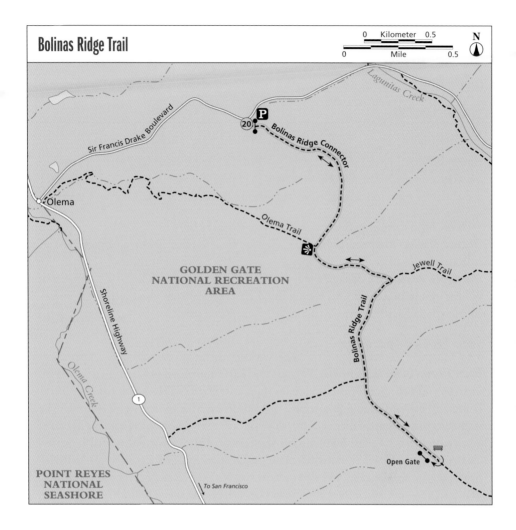

## Bolinas Ridge Trail

## Miles and Directions

**0.0**  Start at the Bolinas Ridge Trail trailhead.

**0.9**  Trail bends left and upward, revealing views of the Tomales Bay to the northwest.

**1.2**  Come to a trail junction where the trail continues straight. There is a grassy pad surrounded by rocky pinnacles on the left of the trail and a fence on the right. Another trail continues on the other side of the fence with an unmarked gate and a narrow wooden walk-through stall. Walk through the narrow stall and turn right on the trail, walking southeast up the rise.

**1.4**  Arrive at the post for the Bay Area Ridge Trail (Bolinas Ridge Trail is part of the Bay Area Ridge Trail system) and signs pointing straight to the Jewell Trail and right to the Randall Trail. Turn right and walk up toward the Randall Trail, going south.

**2.4** Arrive at a cattle gate. There will be a picnic table on the left. This is the highest point for the hike. Elevation 780 feet. **GPS:** N38 01.47' / W122 45.21' Breathe in the views. Treat yourself and your dog to a snack and water. Go back to the trailhead the way you came.

**4.8** Arrive back at the trailhead.

## Creature Comforts

*Fueling Up*

**Bovine Bakery** (11315 CA 1, Point Reyes Station 94956; 415-663-9420) has organic pastries and breads. Visit **Cowgirl Creamery** (80 Fourth St., Point Reyes Station 94956) for artisan cheeses to complement your Bovine Bakery picnic goods.

*Resting Up*

**Historic Mankas Inverness Lodge,** 30 Callendar Way, Inverness 94937; (415) 669-1034; mankas.com.

**Olema RV Resort and Campground,** 10155 CA 1, Olema 94950; (415) 663-8106; olemacampground.com. This campground has 187 sites (107 tent sites) that sit on thirty wooded acres.

## Puppy Paws and Golden Years

**Point Reyes National Seashore,** Point Reyes Station, 94956; (415) 464-5100; www .nps.gov/pore. Kehoe Beach Trail, 0.06 mile one way off Pierce Point Road in the National Seashore, is the only "trail" you can share with Pooch (on leash). Having said that, you can walk on paved roads with dogs, and there are two other beaches you can access with your dog on leash via a paved path—Point Reyes Beach North and Point Reyes Beach South off Sir Frances Drake Boulevard. Point Reyes National Seashore is a unique gem, and Fido might enjoy a relaxed scenic drive through the National Seashore, watching California cows wander the green meadows and getting high on the thick, rich Pacific headland scents gushing in through the open window. On a cool day with adequate ventilation and a sunshield on the windshield to keep him safe and comfortable, he might welcome a short nap in the car while you check out the Point Reyes Lighthouse or learn more about geology and the famous San Andreas Fault zone in the Bear Valley Visitor Center. In **Point Reyes Station,** at the junction of Third and C Streets, there's a wetland meadow with a COUNTY PARK sign and ambiguous connection to the National Seashore. The good news is that it is an off-leash open space trail. Your dog will be as intrigued as you to watch vultures line up on the fence posts to warm their spread wings in the early morning sun.

# 21 Wolf Ridge Rodeo Beach Loop

This is a scenic Marin Headlands loop that takes you on a "voice control" route so responsive dogs can sniff and gallivant off leash while you enjoy the views stretching above the Gerbode and Tennessee Valleys east and up and down the rugged coastline. Perks include historic bunkers and batteries along the way for military history buffs, and dogs will wag at the thought of romping off leash on Rodeo Beach as you close the loop along the lagoon back to the trailhead.

**Start:** From the west end of the visitor center parking lot on Field Road on the Coastal Trail
**Distance:** 5.4-mile loop
**Approximate hiking time:** 3 hours
**Difficulty:** Moderate
**Trailhead elevation:** 59 feet
**Highest point:** 884 feet
**Best season:** Year-round
**Trail surface:** Dirt, asphalt, gravel, and sand
**Other trail users:** Mountain bikers and equestrians
**Canine compatibility:** Voice control
**Land status:** National Park
**Fees and permits:** None
**Maps:** USGS Point Bonita; Golden Gate National Recreation Area Marin Headlands
**Trail contacts:** Golden Gate National Recreation Area, Fort Mason Bldg. 201, San Francisco 94123; (415) 561-4700; www.nps.gov/ goga. Marin Headlands Visitor Center, GGNRA, Bldg. 948, Fort Barry, Sausalito 94965; (415) 331-1540
**Nearest town:** Sausalito
**Trail tips:** There is no water on the trail after you leave the facilities at the visitor center, and no dogs are allowed in the freshwater lagoon, so bring plenty of water for Pooch. The visitor center is an excellent educational starting point for information, maps, and books, but budget cuts have resulted in limited hours of operation for many public land visitor centers. It is best to call ahead if you need information. Also the maps may not reflect the current dog policy, since these undergo constant revisions and rarely do changes lean in favor of dogs. What tent camping is available at the Marin Headlands does not allow dogs.

**Finding the trailhead:** From Highway 101 north of the Golden Gate Bridge take the Alexander Avenue exit 442. Drive 0.1 mile to Bunker Road. Turn left on Bunker Road/Tunnel Route. Drive 2.6 miles to Field Road, then turn left onto Field Road. Drive 0.1 mile to the visitor center parking lot on the right-hand side of the road. The trailhead is at the west end of the parking lot, to the right of the bathrooms. **GPS:** N37 49.84' / W122 31.51'

## The Hike

The Marin Headlands hills and estuaries were the lands of plenty for the Miwok before they were settled by Spanish and Mexican ranchers, followed by dairy farmers said to have immigrated from the Portuguese Azores. From the 1890s through World Wars I and II and the Cold War, the Marin Headlands were a strategic site for national defense. Evidence of the Headlands military history is visible on many of the ridges,

*Descending southward toward Rodeo Beach*

where fortifications including missile sites, bunkers, gun batteries, and observation sites were installed. Some have been preserved as part of the area's historic legacy, and many nonprofit organizations operate from some of the military buildings maintained for their historic significance.

The Nike Missile Site was restored as a museum and provides a unique opportunity to educate visitors about Cold War tools. The Hostel at Fort Barry, the Marine Mammal Center, Headland Center for the Arts, and the Marin Headlands Visitor Center are examples of military buildings being put to public use.

The Golden Gate National Recreation Area was established in 1972, and a combination of flukes, zoning controversies, timely protests by conservation activists, public awareness, and law suits resulted in the Marin Headlands land being rescued from being developed as the "Marincello" planned community. The 2,000-acre chunk was purchased from the Gulf Oil Corporation by the Nature Conservancy and transferred to the newly created Golden Gate National Recreation Area. Three of the people at the forefront of the battle to halt the development of the Headlands became the founders of the Trust for Public Lands, which operates across the United States.

The Marin Headlands is in the Golden Gate National Recreation Area, and the latter is recognized as the Golden Gate Biosphere Reserve by the United Nations. The Headlands' ridges and valleys provide excellent habitat for deer, mountain lions, foxes, coyotes, wild turkeys, rabbits, raccoon, and skunks. The Headlands are known for their abundant numbers of raptor visitors in the fall, and the top of Hawk Hill is a popular lookout for hawks, falcons, eagles, vultures, osprey, and harriers. Volunteers with the Golden Gate Raptor Observatory keep busy banding, counting, and tracking during the fall migration. Pelicans, grebes, egrets, and herons also travel through the Headlands. Harbor seals live in the Headlands' waters year-round, while gray whales swim by in spring and fall.

Geologically, the North American and Pacific Plates' 100-million-year-old tectonic rub has pushed sandstone, basalt, and shale deposits north from as far south as what we know as Los Angeles.

It's difficult to believe that you hike with your dog in a "national park," let alone off leash, yet this is one of the privileges of hiking in Golden Gate's urban national park on this loop from the visitor center. The trail is easy to follow from the west end of the parking lot next to the bathrooms. In barely 150 feet you turn right on Lagoon Trail, walk down fifty steps, and follow the narrow trail that parallels the road and cross the bridge. Walk across the road in the crosswalk up to the fire road gate to the interpretive sign and you will find the trailhead for the Miwok Trail. The trail gradually wends through grasslands for the first couple of miles, with bush lupine and poppies dotting the slopes in spring.

Coastal weather is most temperamental in the summer, when it can be hot in the shelter of the lower slopes and fiercely windy with fog chilling on the exposed spines and ridges. Expect a stiff breeze on the oceanfront ridges most of the year. On this hike you are mostly protected from the winds until you turn left onto the Wolf Ridge Trail, where it snakes more steeply for about 0.5 mile and emerges at the highest point at a fork for Tennessee Valley and Muir Beach downhill to the right. Bear left and make an immediate right, following the signs for the Coastal Trail to Rodeo Beach along the remnants of an old paved road. The trail overlooks Rodeo Lagoon and Beach. Watch for poison oak mimicking the California blackberry vines.

For the next mile the trail continues downhill as you follow the signs for the Coastal Trail. The views across the entrance to the bay to San Francisco's southern shores are spectacular. On a clear day the Golden Gate Bridge's majestic curve is a sight that never ceases to inspire. There has been much erosion, and parts of the old military settlement's paved roads have crumbled and slid off the edge of the Headlands, so the trail detours up rough rocky stitches past cement bunkers before going down ninety-five steep steps and merging with the paved road before passing Battery Townsley on your right.

At 4.1 miles you come to a trail junction indicating a HIKER'S ROUTE going right and a BIKE ROUTE going left to Rodeo Beach along the Coastal Trail following the paved road. The hiker's route looks more inviting, but the bike route on the left is the trail that officially allows dogs on this loop. You will be on the charcoal

# Wolf Ridge Rodeo Beach Loop

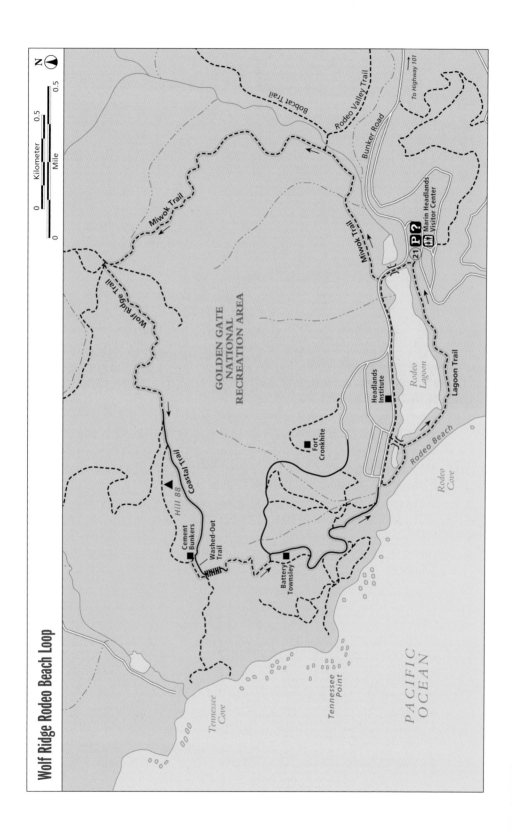

sands of Rodeo Beach in less than 0.5 mile. From here it's just an easy mile across the beach and up the Coastal Trail at the south end of the beach with the lagoon on your left to reach the trailhead in the visitor center parking lot.

## Miles and Directions

**0.0**  Start at the Coastal Trail trailhead at the west end of the visitor center parking lot and walk 150 feet to the Lagoon Trail junction and turn right on Lagoon Trail.

**0.1**  Walk across the bridge.

**0.2**  Arrive at a crosswalk. Walk across the road.

**0.22**  Come to a fire road gate, the Miwok Trail trailhead, and the Gerbode Valley interpretive sign. Walk around the gate and continue walking on the fire road following the Miwok Trail.

**0.7**  Come to the trail junction for the Bobcat Trail on the right. Continue straight on the Miwok Trail.

**1.9**  Come to a trail junction for the Wolf Ridge Trail on the left. Turn left onto the Wolf Ridge Trail and walk up the single-track trail snaking up the slope with a few short-lived steep stretches.

**2.6**  Come to a fork and the highest point on the hike. **GPS:** N37 50.58'/ W122 32.14' The Coastal Trail to the Tennessee Valley and Muir Beach drops down a single track going right. Bear left to where the trail merges with the remnants of an asphalt road on the spine of the hill. Turn right and walk downhill on the asphalt corridor along the Coastal Trail to Rodeo Beach. The trail overlooks Rodeo Lagoon and the beach.

**3.1**  Follow the signs for the Coastal Trail up an eroded rocky stretch past WW II cement bunkers on your right. Savor the views across to Lands End to the south across the entrance to San Francisco Bay.

**3.3**  Come to T junction where the trail meets an old asphalt road at the bottom of ninety-five steep wooden steps. Turn right to continue on the Coastal Trail downhill.

**3.4**  Turn left to follow the Coastal Trail downhill.

**3.6**  The trail merges with an asphalt road. Follow signs for the Coastal Trail.

**3.8**  Battery Townsley will be on your right.

**4.1**  Come to a trail junction for the Coastal Trail (hiker's route goes right and bike route goes left). Turn left and follow the bike route on the asphalt road to Rodeo Beach. Dogs are permitted on the bike route.

**4.3**  Come to a trail junction. The hiker's route comes in from the right.

**4.5**  Arrive at Rodeo Beach. Take time to let Rover spin his wheels on the long stretch of sand and surf. Enjoy a snack before leaving the beach.

**4.7**  Come to a bridge on your left at the north end of the lagoon. The bridge is the alternate route from the Coastal Trail when the channel of water flows to the ocean and walking across the beach at the surf line is not possible. Continue tracing the lagoon, walking south away from the bridge.

**4.9**  Arrive at the trail marker for the Coastal Trail to the visitor center. Walk uphill along the Coastal Trail above the lagoon to complete the loop hike.

**5.4**  Arrive back at the trailhead in the visitor center parking lot.

## Fueling Up

**Cavallo Point Lodge** (601 Murray Circle, Sausalito; 888-651-2003; cavallopoint.com) has a deck for outdoor breakfast, lunch, and dinner with Pooch.

## Resting Up

**Cavallo Point Lodge,** 601 Murray Circle, Sausalito; (888) 651-2003; cavallopoint.com. The historic Fort Baker has successfully morphed into a luxury ecolodge while preserving its historic military character. It's as much a dog's bark as it is the cat's meow in terms of its pooch perks, idyllic location in the Golden Gate National Recreation Area steps away from the Coastal Trail, and a scenic walk from Sausalito. If you and Pooch feel you deserve a splurge, this is the place to indulge.

**Inn at the Presidio,** 42 Moraga Ave., San Francisco 94129; (415) 800-7356; innatthe presidio.com. This is another luxurious choice for hikers with a pooch. The inn is steeped in history with nature at your doorstep.

*Rodeo Beach*

# Sierra Nevada

T he Sierra Nevada in Eastern California extends from the Cascade Range in the north 400 miles south to the Transverse Range. It's heavily forested west side rises gently from California's Central Valley, dropping off abruptly on the east side at the Basin Ranges, revealing granitic escarpments, peaks, and palisades cradling crystalline lakes in narrow stream-fed canyons.

The Sierra Nevada has over 200 warm sunny days a year, golden autumns, and snowstorm winters in the higher elevations. Population centers and agricultural land in the lower valleys depend on the snowpack and gradual spring melt in the rivers and streams to fill the reservoirs for the rest of the year, since "it never rains in California" as the song goes, except during the winter months.

The Sierra Nevada embraces several national forests and wilderness areas, including Plumas, Tahoe, Eldorado, Humboldt-Toiyabe, Stanislaus, and Inyo National Forests and Bucks Lakes, Granite Chief, Desolation, Mokelumne, Carson-Iceberg, Hoover, Ansel Adams, and John Muir Wilderness Areas. The Sierra Nevada is a kingdom of pristine lakes, streams, and wildflower-cloaked meadows that attracts hikers, fishers, and nature contemplators from all over the world.

Within the Sierra Nevada are Mount Whitney, the highest mountain in the Lower 48 at 14,495 feet; Lake Tahoe, the largest alpine lake in North America; precious groves of giant sequoias; and Northern Sierra's Yosemite National Park's sheer granite walls draped in breathtaking waterfalls.

Like most of California's mountain ranges, the Sierra Nevada's rich resources supported Native Peoples for thousands of years, because they learned to live in harmony with the rhythm of her seasons and respect the indomitable. Many an explorer, fur trader, pioneer, and fortune seeker underestimated the power of Mother Nature and perished trying to conquer the colossal mountain barrier. Many of the hiking trails and developed recreation sites you enjoy with your dog were established along ancient paths traveled by Native Americans and historic routes blazed by early emigrants.

# 22  Mill Creek Trail

This dirt trail tracing the eastern shore of Bucks Lake (a natural-looking reservoir cradled by forested slopes of pine and fir) on the way to the Mill Creek Campground makes an excellent jaunt for hikers and pooches who long for a pleasant, generally flat hike with lots of opportunities for cooling dips where the trail hugs the shoreline. The pine, fir, and aspen woodland provides shade with good views of the lake, and spring wildflowers give the fern groves a splash of color.

**Start:** From Mill Creek trailhead
**Distance:** 10.3 miles out and back
**Approximate hiking time:** 4.5 hours
**Difficulty:** Moderate because of length
**Trailhead elevation:** 5,220 feet
**Highest point:** 5,309
**Best season:** Early summer to early fall
**Trail surface:** Dirt trail
**Other trail users:** Horses and mountain bikes (except where the trail skirts the wilderness)
**Canine compatibility:** Voice control
**Land status:** National Forest; Wilderness
**Fees and permits:** None
**Maps:** USGS Bucks Lake; Plumas National Forest

**Trail contacts:** Plumas National Forest Mount Hough Ranger District, 39696 CA 70, Quincy, CA 95971; (530) 283-0555; www.fs.fed.us
**Nearest town:** Quincy
**Trail tips:** The flow out of Mill Creek, depending on the winter snowpack, will determine whether you can hike all the way to Mill Creek Campground across the creek or if you will have to turn around at 4.7 miles before the creek crossing. If the creek is safe to cross, you have the option of driving to Mill Creek Campground along Bucks Lake Road to camp (no day-use parking) and then hiking the out-and-back trail from the campground rather than from the Mill Creek trailhead on Bucks Lake Road.

**Finding the trailhead:** From Quincy on CA 70/89 turn west toward Bucks Lake. Turn onto CR 119 and follow the signs for Bucks Lake. Drive 14.0 miles to the parking area on the right shoulder of the road for the Mill Creek trailhead. **GPS:** N39 53.06 / W121 08.97'

## The Hike

Bucks Lake in Plumas National Forest was created by building the Bucks Storage Dam in 1928 on Bucks Creek, a tributary to the Feather River. The flooded land was originally the site of a ranch dating back to 1850. The town on the south shore of the lake by the same name is registered as a California Historical Landmark.

Although Bucks Lake is a human-made reservoir with a dam, it is surprisingly natural looking and not overdeveloped. The west shore has a couple of lodges, marinas, campgrounds, and summer cabins. Even motorized recreation on Bucks Lake (motor boats and water skiing) isn't the intrusive nuisance you would expect.

The east shore of the lake is pristine, and the Mill Creek Trail is a lovely trek. With the exception of a 0.5-mile stretch where the trail cuts across a forested headland,

*Trail along Bucks Lake*

the lake and mountains across the lake are always within sight, and the trail hugs the shoreline close enough for you and Pooch to stop for dips from several beachheads and along tucked-away inlets. The beauty of this hike is that if a particular granite-slab perch above the lake calls to you, an inlet beach seems especially alluring, or your dog is so euphoric from the forest smells and lakeside romping within the first mile or two, you are free to call any part of this trail your destination.

The southern end of Bucks Lake is narrow but quickly widens to reveal a panorama of mountains across the larger body of water. The first couple of miles showcase lush fern groves beneath the canopy of pine, fir, and some aspen and occasional cedar. Snowbush and manzanita shrub are dappled with purple Sierra daisies, white ranger buttons, crimson columbines, and Sierra gooseberry.

At 2.0 miles the trail climbs gently and briefly, and a forested slope on your left obscures the view of the lake for about 0.5 mile as the trail cuts across a forested headland, which is where you and Pooch briefly set foot and paw in the Bucks Lake Wilderness. The trail skirts Bucks Lake Wilderness at this point and enters the wilderness for a short stretch. The lake reappears on your left at an inlet where you will pass two designated campsites.

The creek crossing at 2.6 miles boasts a lovely cascade that is sure to lure any water-loving dog on a hot summer day. Just across the creek at the trail junction and to your right about 50 feet away is a WILDERNESS BOUNDARY sign on the tree.

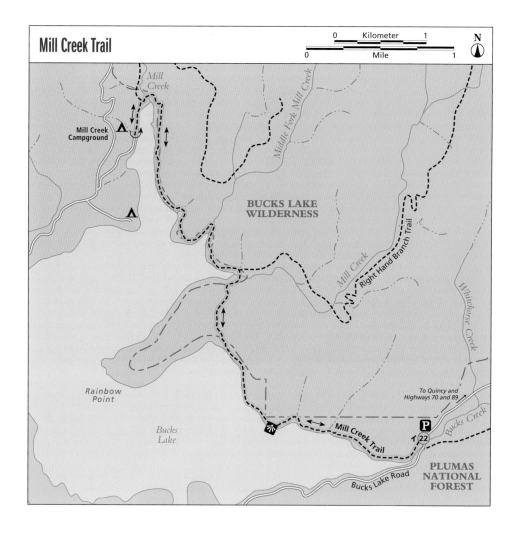

## Mill Creek Trail

Mill Creek

Mill Creek Campground

BUCKS LAKE WILDERNESS

Middle Fork Mill Creek

Mill Creek

Right Hand Branch Trail

Whitehorse Creek

Rainbow Point

To Quincy and Highways 70 and 89

Bucks Lake

Mill Creek Trail

Bucks Creek

22

Bucks Lake Road

PLUMAS NATIONAL FOREST

0    Kilometer    1
0    Mile    1

N

Although the trail narrows from here on with some more primitive stretches, it is well worn and the lake will always be on your left until you turn around at Mill Creek Campground.

At 4.5 miles cross a babbling brook, and 0.2 mile up the trail, Mill Creek, the main inlet into Bucks Lake, comes in from your right. This is where a light or heavy winter will determine if the creek is safe to cross to Mill Creek Campground or if this will be your turnaround point. Fortuitously, a recent fallen sugar pine now serves as a natural footbridge to help keep your feet dry.

Once you cross the creek, the trail continues straight up a hill for 0.1 mile to a trail junction and the boundary for the Bucks Lake Wilderness on the right. Mill Creek Campground, your destination and turnaround point, is to the left 0.3 mile ahead.

If you want to go down to the beachhead at the lake below, look for the trail on the left just short of a log footbridge and a sign for Mill Creek Trail and Chuck Rock.

Mill Creek Campground does not have a day-use area. Have fun and turn around the way you came.

## Miles and Directions

**0.0** Start at the Mill Creek Trail trailhead.

**1.2** Come to a viewpoint overlooking the lake.

**2.6** Come to a creek crossing with a cascade inviting your pooch for a soak.

**2.65** Reach a trail junction across the creek for the Right Hand Branch Trail. Notice the WILDERNESS BOUNDARY sign posted on a tree about 50 feet to your right. Bear left and continue walking along the lake.

**4.5** Come to a stream. Walk across the stream.

**4.7** Reach Mill Creek flowing into Bucks Lake from the northwest. Walk across Mill Creek if the water is not too high or too fast, which depends on the season and the winter's snowpack. Walk straight uphill on the other side of the creek.

**4.8** Come to a trail junction. You will see a BUCKS LAKE WILDERNESS sign on your right. Turn left and continue walking with the lake on your left.

**5.15** Reach Mill Creek Campground. This is your turnaround point. **GPS:** N39 54.76' /W121 11.22' Take the time to go down to the lake on the beach below. Turn around and go back the way you came.

**10.3** Arrive back at the trailhead.

## Creature Comforts

### Fueling Up

**Bucks Lakeshore Resort** (16001 Bucks Lake Rd., Quincy 95971; 530-283-2848; buckslakeshore.com) has dog-friendly outdoor seating by the parking lot. **Quincy Natural Foods** (269 Main St., Quincy 95971; 530-283-3528; qnf.weebly.com) is a well-stocked little grocery store with some prepared foods as well as organic breads and pastries from its onsite bakery. You and your pooch can enjoy a leisurely snack at one of the outdoor tables.

### Resting Up

**Mill Creek Campground** (Forest Service) off Bucks Lake and FR 33 has seven sites for tent/RV spaces.

**Bucks Lakeshore Resort** (16001 Bucks Lake Rd., Quincy 95971; 530-283-2848; buckslakeshore.com) has tent and RV camping as well as dog-friendly cabins.

# 23 Round Lake/Bear Lakes Loop

This easy, enchanting, well-marked trail begins in a pine forest before crossing a rainbow-palette wildflower-laden meadow (blooms peak in late spring and early summer) before weaving and undulating past six picturesque lakes with granitic backdrops. Although the elevation change is slight, the trail's exposed sections provide panoramic views. This is a hike you and your pooch will replay in your dreams for a long time.

**Start:** From Round Lake Trail trailhead
**Distance:** 4.7-mile loop
**Approximate hiking time:** 2.5 hours
**Difficulty:** Easy
**Trailhead elevation:** 6,600 feet
**Highest point:** 6,859 feet
**Best season:** Early summer to early fall
**Trail surface:** Dirt trail with intermittent rocky sections
**Other trail users:** Horses
**Canine compatibility:** Voice control
**Land status:** National Forest
**Fees and permits:** None

**Maps:** USGS Gold Lake; USFS Plumas National Forest
**Trail contacts:** Plumas National Forest Beckwourth Ranger District, 23 Mohawk Highway Rd., Blairsden 96103; (530) 836-2575; www .fs.usda.gov/plumas
**Nearest town:** Graeagle
**Trail tips:** The hike is strictly a day hike, since there is no camping permitted along any of the lakes on this loop. If you wish to make an overnight trip in this area, check with the ranger district listed in the Trails contacts section for details on which lakes in the Basin area allow camping and what permits may be required.

**Finding the trailhead:** From Graeagle drive 1.0 mile south on CA 89 onto FR 24/Gold Lake Forest Highway and follow the signs for the Lakes Basin (FR 24 is unmarked until you make the turn and are actually on it). Drive 7.5 miles on FR 24 and turn right at the sign for Round Lake Trail and Gold Lake Lodge just past the SIERRA COUNTY LINE sign on the right. ROUND LAKE TRAIL and GOLD LAKE LODGE signs are on the left side of FR 24. Drive into the parking lot at the end of the road. There is a vault toilet on the left, and the sign for Round Lake Trail is to the right of the parking lot. **GPS:** N39 41.58' / W120 39.39'

## The Hike

The Lakes Basin is a relatively small concentrated paradise of lakes, buttes, and peaks accessed via the scenic Gold Lake Forest Highway in the northeast corner of the Plumas National Forest's million-acre spread.

The story of this tranquil corner of the Sierra Nevada is steeped in gold fever history. The Maidu called the region home in summer for thousands of years, until fortune hunters lured by rumors of lakes lined in gold displaced them. These days the picturesque lake-strewn region bordered by sprawling meadows to the east and dotted with historic mining outposts that have been turned into quaint tourist recreation basecamps is all about hiking and fishing in the summer. Whether you are camping or

*Round Lake*

bunking in one of the cozy old cabin resorts, the Lakes Basin is dog-friendly Plumas County's outdoor recreation jewel.

This loop is one of the most popular hikes in the Lakes Basin and for good reason. From spring to midsummer the spectacle of wildflowers in the meadows along the first 0.5 mile is an exceptional treat, from pink nettle-leaf horsemint and scarlet Indian paintbrush to the purple trumpet penstemon and white corn lilies.

The plant zones that transition from deep green conifer forest to sub-alpine shrubs and thickets, mixed in with manzanita on the exposed plateau and willow by the lake sides, provide visual variety against the granitic backdrop. At 0.8 mile the trail climbs out of the pine forest to more exposed windswept manzanita brush and becomes rockier.

You will spot your first lake in less than 1.0 mile and will come to a lake about every 0.5 mile until you close the loop. Although the setting is wild and pristine, another aspect that makes this hike unique are the signs with names and elevations at every lake, along with tidbits of natural and cultural history.

The first of these markers is at the 1.8-mile trail junction and site of the remains of an old gold mine and stamp mill that burned down in 1935.

At 2.6 miles the Silver Lake sign gives you a taste of geology 101, describing it as a "cirque lake" scooped out by glacial activity.

*Silver Lake*

The view overlooking Long Lake at almost 3.0 miles is one of the biggest wow factors of this hike. It says "big is beautiful," and even in this small pocket of wildness cradled by communities, the sheer wall plunging into the lake on the northwest shore speaks to the majesty of the Sierra's colossal indomitable kingdom.

Any of the lakes make splendid picnic stops and cooling-off breaks for your pooch.

## Miles and Directions

**0.0** Start at the Round Lake Trail sign.

**0.2** Come to a fork on the trail with a sign for Round Lake 1¾ with an arrow pointing to the left and Bear Lake ½ with an arrow pointing to the right. Turn left to hike the trail in a clockwise direction before looping back from Bear Lake this fork.

**0.9** You get your first view of Big Bear Lake and the granite necklace that hugs the Lakes Basin below on your right.

**1.4** Come to an unnamed pond on the right.

**1.7** Come to a viewpoint overlooking Big Bear Lake.

**1.8** Come to a historical marker for the Round Lake Gold Mine overlooking Round Lake and a trail junction with signs for the Pacific Crest Trail (PCT) and Silver Lake. Turn right on the downhill trail toward Silver Lake ¾.

# Round Lake/Bear Lakes Loop

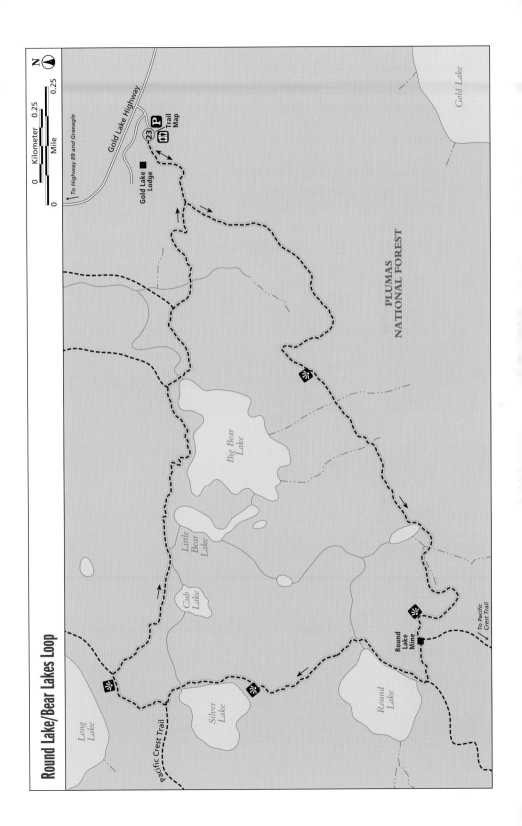

**2.0** Arrive at Round Lake at the base of a granite butte.

**2.4** Come to a view of Silver Lake on the left below.

**2.6** Arrive at Silver Lake.

**2.7** Come to a trail junction with signs for the PCT, Mount Well, and Bear Lakes. Bear right heading north toward Bear Lakes.

**2.9** Reach a viewpoint for Long Lake.

**2.95** Come to a fork on the trail and a sign for CUB LAKE, BIG BEAR LAKE, AND LAKES BASIN CG. Turn right and descend toward Cub Lake and Big Bear Lake.

**3.2** Arrive at Cub Lake on your right.

**3.3** Come to Little Bear Lake on your right.

**3.6** Arrive at Big Bear Lake on your right.

**3.9** Reach a trail junction for Gold Lakes Lodge and Round Lake trailhead. Turn right. Big Bear Lake will still be on your right.

**4.1** Reach a trail junction and turn right to Round Lake trailhead.

**4.4** Come to a trail junction and sign for ROUND LAKE TR HD stapled to a post. Turn right to Round Lake trailhead.

**4.5** Reach the trail junction that completes the Lakes Loop. Continue walking straight back 0.2 mile to the trailhead the way you came.

**4.7** Arrive back at the trailhead.

## Creature Comforts

*Fueling Up*

**Graeagle Outpost,** 7358 CA 89, Graeagle 96103; (530) 836-2414; graeagleoutpost .com. Open every day of the year. Summer food service is offered from 7 a.m. to 6 p.m., and on Wednesday evening you and Pooch can enjoy live music and pizza on the deck.

**Nakoma Golf Resort and Spa,** 348 Bear Run off A 15, Clio 96106; (530) 832-5067; nakomagolfresort.com.

**Chalet View Lodge,** 72056 CA 70, Portola 96103; (530) 832-5528; chaletviewlodge .com.

*Resting Up*

**Gray Eagle Lodge,** 5000 Gold Lake Rd., Graeagle 96103; (800) 635-8778; grayeagle lodge.com.

**Chalet View Lodge,** 72056 CA 70, Graeagle 96103; (530) 832-5528; chaletviewlodge .com.

**Nakoma Golf Resort and Spa,** 348 Bear Run off CA 89 and CR A-15, Clio 96106; (530) 832-5067; nakomagolfresort.com. This Frank Lloyd Wright–designed resort recently re-opened under new dog-loving ownership and management. Four of the twelve architecturally unique villas welcome dogs.

*Big Bear Lake*

**Clio's River's Edge RV Park,** 3754 CA 89, Clio 96106; (530) 836-2375; riversedgervpark .net. This is one of the best-maintained and spacious RV campgrounds (there are no tent sites), and it has access to the Feather River.

**Plumas-Eureka State Park,** CR A-14/Graeagle-Johnsville Road, off CA 89; (530) 836-2380; www.parks.ca.gov, www.reserveamerica.com. This state park has tent and RV sites (no hookups), a visitor center/museum, and a historic mining camp.

**Lakes Basin Forest Service Campground, Plumas National Forest** on Packer Lake Rd. off of Gold Lake Rd., Graeagle; (530) 836-2575, (877) 444-6777; www.reservations .gov

## Puppy Paws and Golden Years

**Graeagle Outpost and Yacht Club on Mill Pond** (530-836-2414; graeagleoutpost.com), at the edge of town, is great for a swim with Pooch or for cruising on a rented paddle-boat or kayak. The path circling the pond is level and scenic with benches and picnic areas for leisurely strolls.

# 24 Feather Falls

On some hikes the journey is as much a highlight as the destination. This is not one of those hikes. Although the trail is relatively undistinguishable with a run-of-the mill mix of deciduous and coniferous woodland, it's easy on your dog's paws. And what dog doesn't love to have his senses flooded with new smells? He won't be impressed by the waterfall or one of the best waterfall-viewing decks in the country, but you will. The Feather Falls National Recreation Trail gives you the opportunity to enjoy this stunning 620-foot waterfall from a unique perspective, thanks to a daring deck design with the added bonus of sharing the experience with your dog.

**Start:** From Feather Falls trailhead
**Distance:** 9.7 miles out and back
**Approximate hiking time:** 5 hours
**Difficulty:** Moderate because of distance
**Trailhead elevation:** 2,500 feet
**Highest point:** 2,500 feet
**Best season:** Year-round; spring is cool and the prettiest season to visit
**Trail surface:** Hard-packed dirt trail with a couple patches of deteriorated pavement
**Other trail users:** Horses and mountain bikes
**Canine compatibility:** On leash
**Land status:** National Forest

**Fees and permits:** None
**Maps:** USGS Brush Creek, Forbestown; USFS Plumas National Forest
**Trail contacts:** Plumas National Forest Feather River Ranger District, 875 Mitchell Ave., Oroville 95965; (530) 534-6500; www.fs.usda.gov/plumas
**Nearest town:** Oroville
**Trail tips:** Bring water. A short trail bridge that allows for a lollipop option is out indefinitely due to budget cuts. The longer trail is the out and back.

**Finding the trailhead:** From CA 70 in Oroville take exit 46 for CA 162 and drive 8.0 miles east on CA 162. Make a right turn onto Forbestown Road and drive 6.0 miles to Lumpken Road. Turn left onto Lumpken Road and drive 10.8 miles to the FEATHER FALLS SCENIC AREA sign. Turn left at the sign and drive 1.5 miles to the parking lot at the end of the road. **GPS:** N39 36.87' / W121 16.00'

## The Hike

Feather Falls Scenic Area in the Plumas National Forest was established in 1965 to preserve 15,000 acres that surround the canyon of the Middle Fork Feather River and three of its tributaries. The centerpiece to the scenic area is the Feather Falls, a 620-foot plunge that looks like a roll of white muslin fabric unfurling over the granite face. Feather Falls is the fourth-highest waterfall in California and sixth-highest in the United States outside of Alaska. The Middle Fork Feather River was one of the first rivers in the country to be designated "Wild and Scenic."

*View of Feather River*

The trail begins at the far end of the parking lot, and the first 200 feet or so are paved. The hike begins on a nourishing note with the sound of water flowing from a nearby creek to feed the riparian habitat on this slope of the forest. Besides a sprinkling of wooden benches (some in disrepair) along the way and a couple of nice wooden footbridges over cascading streams in the first two miles, the trail itself isn't rich in outstanding characteristics until it opens up for a view of Bald Black Dome across the precipitous canyon about halfway to beautiful Feather Falls. The falls are in a uniquely dramatic setting, and the viewing deck, which clutches the top of a rocky nob, is connected to the mountain by a footbridge; it looks like it is suspended above the canyon.

Dogs aren't into waterfalls, nor are they impressed by edgy viewing-deck designs, but there will be plenty of tail wagging going on as her senses get flooded from the rich odors floating under the deciduous woodland canopy of bay, oak, and madrone mixed with pine and fir trees. Ferns, Manzanita, and wild blackberry abound as the trail gradually wends down the canyon.

There are two footbridges over creeks, one at 1.2 miles and the second at 1.7 miles over Frey Creek. The latter is the lovelier of the two, with a cascade on the right offering you and Pooch refreshing dipping pools. The rest of the way is dry, so be sure to have plenty of water to hydrate yourself and Pooch to the falls and back.

At 2.5 miles, where the trail reveals expansive views of the Middle Fork Feather River canyon walls and an interpretive sign compares the geology of Bald Black Dome across the canyon to Yosemite National Park's famous Half Dome, the trail begins to hug the slope and the vegetation changes to a scrubbier, drier woodland.

At 4.2 miles you come to an unmarked trail junction with a bench on the left side of the trail. Walk uphill on the trail to the right and up the switchbacks. The trail transitions to a path of deteriorated concrete, indicating that you are on the last stretch to the viewpoint.

The sound of water filters around the bend, and at 4.6 miles you reach the first overlook. Follow the trail along the metal guardrail, bear left, and step down, always following the guardrail, and ignore the concrete steps going up to the right. Follow the trail downhill for about 0.2 mile and prepare to be awed as you walk down the stairway and over a timber gangway to the diamond-shaped viewing deck anchored to a granite nob. The design and location of the deck is as astounding as the view of the falls and the narrow rugged river canyon below. It's a great spot to have a picnic and take time to savor the experience before going back the way you came.

## Miles and Directions

**0.0**  Start at the Feather Falls trailhead.

**0.3**  Come to a trail fork with a sign for Falls 3.3 miles to the left and 4.5 miles to the right. Bear right on the 4.5-mile trail.

**0.7**  Come to a bench on the right.

**1.2**  Come to a footbridge across a stream.

**1.7**  Come to a footbridge over Frey Creek and an interpretive sign about riparian habitats.

**2.5**  Reach the viewpoint for Bald Black Dome and an interpretive sign explaining the geology of the dome.

**4.2**  Come to a trail junction and a bench on the left. Turn right and walk uphill away from the bench and follow the switchbacks up the slope and along the remnants of a previously paved path.

**4.6**  Reach the first falls overlook, where the trail is bordered by a metal guardrail.

**4.7**  Come to an unmarked fork with a couple of concrete steps going uphill to the right. Bear left and continue following the trail and metal guardrail downhill to a stairway and a gangway to the main and most impressive viewing deck.

**4.85**  Reach the viewing deck dropped atop a granite nob and let the view take your breath away. The falls are to the north, and the Middle Fork Feather River flows south along the canyon floor. Snap some shots of Bowser looking at the falls, hydrate, and enjoy a scenic snack before going back the way you came. Elevation 1,930 feet. **GPS:** N39 38.51' / W121 16.50

**9.7**  Arrive back at the trailhead.

## Creature Comforts

### Resting Up

**Feather Falls Forest Service Campground** at the trailhead has five tent sites. It's nothing more than convenient. Contact the Feather River Ranger District at (530) 534-6500. There are a few dog-friendly motels in **Oroville.**

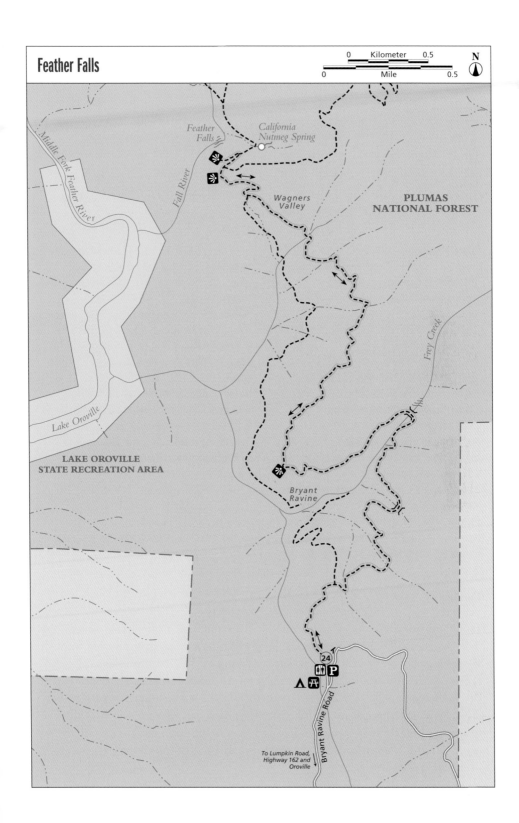

# Feather Falls

0  Kilometer  0.5

0  Mile  0.5

N

Middle Fork Feather River

Feather Falls

California Nutmeg Spring

Fall River

Wagners Valley

PLUMAS NATIONAL FOREST

Frey Creek

Lake Oroville

LAKE OROVILLE STATE RECREATION AREA

Bryant Ravine

24

Bryant Ravine Road

To Lumpkin Road, Highway 162 and Oroville

# 25 Sagehen Creek Trail

This easy flat trail is every dog's dream, and there's something in it for you, too. The gurgling waters of Sagehen Creek escort you visibly almost all the way to Stampede Reservoir and frequently swirl just one paw stride away for a cooling splash. Whereas the plentiful pines and aspens offer shade over the initial 1.5 miles, the last stretch across the sundrenched meadow blooms with eye-popping perrywinkle blue camas lilies in spring. Bowser will be euphoric at the chance to sprint across the grassland in spring, summer, or fall.

**Start:** From the parking area off CA 89, just after the unmarked Sagehen Creek bridge

**Distance:** 5.6 miles out and back

**Approximate hiking time:** 2.5 hours

**Difficulty:** Easy

**Trailhead elevation:** 6,151 feet

**Highest point:** 6,151 feet

**Best season:** Early summer to early fall

**Trail surface:** Dirt trail with a little rock

**Other trail users:** Horses, mountain bikes

**Canine compatibility:** Voice control

**Land status:** National Forest

**Fees and permits:** None. This is a "user-created trail" that does not officially appear on any maps. But be aware that because it is on national forest land, it is subject to the same rules and regulations as any other national forest trail regarding campfire permits.

**Maps:** USGS Hobart Mills; USFS Tahoe National Forest

**Trail contacts:** Tahoe National Forest Truckee Ranger District 10811 Stockrest Springs Rd., Truckee 96161; (530) 587-3558 (ask to speak to "recreation staff"); www.fs.usda.gov/tahoe

**Nearest town:** Truckee

**Trail tips:** As a "user-created trail," there are no trailhead signs or trail markers and no toilets or other facilities on this hike. The creek is a great splash zone for your dog, but be sure to carry drinking water.

**Finding the trailhead:** From Truckee on I-80, take the exit for CA 89 north toward Sierraville (exit 188B). Drive 7.2 miles and turn right into the parking area immediately after the unmarked Sagehen Creek bridge. **GPS:** N39 26.05' / W120 12.30'

## The Hike

In addition to a bounty of high-country hikes and a rich pioneering history, the Tahoe National Forest in the Sierra Nevada has some gems only revealed through the local grapevine. Sagehen Creek Trail to Stampede Reservoir outside of Truckee is one of those. What it lacks in views across to precipitous peaks or climbs to lakes in the shadow of granite cirques, it makes up for with its serene setting, unusual botanic display, and amazing expanse of flat grassy land made to order for pooches who live to get high on running in circles. This is a very pretty hike and an opportunity to appreciate the contrast between the rugged high country and this more gentle side of the Sierra Nevada.

*Enjoying the walk along the trail*

This trail is soft on the paws and easy on the eyes with its slopes and glade carpeted in mule's ear and highlighted by occasional tall, graceful blooms of orange pine drops and bouquets of red Indian paintbrush. The explosion of purple camas lilies in spring is what brings wildflower enthusiasts to the meadow.

Once you park the car, it's just a matter of walking between the two boulders and following the trail for 2.8 miles to the shores of Stampede Reservoir. The shoreline can vary from 2.0 to 3.0 miles down the trail depending on water levels from dry or wet winters.

The trail is narrow and traces the creek for the first mile. Road noise is soon replaced by the gurgle of the creek as it meanders toward the reservoir, flooding a willow meadow along the way before morphing into a snaking ribbon across the vast meadow partly swallowed by the reservoir. The backdrop of undulating green-forested mountains in the distance helps create a peaceful relaxing cadre for you and your dog to enjoy fresh air, open space, and quality time at a leisurely pace.

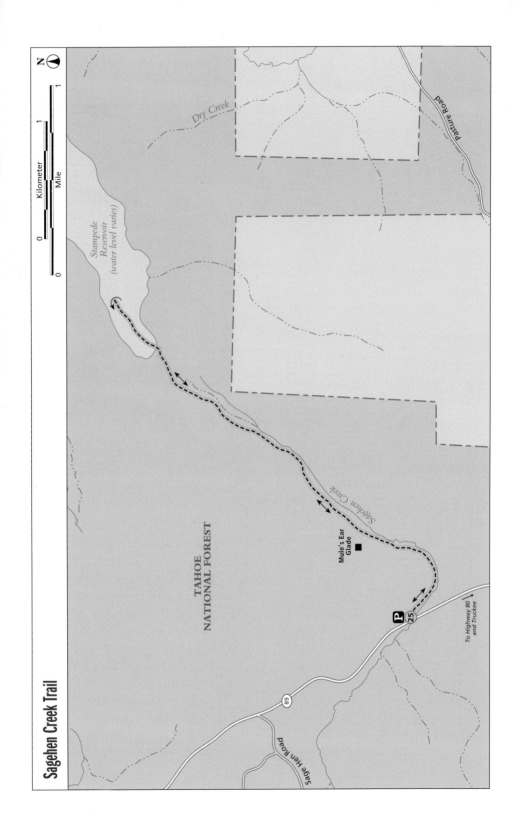

Sagehen Creek Trail

*Headed toward Stampede Reservoir*

## Miles and Directions

**0.0**  Start at the unmarked trailhead between two boulders on Sagehen Creek.

**0.6**  The trail is carpeted with mule's ear on the slopes as far as the eye can see.

**2.8**  Come to the shores of Stampede Reservoir. Soak up the view across the water to the forested mountains and take time to stroll the meadow with your dog before going back the way you came. Elevation 5,947 feet. **GPS:** N39 27.47' / W120 10.41'

**5.6**  Arrive back at the trailhead.

## Creature Comforts

### Fueling Up

**Wild Cherries Coffee House,** 11429 Donner Pass Rd., Truckee, 96161; (530) 582-5602; wildcherriescoffeehouse.com.

**Taco Station,** 11782 Donner Pass Rd., Truckee, 96161; (530) 587-8226.

**FiftyFifty Brewing Company,** 11197 Brockway Rd., Truckee, 96161; (530) 587-2337.

**Ritz-Carlton, Lake Tahoe,** 13031 Ritz Carlton Highlands Court, Truckee 96161; (530) 562-3000; ritzcarlton.com. The Ritz hosts a summer afternoon "Yappee Hour."

*Resting Up*

**Donner Memorial State Park,** 12593 Donner Pass Rd., Truckee, 96161; (530) 582-7892; www.parks.ca.gov. There are many lovely campgrounds (most are Forest Service) around Truckee, but most off I-80, even when boasting riverside settings, will be spoiled by road noise. The quietest campsites are at the rear of the campground. Dogs on leash are also welcome to the day-use areas of the park. This park's location at the east end of beautiful but mostly privately developed Donner Lake happens to be scenic as well as historic. The **Emigrant Trail Museum** at the Donner Memorial State Park Visitor Center has exhibits and a short film reviewing the pioneering history of the area, including the tragic tale about the infamous "Donner Party" from the winter of 1846. The park was established on the site where members of the Donner Party of emigrants met their demise as they traveled from the Midwest to begin new lives in California.

**Cedar House Sport Hotel,** 10918 Brockway Rd., Truckee 96161; (530) 582-5655; cedarhousesporthotel.com.

**Inn at Truckee,** 11506 Deerfield Dr., Truckee 96161; (530) 587-8888; innattruckee .com.

**Ritz-Carlton, Lake Tahoe,** 13031 Ritz Carlton Highlands Court, Truckee 96161 (off of CA 267 between Truckee and Tahoe Vista on Lake Tahoe's north shore); (530) 562-3000; ritzcarlton.com. The Ritz offers pooch pampering plus!

## Puppy Paws and Golden Years

**Donner Camp Day-Use Area,** 2.5 miles north of Truckee on the east side of CA 89, is the historic site where some members of the distressed Donner Party spent the winter. Soak up some California pioneer history while sharing a picnic with Pooch on the way back from Sagehen Creek. Call Tahoe National Forest Truckee Ranger District at (530) 587-3558.

# 26 Loch Leven Lakes Trail

The granitic and root-laced trail zigzagging to the crest before dropping down to the first of the three Loch Leven Lakes won't necessarily wow you. It's a narrow, mostly rocky trail that starts on exposed granite slabs before slipping under the cool shade of pines for part of the way. A sprinkling of scarlet Indian paintbrush and delicate lavender daisies add color to the manzanita bushes. I-80 will come in and out of view, and the hum of the highway won't hush until you drop down to Lower Loch Leven Lake. But the second you catch a glimpse of Lower Loch Leven, the first of three picturesque glacier-carved lakes suspended on a granite plateau, you will understand why this is a popular day hike and an enchanting overnight. The lakes are favorite plunging pools for hikers and their dogs, and the granite slabs will beckon you and your dog to scamper up to enjoy a scenic picnic.

**Start:** From the Loch Leven Lakes Trail trailhead
**Distance:** 8.6 miles out and back
**Approximate hiking time:** 5 hours
**Difficulty:** Strenuous because of the rocky terrain
**Trailhead elevation:** 5,797 feet
**Highest point:** 6,882 feet
**Best season:** Summer to fall
**Trail surface:** Rock, roots, and granite with some dirt stretches;
**Other trail users:** Hikers and dogs only
**Canine compatibility:** Voice control
**Land status:** National Forest
**Fees and permits:** None for day hikes; campfire permits for overnights subject to seasonal district regulations

**Maps:** USGS: Cisco Grove and Soda Springs, CA; USFS Tahoe National Forest
**Trail contacts:** Tahoe National Forest, American River Ranger District, Foresthill Ranger Station, 22830 Foresthill Rd., Foresthill 95631; (530) 367-2224; www.fs.usda.gov/tahoe
**Nearest town:** Truckee
**Trail tips:** Unless your dog is a veteran of coarse and rocky surface hiking, this is not the trail to test the toughness of his paws. If ever there was a trail that screamed for booties, this is it. Don't leave home without them, and put them on your dog's feet before he shows signs of tender tootsies—or risk having to carry him on the way back.

**Finding the trailhead:** From central Truckee take the I-80 exit (exit 186) and drive 17.5 miles west on I-80. Take the Big Bend/Rainbow Road exit (exit 168), to turn left toward Big Bend, bear right, and drive 1.0 mile to the parking area with the vault toilet on your right. **GPS:** N39 18.56' / W120 30.94'

## The Hike

Not all regions in the Sierra Nevada are created equal. It could be argued that the two major interstate highways, I-50 and I-80, are scars across the face of the stunning Sierra Nevada in the Lake Tahoe Basin and Tahoe National Forest region. Yes, the

*High Loch Leven Lake*

highways have ploughed the way for ski resorts and some runaway development, and the road noise intrudes on campgrounds that would otherwise be considered "idyllic." But iconic Lake Tahoe surrounded by crests and peaks remains a unique jewel, and the region is a rich cauldron of emigrant and gold rush history steeped in legendary exploits as well as pioneering tragedies. Ironically, the two interstate highways are also convenient gateways to fabulous dog-friendly hikes in the Tahoe National Forest and surrounding wilderness areas.

The Loch Leven Lakes hike is just one of many of these easily accessed excursions. *Loch* is a Gaelic word for lake, and it is a fitting name for these lovely organic bodies of fresh water tucked atop a granitic plateau.

The narrow Loch Leven Lakes Trail begins with an east-to-west zigzag upward across exposed lichen-dappled granite slabs. Watch for the rock cairns and two orange stakes as you walk the first 200 feet to help locate the sharp turn east on the trail.

I-80 comes in and out of view for the first mile, until your eyes refocus on the railroad tunnel high up across the canyon. That stitch of rail makes the history of the first transcontinental railroad come to life. The railroad and its impressive snowshed tunnels were built by Chinese laborers during the construction of the transcontinental railroad of 1860.

At 1.2 miles leash your dog after you cross the wooden footbridge, as you will cross railroad tracks 0.2 mile ahead. The trail continues across the railroad tracks and climbs into the shade of the forest. The trail remains mainly a rocky route, with roots sometimes requiring some fancy footwork; booties are definitely in order for your pooch. Both you and your dog will welcome the occasional rock-free stretches of dirt trail. Take advantage of the shadier sections for rest and water breaks. Notice the wild roses and Indian paintbrush mingling with the manzanita bush

At 2.5 miles the trail approaches a plateau and the views open to surrounding ridges. Imagine a few patches of late spring snow, and you could be standing in the middle of a Bev Doolittle painting. The hum of the interstate will finally be replaced by the sound of the breeze brushing the treetops.

You reach the open crest of the ridge just under 3.0 miles, before the short, steep descent to Lower Loch Leven. Those beautiful Lock Leven Lakes are your payoff. Whether you make Lower, Middle, or High Loch Leven your destination, all three make excellent stops for a swim and a picnic perched on a granite slab on this glaciated plateau that makes these lakes appear to be floating in the sky. Lower Loch Leven is a good time to check on your dog's paws and decide if you want to continue another 0.5 mile to Middle Loch Leven and the last mile to High Loch Leven.

You will come to a couple of straightforward forks on the trail between Lower Loch Leven and High Loch Leven; lakeshores will always be on your left.

## Miles and Directions

**0.0**  Start at the Loch Leven Lakes Trail trailhead across the road from the parking area and vault toilets. Walk 200 feet before the trail makes a sharp left turn across a granite slab.

**0.2**  Come to the Loch Leven Lakes Trail sign nailed to a pine tree. You will see I-80 on your left.

**0.3**  Enter a fern grove shaded in a fir forest.

**0.7**  Come to a pond on your left.

**1.1**  Come to a yellow and black striped sign marking underground cables on your right. You will see the railroad across the canyon.

**1.2**  Cross a wooden bridge and enter a lush shaded stretch of aspen and mixed conifers.

**1.4**  Come to railroad tracks. Walk across the tracks and continue on the trail climbing up into the forest.

**2.9**  The trail crests, and views open to surrounding ridges before a short, steep descent.

**3.0**  Arrive at Lower Loch Leven Lake.

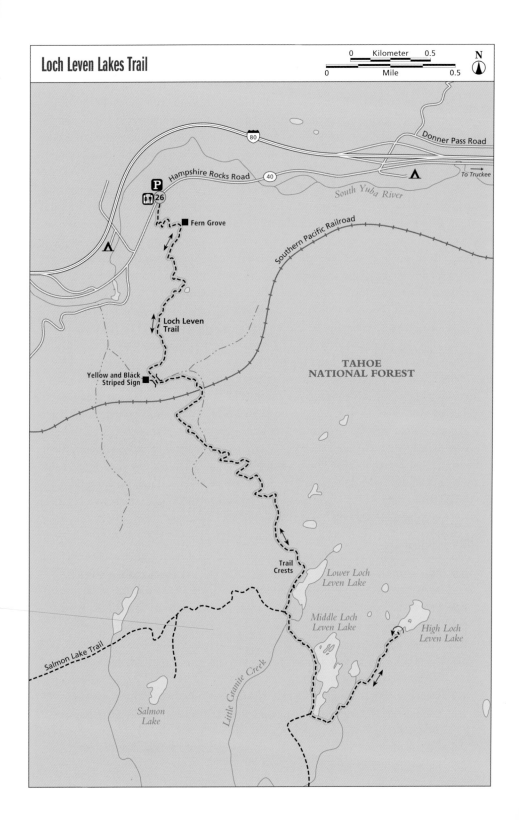

**3.2** Come to a fork with a Middle Loch Leven Lake ¼, Cherry Pt. ½, High Lock Leven Lake 1 trail sign. The unmarked trail to the right leads to Salmon Lakes. Continue straight toward Middle and High Loch Leven Lakes.

**3.5** Arrive at Middle Loch Leven Lake and a sign for Middle Loch Leven Lake that hangs on a rope from a tree.

**3.8** Come to a fork on the trail and a Horse Flat 3, Big Granite 3, North Fork of the American River 8 sign. Bear left around the head of Middle Loch Leven Lake.

**4.3** Arrive at High Loch Leven Lake. **GPS: N39 17.13' / W120 29.89'**

**8.6** Arrive back at the trailhead.

## Creature Comforts

### Fueling Up

**New Moon Natural Foods,** 11357 Donner Pass Rd., Truckee 96161; (530) 587-7426; newmoonnaturalfoods.com

**Wild Cherries Coffee House,** 11429 Donner Pass Rd., Truckee 96161; (530) 582-5602.

**Taco Station,** 11782 Donner Pass Rd., Truckee 96161; (530) 587-8226.

**FiftyFifty Brewing Company,** 11197 Brockway Rd., Truckee 96161; (530) 587-2337.

**Ritz-Carlton, Lake Tahoe,** 13031 Ritz Carlton Highlands Court, Truckee 96161; (530) 562-3000; ritzcarlton.com. The Ritz hosts a summer afternoon "Yappee Hour."

### Resting Up

**Donner Memorial State Park,** 12593 Donner Pass Rd., Truckee 96161; (530) 582-7892; www.parks.ca.gov. There are many lovely campgrounds (most are Forest Service) around Truckee, but most off I-80, even when boasting riverside settings, will be spoiled by road noise. The quietest campsites are at the rear of the campground. Dogs on leash are also welcome to the day-use areas of the park. This park's location at the east end of beautiful but mostly privately developed Donner Lake happens to be scenic as well as historic. The **Emigrant Trail Museum at the Donner Memorial State Park** has exhibits and a short film that reviews the pioneering history of the area, including the tragic tale about the infamous "Donner Party." The park was established on the site where members of the Donner Party of emigrants met their demise while traveling from the Midwest to begin new lives in California in 1846. **Hampshire Rocks Forest Service Campground** (530-265-4531; www.reservations.gov) is off I-80 from the Big Bend exit 168 on the way to the Lock Leven Lakes Trail trailhead parking area. There are tent and RV sites (no hookups) on the South Fork of the Yuba River. **Lost Trail Lodge** (8600 Coldstream Rd., Truckee 96161; 530-320-9268; losttraillodge.com) is 4.0 miles down the road off of Donner Pass Road. It offers a common kitchen for self-catering. Other options include **Cedar House Sport Hotel** (10918 Brockway Rd., Truckee 96161; 530-582-5655; cedarhousesporthotel.com) and **Inn at Truckee** (11506 Deerfield Dr., Truckee 96161; 530-587-8888; innattruckee.com). The **Ritz-Carlton** (ritzcarlton.com) is located off of CA 267 between Truckee and Tahoe Vista on Lake Tahoe's north shore. The hotel offers pooch pampering plus!

# 27 Five Lakes Trail

This moderate scenic hike between two popular ski resorts climbs across an exposed granitic landscape before entering the Granite Chief Wilderness, where you and Pooch can enjoy the sights and refreshing coolness of one or all three of the five lakes along this popular trail.

**Start:** From the Five Lakes Trail trailhead
**Distance:** 4.8 miles out and back
**Approximate hiking time:** 2.5 hours
**Difficulty:** Moderate
**Trailhead elevation:** 6,575 feet
**Highest point:** 7,575 feet
**Best season:** Summer to fall
**Trail surface:** Dirt trail with some rock and granite
**Other trail users:** Horses
**Canine compatibility:** Voice control
**Land status:** National Forest; Wilderness
**Fees and permits:** None
**Maps:** USGS Tahoe City, Granite Chief; USFS Tahoe National Forest; Granite Chief Wilderness
**Trail contacts:** Tahoe National Forest, Truckee Ranger Station, 9646 Donner Pass Rd., Truckee 96161; (530) 587-3558; www.fs.usda.gov/tahoe

**Nearest town:** Tahoe City
**Trail tips:** The information board at the trailhead says that "dogs are discouraged" because of stress to wildlife and because dogs may bother people who do not enjoy them. It also says that dogs are prohibited in certain areas of the Five Lakes during fawning season, from May 15 to June 15. The hike described here does not go into the restricted area and was recommended by a couple of rangers who hike with their dogs. On a sunny July Saturday, we met at least twenty well-behaved dogs off leash between 9 a.m. and 11a.m. Evidently this is a favorite jaunt of many dogs and their owners, and it's a perfect opportunity for you and your dog to be ambassadors for all the responsible dog owners with well-mannered dogs who hike in wilderness areas.

**Finding the trailhead:** From Tahoe City drive 3.7 miles north on CA 89. Turn left on Alpine Meadows Road toward Alpine Meadows Resort and drive 2.0 miles to the trailhead on the right-hand side of the road across from Deer Park Road. Park on the shoulder. **GPS:** N39 10.76' / W120 13.78'

## The Hike

The Granite Chief Wilderness's 25,000 acres in the Tahoe National Forest is not California's largest wilderness, nor does it abound with lakes like some regions of the Sierra Nevada, but its cirques and hanging valleys and the fact that the headwaters of the 119-mile-long American River and several other major tributaries drain in this glaciated wilderness give it status. Ironically the wilderness was named for the 9,000-foot Granite Chief Peak to the north, which was excluded from the wilderness after lobbying private landowners expressed fear of invasion by too many hikers.

Fans of extreme sports should know that the grueling Western States 100-mile endurance run crosses parts of the Granite Chief Wilderness.

*The furthest of the Five Lakes*

It is not unusual to find good hikes near ski hills, but few offer a relatively short scenic trail to a lake setting in a wilderness area accessible from the shoulder of a paved road on the outskirts of a resort town as bustling as Tahoe City. That's what makes the Five Lakes Trail in the Five Lakes Basin near the center of the Granite Chief Wilderness different.

You park your car on the shoulder just short of the Alpine Meadows Resort and start the climb in mostly exposed terrain. Crimson columbine and Indian paintbrush brighten up the mountain chaparral mixed with manzanita and snowbush that dominate the steep slopes until you reach the first patch of forest at 0.5 mile. You and your dog should take advantage of the occasional trees over the next mile to hydrate in the shade.

As the trail climbs, it overlooks the Alpine ski bowl for the first mile. At 1.2 miles a sign on a tree alerts you that you are crossing private property as the slope-side trail skirts the granite canyon on your left. This stretch of the trail is exceptionally scenic where the elements have sculpted granite slabs, stacks, and some outcrops that look like granite dough balls clinging to the slopes.

In less than 0.5 mile, you enter the Granite Chief Wilderness. You then pass a meadow that is purple with aster before catching a glimpse of your first lake through the trees on the left at 1.8 miles. Bear left at the trail junction ahead, and at 2.1 miles you see a sign for Five Lakes posted on a tree to your left, indicating that you are entering the Five Lakes area. The sign also advises hikers that camps and stock animals should be no closer than 600 feet from the lakes. The first of the Five Lakes is on your left. This is a good spot for a dip, but the best picnic perch is still ahead.

Continue to the lake's outlet just left of the unmarked trail junction. Walk across the lake's outlet, which may be obscured by willow. Follow the trail across the outlet and come to a bluff with a lovely view to the east of the two most accessible of the five lakes. You are standing on the backside of Squaw Valley, and some of the ski resort's lifts are visible on the ridge to the north. This bluff overlooking two lakes is your destination. You and Pooch can enjoy a snack and take time to explore along the shore below before going back the way you came.

## Miles and Directions

**0.0**  Start at Five Lakes Trail trailhead.

**1.2**  Reach private property boundary.

**1.6**  Enter Granite Chief Wilderness.

**1.8**  Come to an unmarked spur leading to the first lake on the left. The trail to the other two lakes continues straight ahead.

**1.9**  Come to a trail junction for the Pacific Crest Trail and Whiskey Camp Trail to the right. Bear left to Five Lakes.

**2.1**  Arrive at the FIVE LAKES sign posted on a tree to the left; the second of the Five Lakes is visible ahead.

**2.2**  Come to an unmarked trail junction. Turn left and walk across the lake's outlet and up the trail.

**2.4**  Reach a bluff overlooking two lakes. This is your turnaround point after you enjoy the setting and a refueling snack. Go back the way you came. Elevation 7,554 feet. **GPS:** N39 10.48' / W120 15.22'

**4.8**  Arrive back at the trailhead.

## Creature Comforts

*Fueling Up*

**New Moon Natural Foods,** 505 West Lake Blvd., Tahoe City 96145; (530) 583-7426; newmoonnaturalfoods.com.

**Dockside 700,** 700 Northlake Blvd., Tahoe City 96145; (530) 581-0303; dockside700 .com. Order your food to go and enjoy the lake view with Pooch at one of the picnic tables.

*Resting Up*

**Tahoe State Recreation Area** (CA 28 on the lake side in Tahoe City) is one of several good campgrounds around Lake Tahoe. This smaller popular campground (about twenty-five tent and RV sites with no hookups) on the North Shore offers

# Five Lakes

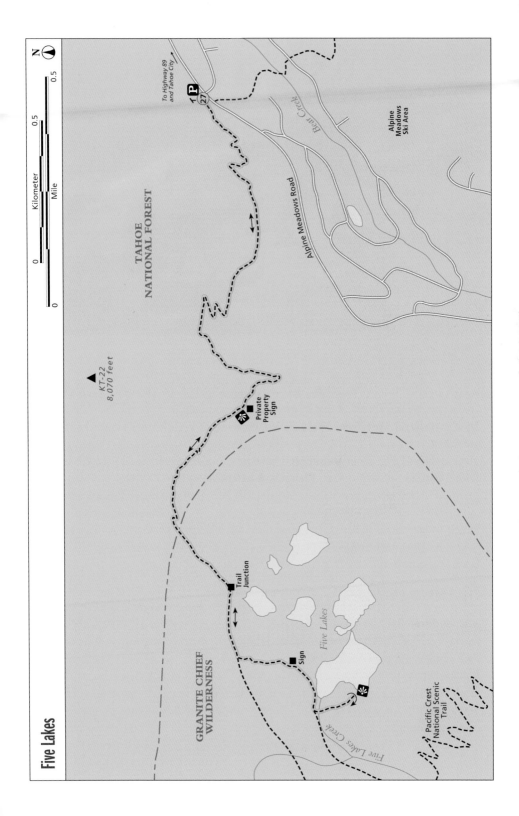

N

Kilometer
0        0.5

Mile
0        0.5

TAHOE
NATIONAL FOREST

KT-22
8,070 feet

To Highway 89
and Tahoe City

P

27

Bear Creek

Alpine Meadows Road

Alpine
Meadows
Ski Area

Private
Property
Sign

GRANITE CHIEF
WILDERNESS

Trail
Junction

Sign

Five Lakes

Five Lakes Creek

Pacific Crest
National Scenic
Trail

*Starting the return hike*

a convenient location to civilized conveniences such as restaurants, supermarkets, and a visitor center, with access to the paved recreational path up the Truckee River. **Ed Z'Berg Sugar Pine Point State Park** (approximately 10.0 miles south of Tahoe City on CA 89; 530-525-7232; www.parks.ca.gov) is a large, well-developed campground with 175 tent and RV sites (no hookups) in a densely forested peaceful setting with 2.0 miles of lake frontage. **Plump Jack Squaw Valley Inn** (1920 Squaw Valley Rd., Olympic Valley aka/Squaw Valley 96146; 530-583-1576; plumpjacksquawvalleyinn .com) caters to luxury-loving dogs and their owners. Other options include **River Ranch Lodge** (2285 River Rd., Tahoe City 96145; 530-583-4264; riverranchlodge .com) and **Tamarack Lodge** (2311 N. Lake Blvd., Tahoe City 96145; 530-583-3350; tamarackattahoe.com).

## Puppy Paws and Golden Years

**Truckee River Raft Company,** 185 River Rd., Tahoe City 96145; (971) 208-7382; truckeeriverraft.com. Rent a raft and float down the Truckee River with time to stop for a plunge and picnic with Pooch.

**Gallery Keoki,** 1850 Village S, Olympic Valley in the Squaw Valley Resort Village; (530) 583-1404; gallerykeoki.com. Your dog will want to check out the dog photography and dream about the Alpine Meadows Avalanche Patrol Team of nine golden retriever pinups.

# 28 Cascade Falls

This is a sweet, short scenic hike to a precipitous waterfall along a wide, soft dirt trail that crosses a sparse coniferous forest before it narrows along exposed terraced granite. It offers views of Cascade Lake, Lake Tahoe, and the surrounding majestic peaks.

**Start:** From the information board at the back of Bayview Campground
**Distance:** 1.6 miles out and back
**Approximate hiking time:** 1 hour
**Difficulty:** Easy
**Trailhead elevation:** 6,895 feet
**Highest point:** 6,933 feet
**Best season:** Summer to fall
**Trail surface:** Dirt and granite
**Other trail users:** Hikers and dogs only
**Canine compatibility:** Voice control
**Land status:** National Forest
**Fees and permits:** None
**Maps:** USGS Emerald Bay; USFS Eldorado National Forest

**Trail contacts:** Eldorado National Forest, Pacific Ranger District 7887, CA 50, Pollock Pines 95726; (530) 644-2349. Taylor Creek Visitor Center, CA 89, South Lake Tahoe 96150; (530) 543-2674; www.fs.usda.gov/ltbmu
**Nearest town:** South Lake Tahoe
**Trail tips:** The trail is narrow between a granite slope and a steep forested drop over the last 0.5 mile. You are likely to meet other hikers, some with dogs, so it is safest to have your canine pal on a harness and leash on this narrower stretch of the trail.

**Finding the trailhead:** From South Lake Tahoe at the intersection of CA 89 and CA 50, drive 7.5 miles north on CA 89. Turn left at the Bayview Campground and drive 0.2 mile to the trailhead parking area at the far end of the campground. The trailhead is set back to the right of the information board, with a large wooden sign at the fork for Cascade Falls and Desolation. Bear left for Cascade Falls. **GPS:** N38 56.61' / W120 06.00'

## The Hike

Lake Tahoe, the largest alpine lake in North America with 72.0 miles of shoreline, was formed two million years ago, and the basin was first inhabited by the Washoe. The history of Lake Tahoe and the basin's discovery by Europeans, settlement, exploitation, and efforts at balancing recreation and development with conservation follows much the same chronology as most of California's spectacularly resource-rich regions. Native Americans greeted European explorers, who were followed by settlers who saw the land and waterways as inexhaustible sources of timber, minerals, and wildlife. The Lake Tahoe Basin was no different.

Lieutenant John C. Fremont was the first European to set eyes on 22.0-mile-long and 12.0-mile-wide Lake Tahoe floating at a 6,000-foot elevation. He was on his second Sierra expedition, and "discovered" the lake on Valentine's Day 1844. The floodgates were opened from that moment of discovery. By 1862 the Department

*Top of Cascade Falls*

of the Interior named the lake "Tahoe," which is in effect a mispronunciation of a Washoe word that means "lake." Lake Tahoe was partitioned between California and Nevada when the latter became a state in 1864. Mining and logging scarred the land in the Lake Tahoe Basin from the 1850s to almost the turn of the twentieth century, when the public began to appreciate Lake Tahoe from another perspective. Several opulent mansions and mega summer homes were built by the financial movers and shakers of the times, several of which are now fabulous historic sites and museums. Efforts by some members of Congress between 1912 and 1918 to designate the area a national park failed. By the 1950s and well into the 1970s, building along the lakeshore, especially on the south shore, ran amuck. The Nevada state line exploded with gambling casinos, and California ski resorts and strip malls were evidence that Lake Tahoe's natural beauty was on the verge of being smothered.

Since the 1980s local grass roots organizations have mobilized to bring attention to the environmental concerns, and development has slowed with much stricter regulations. In 1973 the creation of the Lake Tahoe Basin Management Unit (LTBMU) by the US Department of Agriculture made "preservation and restoration of the Lake Tahoe watershed ecosystem" its primary mission. The LTBMU oversees 191,000 acres of public land interlaced with private land and is responsible for maintaining all

*View of Cascade Lake and Lake Tahoe*

the recreational opportunities that make the peak-cradled Lake Tahoe area so popular. The LTBMU is also charged with protecting natural historic and cultural sites in the basin. In addition to national forests, the basin has several state parks that protect miles of beachfront for public recreational access.

Cascade Falls, in the Eldorado National Forest of the Lake Tahoe Basin, has views of Lake Tahoe's approximate 1,600-foot-deep glacial age phenomenon, and it is a delightful trail for you and your dog from the get-go. The wide trail with soft, sandy dirt under Pooch's paws begins in a sparsely forested clearing for the first 0.2 mile. Then it rises over polished granite and opens up to soaring views of Cascade Lake in the foreground on your left below and majestic Lake Tahoe in the background. Mount Tallac and the colossal granite peaks are straight ahead.

The granitic landscape is interrupted by mountain chaparral with manzanita, snowbush, and an occasional splash of wildflower color.

At 0.4 mile the trail narrows and descends gently along the granite slope on your right, and there's a steep drop covered in mountain chaparral all the way to Cascade Lake below. The trail soon rises over granite steps, and Lake Tahoe returns into sight behind you.

Watch for the trail sign on the granite slab at 0.7 mile and follow the arrow to the falls. The visible trail peters out over granite, but keep walking to the large, flat granite bench, where you can see the water plummeting over the sheer face. Cascade Creek tumbles down the swale above the face between Mount Tallac to the southeast and Maggies Peaks to the west.

Leash your dog before stepping closer for a view of the falls. After a good look and some photos, walk back up away from the falls to other granite slab perches for a snack. This spot near the creek is a great place to spend time letting your spirit soar and your pooch sniff around the green patches of shrubbery. The return trip to the trailhead will continue to enchant you with views of the lakes.

## Miles and Directions

**0.0** Start at the Cascade Falls and Desolation Wilderness trailhead. Cascade Falls is to the left.

**0.2** Come to a rise and view of Cascade Lake and Lake Tahoe to the left.

**0.6** Trail climbs over terraced granite.

**0.7** Come to a trail junction with a sign for CREEK with an arrow pointing right and FALLS with an arrow pointing downhill. Continue walking down across the granite slab. This is a good place to leash your dog, as the falls drop down a sheer face just ahead on your right.

**0.8** Reach the top of Cascade Falls plummeting down the precipitous granite face on the right. Enjoy the view and go back the way you came, taking time for a snack and a scamper on the granite slabs set safely back from the falls.

**1.6** Arrive back at the trailhead.

## Creature Comforts

### Fueling Up

**Camp Richardson Resort,** 1900 Jameson Beach Rd., South Lake Tahoe 96150; (530) 541-1801; camprichardson.com. This resort is located off of CA 89, 2.5 miles north of the CA 50 and CA 89 junction on the lake side of CA 89. Resupply from the general store or the coffee and confectionery shop, or stop by the ice cream parlor for Fido's favorite flavor (anything but chocolate, since it is toxic for dogs).

### Resting Up

**Bayview Campground,** (530) 543-2694 or (530) 544-5994. This is a small Forest Service campground (first-come, first-served) at the trailhead for Cascade Falls and the Desolation Wilderness.

**D. L. Bliss State Park,** (530) 525-7277; www.parks.ca.gov. The campground has 168 sites for tents and RVs (no hookups) on Lake Tahoe, just north of the trail for Cascade Falls.

**Fireside Lodge B&B,** 515 Emerald Bay Rd., South Lake Tahoe 96150; (530) 544-5515; tahoefiresidelodge.com.

South Lake Tahoe also has several **dog-friendly motels.**

## Puppy Paws and Golden Years

**Camp Richardson Marina,** 1900 Jameson Beach Rd., South Lake Tahoe 96158; (530) 541-1801. Boat rentals offer some "on water" sightseeing.

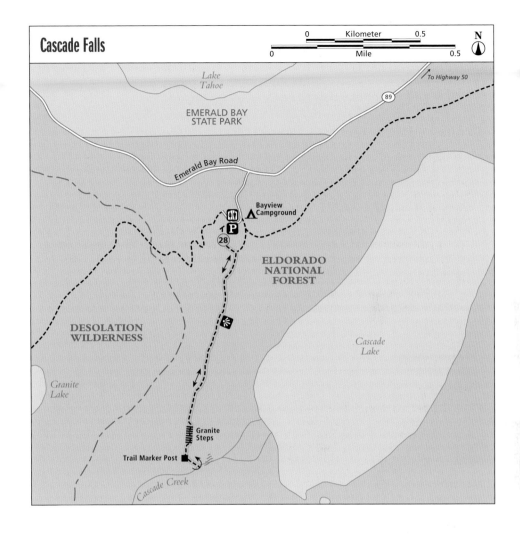

**Cascade Falls**

Lake Tahoe

EMERALD BAY STATE PARK

To Highway 50

89

Emerald Bay Road

Bayview Campground

28

ELDORADO NATIONAL FOREST

DESOLATION WILDERNESS

Cascade Lake

Granite Lake

Granite Steps

Trail Marker Post

Cascade Creek

**Kiva Beach,** just north of Camp Richardson Resort, is one of a few Lake Tahoe beaches where dogs can stroll with their owners. But they must be on leash to protect the local wildlife from harassment. Visit **Taylor Creek Visitor Center** (**GPS:** N38.9356' / W120.0530'; 530-543-2674) on CA 89 3 miles north of South Lake Tahoe on the lake side.

The **Tallac Historic Site** (three lavish summer estates from the turn of the twentieth century) between Camp Richardson and Taylor Creek Visitor Center has multiple paths and is a pleasant "travel back in time" stroll. In August you can enjoy the annual Vintage Faire with Fido on the grounds of Tallac. Contact the Tahoe Heritage Foundation for details (2435 Venice Drive, #108, South Lake Tahoe 96158; 530-544-7383; tahoeheritage.org; Tallac Historic Site: 530-541-5227).

# 29 Lake Aloha

The scenic fifteen-minute boat taxi across Echo Lake to the trailhead is just a teaser for the mesmerizing hike ahead along one of the prettiest sections of the Pacific Crest Trail (PCT) in the western Sierra, which also happens to run along the Tahoe Rim Trail (TRT) on this stretch. The trail climbs gradually above Echo and Tamarack Lakes over a granite terrace laced with mountain chaparral for 2.0 miles before crossing a wildflower meadow and continuing through patches of hemlock, fir, and pine forests. The trail offers glimpses of other lakes and ponds along the way before revealing Lake Aloha's magnificently stark, smooth granite, island-dotted panorama.

**Start:** From the Upper Echo Lake boat landing where the water taxi drops you off.
**Distance:** 7.9-mile lollipop, after the 3.0-mile boat ride (approximately 15 minutes)
**Approximate hiking time:** 4 hours plus round-trip boat shuttle
**Difficulty:** Moderate
**Trailhead elevation:** 7,418 feet
**Highest point:** 8,344 feet
**Best season:** Memorial Day to Labor Day (boat-shuttle season varies depending on winter snow conditions)
**Trail surface:** Rock and dirt: The first 2.0 miles are granite slabs and granite rock
**Other trail users:** Horses
**Canine compatibility:** Voice control
**Land status:** National Forest; Wilderness
**Fees and permits:** Free mandatory Wilderness permits for day hikes and fee Wilderness permits for overnights. Desolation Wilderness sees more visitors per acre than any forest in the country.
**Maps:** USGS Echo Lake, Pyramid Peak; Eldorado National Forest; Desolation Wilderness
**Trail contacts:** Summer—Taylor Creek Visitor Center, CA 89, 3.0 miles north of South Lake Tahoe/6.0 miles south of Emerald Bay; (530) 543-2674. Year-round—Lake Tahoe Basin Management Unit, Supervisor's Office, 35 College Dr., South Lake Tahoe 96150; (530) 543-2600; fs.usda.gov/ltbmu (lake tahoe management unit); Echo Chalet and boat taxi information for Lake Aloha (schedule and fees), echochalet.com/taxi.htm
**Nearest town:** South Lake Tahoe
**Trail tips:** Confirm the boat taxi schedule for your return

**Finding the trailhead:** From South Lake Tahoe at the intersection of CA 89/50, drive 9.7 miles on CA 50 west to Johnson Pass Road. Turn right onto Johnson Pass Road (Echo Camp sign is on the left side of CA 50). Drive 0.5 mile on Johnson Pass Road to Echo Lake Road, turn left onto Echo Lake Road, and drive 1.0 mile down to the marina parking lot by Echo Chalet. (Hikers using the boat taxi can park by the marina). Purchase your ticket at the booth by the dock (dogs are an extra fee) ($12 and $5). Hop on the boat to the Upper Echo Lake boat landing. The unnamed trailhead is to the right of the information board across from the boat landing. **GPS:** N38 50.80' / W120 04.71'

*Hikers disembark from the boat taxi at the trailhead.*

## The Hike

Echo Lakes is the gateway to the Lake Aloha Trail in Eldorado National Forest's almost 600,000 acres. The Eldorado National Forest was actually established with a portion of land from the Tahoe National Forest in 1910. Echo Lakes are a set of glacial twin lakes in a stunning granite setting. The original stream that connected the pair of lakes was diverted for mining operations, and the dam raised the lakes' water level to create the channel that makes it possible for the boat taxi to ferry hikers and backpackers to the farthest shore for shorter access to the PCT and trails into the Desolation Wilderness, as long as winter snowmelt provides high-water conditions in the channel. The length of the boat taxi season varies according to water levels.

The Washoe occupied the Echo Lakes area prior to the arrival of fur trappers, miners, and settlers who opened up a trade route. Visitors began to recreate in the Echo Lakes Basin in the 1920s, and the chalet that was built in 1939 continues to offer cabin rentals and supplies to hikers and backpackers. It also operates the seasonal boat taxi.

Lake Aloha began as a natural shallow granite basin formed by glacial activity and filled by snowmelt. It is the largest alpine lake in the Desolation Wilderness. The first

*Lake Aloha*

dam was built in 1875 to control seasonal water flow. What is left of the dam activity that took place prior to 1969, when the area of the Eldorado National Forest first set aside as a "primitive" area was officially designated as the Desolation Wilderness, is relatively inconspicuous. It is actually only visible when you return to the trailhead following the lollipop route back along the eastern shore walking south. The first view of broad Lake Aloha's smooth granite giant stepping-stone-like islands against the backdrop of a stunningly stark granite crest is such a breathtaking panorama, you have to believe Mother Nature was the artist. Although the idea of a dam seems incongruent with this awe-inspiring desolate wilderness, it does not diminish the setting's unique and extraordinary beauty.

The boat taxi is an exciting and very scenic way to start your adventure to Lake Aloha with your dog as you cruise across Lower Echo Lake and through a narrow idyllic channel to Upper Echo Lake. You will see cabins on the southwest shore of Echo Lakes as you taxi along. The first cabin at Echo Lakes dates back to 1872, and since the Forest Service offered leases for summer homes in the 1920s, 121 cabins without phone or electricity have been built above the lake, a few of which are on private property. Access is by boat or trail. Cabin owners are proud to tell you that they have formed an association that supports the Forest Service in protecting the delicate environment around the lake.

Within less than twenty minutes, you are landing at the foot of the trailhead across from the dock and to the right of the information board. The trailhead is unnamed at this point, but 400 feet up the hill, the trail merges with the PCT and TRT to Lake Aloha.

Although the first 2.0 miles up along an exposed granite slope is slow going, because the trail is mostly granite slabs and granite rock, it's just gives you more time to soak up the scenery. The green veins of mountain chaparral mixed with manzanita, snowbush, and other windswept shrubbery highlighs the pale of the granite. Both Lower and Upper Echo Lakes remain visible behind you for the first mile, and Tamarack Lake appears on the left below about 1.0 mile up the trail. No matter how striking the views as you move through this granite kingdom, it won't make your dog's paws feel any better, so have him wear booties for the first couple of miles.

At 0.7 mile you enter the Desolation Wilderness, and from here on you come to several trail junctions for nearby lakes before reaching Lake Aloha. Follow the PCT and LAKE ALOHA signs.

At about 1.8 miles you come to a lush glen bursting with purple asters, blue lupine, and red Indian paintbrush and interrupted by gnarly element-battered pines and clusters of shaggy, droopy hemlock trees.

At 2.6 miles Lake Margery comes into view on your right as you cross a swale of boulders. About 0.3 mile ahead you come to a fork with an option for Lake Aloha on a left trail or Lake Aloha along the PCT trail. This is the beginning of your lollipop. Bear right to stay on the PCT to Lake Aloha, and you return to this fork from the other trail to close your lollipop on the way back from Lake Aloha.

Notice the rock pond on your left just past the Lake Aloha fork and another pond on your right as you pass the Lake Lucille junction at 3.1 miles. Lake Aloha appears on your left in another 0.5 mile, just short of the Mosquito Pass trail junction.

Prepare to be wowed at 3.7 miles when you reach the shores of Lake Aloha's unusual beauty. Smooth, barren granite islands float on the water, and sculpted granite arms reach into the lake. A granite rampart braces the lake on its western shore, and a ring of evergreens cradle the eastern shore. You can see the cleavage where Mosquito Pass cuts its way to the northwest.

This is a place you and Pooch want to absorb. Sit for a snack before you turn left to walk south along the eastern shore. The lake will be on your right as you loop back to the PCT where the Lake Aloha Trail merges in back at the 2.9-mile point.

At 4.5 miles bear left at the unmarked fork on the trail and continue uphill toward Echo Lake at the next trail junction. Bear left again to Echo Lake at 4.65 miles.

You merge back with the PCT at 5.1 miles, and turn right to close the lollipop and head back to the trailhead the way you came. The views will be as enchanting on the way back, and it will seem as though you are seeing it all for the first time. Remember to stop and hydrate yourself and your dog frequently and use the occasional shade for rest stops. The exposed granite slope on the last couple of miles down to the trailhead can be beastly on a summer afternoon. Once you are back at the trailhead, call the boat taxi from the shelter next to the dock if no one else is waiting for the boat.

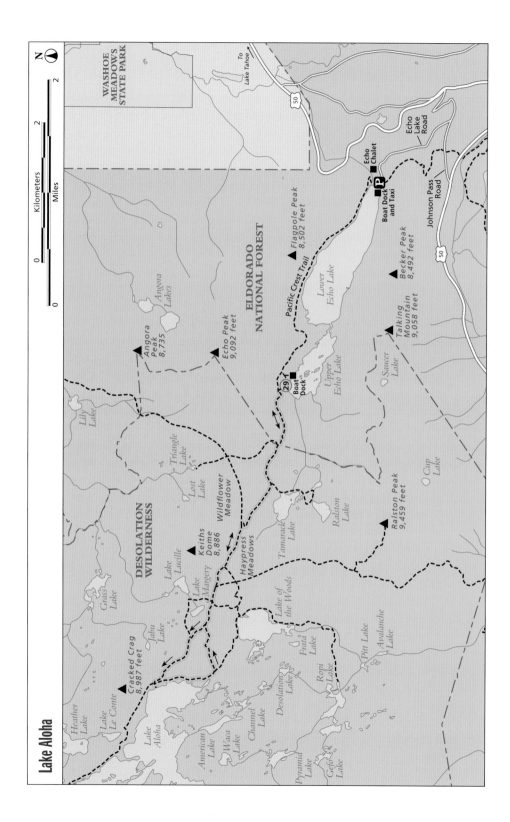

Lake Aloha

## Miles and Directions

**0.0**  Start at the trailhead right of the information board just across from the Upper Echo Lake boat landing. Walk 400 feet uphill and merge with the PCT and TRT.

**0.7**  Enter the Desolation Wilderness. Come to a trail marker for the PCT and trail junction for Triangle Lake and Lake Aloha. Walk straight on the PCT to Lake Aloha.

**1.2**  Come to a trail junction for Tamarack Lake on the left. Continue straight on the PCT to Lake Aloha.

**1.8**  Come to another trail junction for Triangle Lake. Continue on PCT straight ahead to Lake Aloha.

**2.2**  Reach a trail junction for Lake of the Woods left. Continue straight on PCT to Lake Aloha.

**2.4**  Reach another trail junction for Lake of the Woods. Continue walking straight on the PCT to Lake Aloha.

**2.5**  Reach a trail junction for Lake Lucille. Continue walking straight on the PCT to Lake Aloha.

**2.9**  Come to a fork where you have a choice to take a left trail to Lake Aloha or continue on the PCT to Lake Aloha. Bear right to continue on the PCT to Lake Aloha. You will lollipop back along the left trail to this junction from Lake Aloha.

**3.1**  Come to a trail junction for Lake Lucille on the left. Continue walking straight on the PCT to Lake Aloha.

**3.7**  Reach a trail junction for Mosquito Pass and the PCT and arrive at Lake Aloha. Head down to the lake for a full-view impact. Elevation 8,122 feet. **GPS:** N38 51.86' / W120 07.75' Choose a granite seat for a snack. Turn left to walk along the lakeshore with the lake on your right as you head back to where the trail will merge with the PCT and the close of the lollipop.

**4.5**  Come to an unmarked trail junction and bear left.

**4.6**  Come to unmarked trail junction and continue along the rising trail toward Echo Lake.

**4.65**  Come to trail junction for Lake of the Woods to the right. Bear left to Echo Lake.

**5.1**  Reach the trail junction for the PCT and Echo Lake. Merge with the PCT and close the lollipop and turn right to Echo Lake, retracing your steps to the trailhead back the way you came.

**7.9**  Arrive back at the trailhead and boat landing.

## Creature Comforts

*Fueling Up*

**Echo Lake Chalet,** (530) 659-7207 (summer number only); echochalet.com. This summer resort has a grocery store, soda fountain, and deli above the boat launch and boat taxi dock.

*Resting Up*

**Echo Lake Chaletlees,** (530) 659-7207 (summer only); echochalet.com. These are eight housekeeping units that were built in 1947.

Other lodging can be found in **South Lake Tahoe.**

# 30 Round Top Lake

The hike to Round Top Lake has the distinction of beginning at the crest of a High Sierra pass in a significantly historic locale next to a visitor center, thereby dropping you and Pooch right in the heart of alpine beauty on the doorstep of a great resource center (Carson Pass Visitor Center), assuming you are in the area on the days and times when the center is manned by volunteers. This hike across a High Sierra plateau offers streams, lakes, wildflowers, views, and the opportunity to make any part of this hike a fabulous destination over a relatively gentle grade with moderate exertion.

**Start:** From the Carson Pass Visitor Center

**Distance:** 7.2 miles out and back

**Approximate hiking time:** 4 hours

**Difficulty:** Moderate, due to elevation

**Trailhead elevation:** 8,584 feet

**Highest point:** 9,390 feet

**Best season:** Summer to early fall

**Trail surface:** Dirt trail

**Other trail users:** Horses

**Canine compatibility:** On leash and voice control

**Land status:** National Forest; Wilderness

**Fees and permits:** Permit for overnight in the wilderness; parking fee

**Maps:** USGS Carson Pass and Caples Lake; Eldorado National Forest; Mokelumne Wilderness

**Trail contacts:** Eldorado National Forest, Amador Ranger District, 26820 Silver Dr., Pioneer, 95666; (209) 295-4251. Carson Pass Visitor Center (volunteer operated); (209) 258-8606; www.fs.usda.gov/eldorado.

**Nearest town:** Markleeville

**Trail tips:** The Carson Pass Visitor Center is a great resource for information about the pioneer history of the region and the connection to iconic scout Kit Carson. There are two vault toilets and a picnic table by the visitor center.

**Finding the trailhead:** From Markleeville on CA 89, drive 6.0 miles to the T junction for CA 88/89. Turn left onto CA 88 and drive 14.5 miles to the summit of Carson Pass. Turn left into the Carson Pass Visitor Center parking lot. The trailhead is to the right of the visitor center. **GPS:** N38 41.69'/ W119 59.36'

## The Hike

Carson Pass, aside from being a scenic route over the Sierra on the "Great Basin Divide" with a river flowing on the east and west flanks (West Fork of Carson River on the east and South Fork of the American River on the west), has roots in early exploration and mapping of the West, the emigrant migration west, the California gold rush, and the American Civil War.

Captain John C. Fremont and famous scout Kit Carson arrived at the summit known as Carson Pass (8,650 feet) with their expedition following their arduous Sierra winter journey of 1844. Pains could have been avoided had they heeded the

*Winnemucca Lake*

better judgment of local Indians who favored a different route. Kit Carson carved his initials and the date in a tree, and that original inscription was removed in 1888 and housed in Sutter's Fort, Sacramento. A permanent plaque marks the summit and location of Kit Carson's tree. Interestingly, Fremont is said to have been the first American to see Lake Tahoe during his Sierra Nevada explorations.

A discharged Mormon battalion returning from the Mexican-American War used the Carson Pass to make their way back to Utah in 1848, just as the rumors of discovered gold fields were beginning to echo across the pass. Carson Pass became a highway of prospectors during the gold rush of 1848 to 1855. By 1861 the spotlight was back on Carson Pass as the shipping route during the Civil War, since the Transcontinental Railway would not be completed until 1869. The visitor center on the summit of the pass is a perfect classroom for history buffs to gorge on the romance and tragedies of early Sierra Nevada exploration.

As you start on the trailhead next to the visitor center, whether or not you decide to detour to Frog Lake after 1.0 mile, call it a hike on the shores of Lake Winnemucca at 1.5 miles or push up the slope to Round Top Lake. The vistas and wildflower blooms surrounding you in the Carson Pass meadow will be one of the most memorable hikes you will share with your dog.

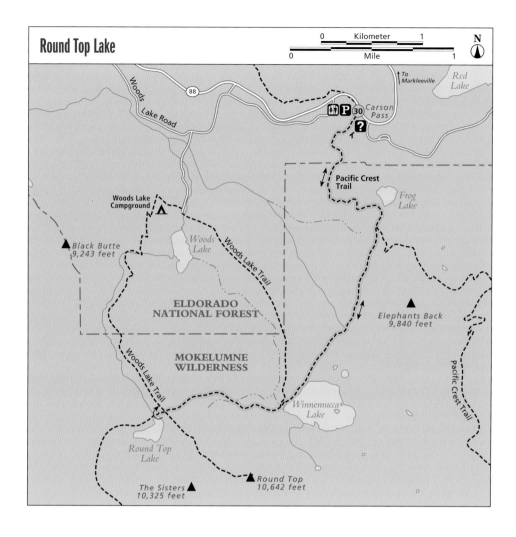

The trail climbs gently and gradually up to the granite canvas highlighted by pine and fir mixed with high-desert sage painted with spring and summer blooms of blue lupine, yellow corn lilies, pink shooting stars, and red Indian paintbrush.

The last stretch of the hike from Lake Winnemucca to Round Top Lake is an exposed uphill, but it lasts less than 1.0 mile before the trail rounds up to the edge of the lake.

## Miles and Directions

**0.0**   Start from the trailhead and information map board to the right of the visitor center.

**0.5**   Enter the Mokelumne Wilderness.

**1.2**   Frog Lake is on your left.

**1.3** Come to a trail junction for the Pacific Crest Trail (PCT) and Lake Winnemucca. Bear right to Lake Winnemucca. You will see Caples Lake in the distance on your right below.

**2.7** Come to a trail junction for Round Top Lake and Woods Lake. Continue straight to Round Top Lake.

**2.75** Arrive at a stream crossing at the outflow of Lake Winnemucca. Cross the stream and continue uphill to Round Top Lake.

**3.6** Come to a trail junction for Woods Lake and Fourth of July Lake. Continue straight as Round Top Lake comes into view. Arrive at the outflow of Round Top Lake a few yards ahead. This is your destination. Elevation 9,338 feet. **GPS:** N38 40.12'/ W120 00.73' This is a scenic spot for your dog to take a dip before heading back the way you came.

**7.2** Arrive back at the trailhead.

## Creature Comforts

### Fueling Up

**Historic Plasse's Resort General Store,** 30001 Plasses Rd., Silver Lake 95666. Stop here for supplies and sundries.

**Markleeville General Store,** 14799 CA 89, Markleeville 96120.

**Stonefly,** 14821 CA 89, Markleeville 96120; (530) 694-9999. This restaurant offers seasonal dishes with wood-fired breads and pizzas for Friday, Saturday, and Sunday dinners.

### Resting Up

**Creekside Lodge,** 14820 CA 89, Markleeville 96120; (530) 694-2511.

**Plasse's Resort,** 30001 Plasses Rd., Silver Lake 95666; (209) 258-8814. Plasse's has tent and RV sites (with water hookups).

**Sorensen's Resort,** 14255 CA 88, Hope Valley 96120; (530) 694-2203; sorensens resort.com.

**Hope Valley Resort and Campground,** 1.25 miles east of CA 88/89 Picketts Junction; (800) 423-9949; hopevalleyresort.com.

**Kirkwood Ski Resort** (1501 Kirkwood Meadows Drive, Kirkwood, CA 95646; kirk wood.com) has a good location off CA 88. Several home and condo owners do rent their places to dog owners. Google "Kirkwood dog-friendly vacation rentals" and follow the links.

**Silver Lake Stockton Family Camp,** off CA 88 (GPS: 29500 Plasse's Road); (209) 227-0082; stocktonfamilycamp.org. Family Camp is at the end of Plasse's Road off CA 88 behind Plasses Resort. Rates include breakfast, dinner, and a bag lunch for the trail; you must bring your own linens for the rustic cabins.

## Puppy Paws and Golden Years

Enjoy a stroll on the shores of Silver Lake or rent a boat (don't forget Pooch's life jacket).

# 31 Hot Springs Falls

It's always a rare occasion when you can walk off the pavement with your dog in a state park. The hike to Hot Springs Falls begins in peaceful Grover Hot Springs State Park's broad grassy meadow before entering the national forest, where the trail passes by a mix of conifers and some deciduous trees with seasonal wildflower blooms before it narrows into a canyon cradled by jagged-ridged granite sentinels. Apart from the sketchy 0.2-mile trek over a granite boulder–strewn rise to the base of the falls, this idyllic trail is well marked and easy to follow.

**Start:** From Hot Springs Cut-off Trail in the Hot Springs Grove parking lot.
**Distance:** 3.6-mile lollipop
**Approximate hiking time:** 2 hours
**Difficulty:** Easy
**Trailhead elevation:** 5,946 feet
**Highest point:** 6,166 feet
**Best season:** Late spring to fall
**Trail surface:** Dirt trail
**Other trail users:** Horses and mountain bikes on parts of the trail
**Canine compatibility:** On leash in the state park; voice control in the national forest
**Land status:** State Park; National Forest
**Fees and permits:** None
**Maps:** USGS Markleeville; Humboldt-Toiyabe National Forest

**Trail contacts:** Grover Hot Springs State Park, P.O. Box 188, Markleeville 96120; (530) 694-2248. Hot Springs Pool information, (530) 694-2249; www.parks.ca.gov/
**Nearest town:** Markleeville
**Trail tips:** Grover Hot Springs State Park Campground is an ideal overnight basecamp for hiking to the falls with Pooch and for you to treat your muscles to an après hike dip in the Grover Hot Springs pool (fee) in the trailhead parking lot. Remember that your dog cannot be left in the campground unattended. She may be ready for a snooze, but only if you can park in the shade with adequate ventilation to keep her cool and comfortable while you take a short soak in the naturally heated therapeutic water.

**Finding the trailhead:** From Markleeville on CA 89, take the Grove Hot Springs Road exit and drive 3.5 miles to the state park entrance. Continue straight past the park entrance and campgrounds to a parking lot beyond the Hot Springs pool. The trailhead is on the north side of the parking lot. **GPS:** N38 41.78' / W119 50.67'

## The Hike

The natural hot springs in Grover Hot Springs State Park have geological as well as historical cultural significance. The hot springs are located on the threshold of the Sierra forest zone and the Great Basin high desert zone. Surface water percolates through cracks in the earth's crust down thousands of feet, where it is heated before absorbing minerals on its bubbly journey back up to the surface. And although there is a little sulfur in the water, there is no rotten-egg smell. The water would be scalding, but the state park regulates the temperature for the hot soaking pool it maintains for the public.

Native Americans were the first to discover these mineral-rich waters. In the 1850s pioneers were sampling the curative powers of the waters, and the property was homesteaded before being leased to a dairy farmer who constructed the first rustic bathhouse. The property was improved over the next couple of decades. In 1959 the California State Parks Department purchased the land and improved the original pools next to the historic cabins and developed a campground at the edge of the scenic meadow that borders the Humboldt-Toiyabe National Forest. The trail to Hot Springs Falls begins in the state park for a short distance before crossing into the vaguely marked forest boundary.

Even if there wasn't a drop of water dripping from the falls, the walk across the meadow would be a special treat. Luckily there is a waterfall throughout the hiking season, but the flow varies depending on the winter snowmelt.

The water that feeds the hot spring pool percolates in various places on the hillside,

*Bridge crossing Hot Springs Creek*

quietly moistening the meadow where grasslands are so lush in places, it is a veritable wetland habitat where birds flutter happily.

Once across the meadow and over the creek's footbridge, the terrain changes to forest and the trail turns left into a narrowing canyon hugged by jagged 10,000-foot peaks and crests peering above the evergreen canopy.

At 0.9 mile bear left at the fork in the trail and follow the trail until it seems to disappear at the foot of a hilly barricade of rough granite boulders and slabs less than 0.5 mile ahead.

# Hot Springs Falls

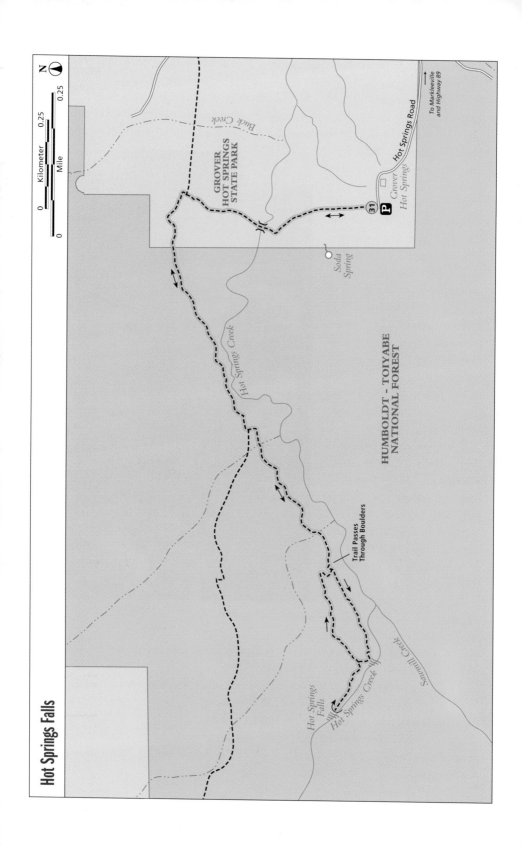

N

Kilometer
0    0.25    0.25

0    Mile    0.25

GROVER
HOT SPRINGS STATE PARK

Buck Creek

Grover Hot Springs Road

31
P

Grover Hot Springs

To Markleeville
and Highway 89

Soda Spring

Hot Springs Creek

HUMBOLDT - TOIYABE
NATIONAL FOREST

Trail Passes
Through Boulders

Hot Springs Falls

Hot Springs Creek

Summit Creek

The falls are on the other side of this mound. Just walk straight up over the boulder scramble and bear left with the creek in sight on your left. This stretch has seen enough boot traffic that you will be able to follow the trail along worn stretches of dirt until you merge back with a dirt trail along the creek. Resist the temptation to cross the creek; the top of the falls is reached from this side of the creek.

At 1.5 mile you come to a pretty cascade pouring through the gap that looks like a hole in the boulder. Continue another 0.4 mile along a series of small pools, and you will see the bigger tumble of water on your left before the last short jaunt to stand above the 30-foot-high or so rush of water into the pool below.

The boulders by the creek make a pleasant rest and picnic stop before you follow the trail back the way you came or follow the trail that crosses the boulder mound closer to the west side of the canyon. The latter trail back is much more discernible on the return than it would have been on the way to the falls. But you can meander over the granite slabs closer to the creek (the creek will be on your right on the return) to merge with the trail you took over the boulders.

*Hot Springs Falls*

## Miles and Directions

**0.0**  Start at the Hot Springs Cut-off trail sign and follow the trail across the meadow.

**0.2**  Reach Hot Springs Creek and a wooden footbridge. Walk across the bridge.

**0.4**  Come to a T junction. The campground is to the right. Turn left and leave the state park property.

**0.9**  Come to a fork and bear left to the falls.

**1.3** The trail seemingly ends at a boulder mound. Continue up the boulder mound and follow the stitches of well-worn path between and around the granite boulders and slabs, keeping the creek in your view below on the left.

**1.5** Merge back in with the creek-side trail and come to a cascade pouring through a gap between boulders.

**1.8** Reach a bench of rough granite where the falls plunge into a pool below. Pick a spot to enjoy a snack before going back the way you came. For a more lollipop hike, walk back along the stitch of a more defined trail that traverses the granite closer to the pool, keeping the creek on your right. The trail eventually merges with the trail you scampered up at the start of the granite mound.

**3.6** Arrive back at the trailhead.

## Creature Comforts

### Fueling Up

**Markleeville General Store,** 14799 CA 89, Markleeville 96120; (530) 694-2448.

**Stonefly,** 14821 CA 89, Markleeville 96120; (530) 694-9999; stoneflyrestaurant.com. This restaurant serves seasonal dishes and wood-fired breads and pizzas for Friday, Saturday, and Sunday dinners.

### Resting Up

**Grover Hot Springs State Park,** 3415 Hot Springs Rd., Markleeville 96120; (530) 694-2248; www.parks.ca.gov. This park offers tent and RV sites (no hookups) in a quiet pine setting with a meadow and mountain backdrop.

**Creekside Lodge,** 14820 CA 89, Markleeville 96120; (530) 694-2511.

# 32 Duck Lake

It would be an exaggeration to call this a "spectacular" hike. It is a pretty forested trail that opens to picturesque mountain scenery. An old rancher's cabin at the edge of a grassy lake is a highlight, which appears on the way to a granite slab at the east end of Duck Lake's riparian meadow. The hike into the Carson-Iceberg Wilderness merits extra points for being conveniently accessed off of Scenic Byway CA 4/Ebbetts Pass Road at a trailhead that is walking distance from two very pleasant Forest Service campgrounds and lovely Lake Alpine.

**Start:** From the Silver Valley trailhead in the Silver Valley Campground
**Distance:** 3.8 miles out and back
**Approximate hiking time:** 2 hours
**Difficulty:** Moderate, because of the uphill climb on the return
**Trailhead elevation:** 7,381 feet
**Highest point:** 7,526 feet
**Best season:** Summer to fall
**Trail surface:** Dirt trail
**Other trail users:** Horses
**Canine compatibility:** Voice control
**Land status:** National Forest; Wilderness
**Fees and permits:** None
**Maps:** USGS Spicer Meadow Reservoir; Stanislaus National Forest; Carson-Iceberg Wilderness
**Trail contacts:** Stanislaus National Forest Alpine Station on CA 4 (1.5 miles east of Bear Valley); (209) 753-2811; Calaveras Ranger District 5519 CA 4, Hathaway Pines 95233; (209) 795-1381; www.fs.usda.gov/stanislaus
**Nearest town:** Markleeville to the east; Arnold to the west
**Trail tips:** Although this trail is in the wilderness, there are cattle grazing here, so if you are in doubt about your dog's behavior around cattle, keep him on leash in the meadow area along the lakeshore. On the map you will see a trail that goes around the lake, and you may read about a trail that goes around the lake or hear from someone that there is a trail that goes around the lake as a 3.0-mile round-trip from the Silver Valley trailhead. Don't get lured into trying to find this trail, as you will only meet frustration and risk getting lost. The trail you see on the national forest and wilderness map does not exist as outlined. First of all, to say there is a trail that loops around the lake suggests that the lake would be visible from the trail. There is a trail that exists as a match to the 3.0-mile round-trip some people talk about. That trail is an unmarked primitive trail that branches off the Rock Lake Trail on the northwest slope and eventually emerges out of the forest along the meadow at the northeast end of the lake. The lake is completely obscured by trees on the northwest side. Furthermore, the stretch that traces the meadow at the forest line is a marsh under normal-precipitation years, when the lake is higher. The hike described here offers you and Pooch the best of Duck Lake along a safe and well-traveled trail.

**Finding the trailhead:** From Angels Camp at the intersection of CA 49 and CA 4, drive 48.0 miles east on CA 4. Lake Alpine Lodge will be on your right, and Lake Alpine will be on your left. Drive 0.05 mile past the lodge and turn right at the Lake Alpine/East Shore sign. Drive 0.05 mile up the road to the Silver Valley trailhead and park on the shoulder. **GPS:** N38 28.84' / W119 59.15'

*Starting out at the Duck Lake trailhead*

## The Hike

The Carson-Iceberg Wilderness was designated as such in 1984. It comprises over 161,000 acres that straddle the crest between Humboldt-Toiyabe and Stanislaus National Forests. The wilderness area is named for the Carson River (named after explorer/scout Kit Carson), which has its headwaters in this wilderness and a distinctive granite formation known as the Iceberg.

You can't talk about this hike or the Carson-Iceberg Wilderness without commenting on the road to get here. Duck Lake is set in the Alpine Lake Recreation Area on the west side of Ebbetts Pass summit. Duck Lake can be accessed from the towns of Markleeville or Arnold. The distance from Markleeville on the east side to the trailhead is approximately the same as the distance from Arnold on the west side. The winding CA 4/Ebbetts Pass Scenic Byway, is most spectacular traveling from Markleeville westward as part of the adventure on the way to a pretty hike.

If you camp, both Pine Martin and Silver Valley Campgrounds have tent sites (the former accommodates larger recreational vehicles), and it's just a hop, skip, and a jump to the Silver Valley trailhead, where the hike begins on a wide dirt trail through a forest of mixed conifers. You enter the Carson-Iceberg Wilderness almost immediately at the rise in the trail before it descends to the meadow and grassy shores of the lake on the left in approximately 1.0 mile, revealing a panorama of rugged crests and mountain chaparral–covered granite ranges.

*Duck Lake and the historic cabin*

You may hear cowbells in the distance, since the meadows and forests around the lake are part of historic grazing lands. You will pass an old rancher's cabin on your left up from the lake; it is a fair distance in dryer years.

Continue on the trail with the lake on your left and, at 1.5 miles, turn left toward the lake on the unmarked spur trail. On a blue-sky day look back toward the northwest end of the lake. You might be lucky enough to catch the lake reflection of the pale late-summer meadow dotted with grazing cattle and the small dark wooden cabin cradled by the backdrop of evergreens beneath a silver granite crest. At that moment you will feel transported into a Swiss alpine painting.

Back on the main trail, to the right, mounds of fractured granite dotted with pines make for a fun side scamper with your pooch.

At 1.9 miles the trail bumps into a large granite slab where the marshy meadow meets the forest across seasonal Duck Creek. The slab is a perfect picnic spot and your turnaround point. If you hike in a dry year or near the end of the season, you and Rover can enjoy roaming the meadow while you exercise the shutter on your camera. Go back to the trailhead the way you came.

## Miles and Directions

**0.0**  Start at the Silver Valley trailhead.
**0.2**  Come to a trail junction for the Emigrant Trail going left. Continue walking to Duck Lake straight ahead.
**0.3**  Enter Carson-Iceberg Wilderness.

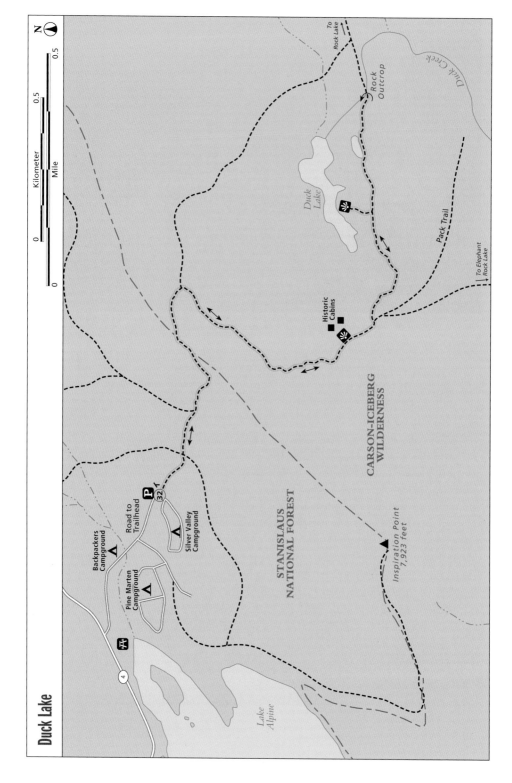

Duck Lake

N

Kilometer
0          0.5
Mile
0          0.5

To
Rock Lake

To
Rock Lake

Rock
Outcrop

Duck Creek

Duck
Lake

Pack Trail

To Elephant
Rock Lake

Historic
Cabins

CARSON-ICEBERG
WILDERNESS

STANISLAUS
NATIONAL FOREST

Inspiration Point
7,923 Feet

Backpackers
Campground

Road to
Trailhead

P

32

Pine Marten
Campground

Silver Valley
Campground

Lake
Alpine

4

**0.6** Come to a trail junction for Rock Lake to the left and Duck Lake straight. Continue walking to Duck Lake.

**1.1** Duck Lake and a meadow with an old cabin will come into view on the left.

**1.2** Come to a trail junction for Elephant Lake to the right and Rock Lake to the left. Continue walking on the trail toward Rock Lake. Duck Lake is on your left.

**1.5** Reach an unmarked spur trail going left to the shore of Duck Lake. Walk left on the spur to the shoreline for a closer view of the lake and the vistas back toward the meadow and cabin. Return to the main trail and turn left.

**1.6** Arrive at the lake.

**1.9** Reach a granite slab at the end of the dirt trail. This is your turnaround point. Take time to enjoy the meadow/marsh setting between you and the lake from your granite perch. This slab makes a great picnic spot for you and Pooch. Go back the way you came. Elevation 7,223 feet. **GPS:** N38 28.44' / W119 58.19'

**3.8** Arrive back at the trailhead.

## Creature Comforts

### Fueling Up

**Lake Alpine Resort**, 4000 CA 4/Ebbetts Pass, Bear Valley 95223; (209) 753-6350; lakealpineresort.com.

**Aria Bakery,** 458 Main St. #B, Murphys 95247; (209) 728-9250; ariabakery.com. This is a must-stop if you are driving up or down Ebbetts Pass on the west side.

**Sierra Hills Natural Foods**, 117 E. CA 4/Ebbetts Pass, Murphys 95247; (209) 728-3402.

### Resting Up

**Lake Alpine Resort,** 4000 CA 4, Bear Valley 95223; (209) 753-6350; lakealpineresort .com. There are four Forest Service campgrounds around Alpine Lake off CA 4 with tent and RV sites. **Pine Marten Campground** is the best maintained and pleasant at the east end of Lake Alpine Contact Calaveras Ranger District, (209) 795-1381; www.fs .usda.gov/stanislaus.

## CATTLE IN THE WILDERNESS

It may seem odd to see cattle in the wilderness. Cattle were grazing on some wild lands back in the 1800s, before the establishment of national rorests and wilderness areas. In wilderness areas where there are cattle, fences are used to manage the grazing area. It can be argued that meadow ecology is a result of long-term grazing and that properly managed grazing can be ecologically sound. Ranchers pay an annual fee for grazing rights based on the number of cattle and months of grazing. Portions of the fees are returned to the counties for infrastructure maintenance.

# 33  Sardine Falls

This is an easy jaunt right from the shoulder of CA 108. The falls are visible from the road as you follow an informal trail along old jeep tracks across a high-desert meadow. The trail merges into a single-track dirt trail through pines and aspen as it climbs a low ridge that leads to the base of frothy Sardine Falls. Because this is a short trek along a relatively flat trail in high country, it is an ideal acclimatization hike and a pleasant setting to hang out with Pooch for a couple hours or more.

**Start:** From Sonora Pass, 0.4 mile west of Sardine Creek
**Distance:** 2.3 miles out and back
**Approximate hiking time:** 1.5 hours
**Difficulty:** Easy
**Trailhead elevation:** 8,783 feet
**Highest point:** 9,081 feet
**Best season:** Summer to fall
**Trail surface:** Dirt trail with grass and some rock
**Other trail users:** Horses
**Canine compatibility:** Voice control
**Land Status:** National Forest

**Fees and permits:** None
**Maps:** USGS Pickel Meadow; USFS Humboldt-Toiyabe National Forest
**Trail contacts:** Humboldt-Toiyabe National Forest, Bridgeport Ranger District, US 395 Bridgeport 93517; (760) 932-7070; www.fs.usda.gov/htnf
**Nearest town:** Bridgeport
**Trail tips:** There is no real inviting spot at the falls for sitting and enjoying a picnic. Best to save that event for the picnic table alongside McKay Creek.

**Finding the trailhead:** From the intersection of Sonora Pass/CA 108 and US 395, drive 12.0 miles west on CA 108. The unmarked trailhead is on the left, 0.4 mile past Sardine Creek Bridge and approximately 100 feet past the no vehicle markers. The trail heads toward the falls in the distance and follows an old jeep track across the meadow. **GPS:** N38 18.90' / W119 36.45'

## The Hike

Sonora Pass is the second-highest pass in the Sierra Nevada at 9,624 feet. Emigrants traveling west were using the pass in the mid-1850s. But it was the mining of gold and silver on the east side that precipitated the improvement of transportation over the pass. By 1865 the dramatic beauty of the Sonora Pass was accessible along a steep winding road.

The Pacific Crest Trail crosses CA 108 at the summit of Sonora Pass and Sardine Meadow. The waterfall is visible from the road just past the summit as you drive east. Sardine Falls is the easiest hike you and your dog will ever enjoy in this rugged remote pocket of the High Sierra.

*Crossing Sardine Creek from the trailhead*

Park your car on the roadside shoulder and head out on the jeep tracks toward the white cascade visible a mile away at the far end of the meadow. The trail will narrow through aspen and pines across a pallet of wildflowers, including scarlet gilia, crimson columbines, and white and pink horsemint.

## Miles and Directions

**0.0** Start at the gravel shoulder 0.4 mile west of Sardine Creek Bridge on the Sonora Pass/CA 108. Walk approximately 400 feet in the meadow to Sardine Creek. Walk across the creek and follow the old jeep tracks toward the falls. McKay Creek, which comes out of Sardine Falls, will be on your left.

**0.5** The trail narrows, and to your left about 100 feet off the trail next to McKay Creek is a picnic table. This is a sweet stop for a snack on the way to the falls or a leisurely picnic on the way back.

**0.7** Come to a seasonal creek and walk across.

# Sardine Falls

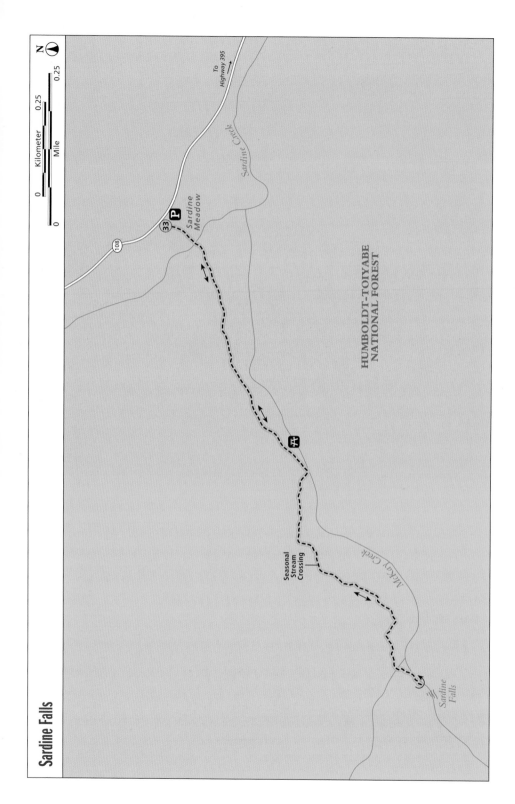

*Returning from Sardine Falls*

**1.0** Walk across another seasonal creek.

**1.15** Arrive at the base of the falls. After enjoying the view, return to the trailhead the way you came.

**2.3** Arrive back at the trailhead.

## Creature Comforts

### *Resting Up*

**Kennedy Meadows Resort and Packstation,** on Sonora Pass/CA 108, Sonora 95370; (209) 965-3911; kennedymeadows.com. This resort opened in 1917 and offers cabins, a general store, and a restaurant.

**Baker Campground,** on Sonora Pass Road/CA 108; www.fs.usda.gov/recarea/stanislaus. Baker is a Forest Service campground.

**Deadman Campground,** Sonora Pass Road/CA 108, Dardanelle, 95314; www.fs.usda .gov/recarea/stanislaus.

**Walker River Lodge,** 100 Main St., Bridgeport 93517 (760) 932-7021; walkerriver lodge.com.

# 34 Pinecrest Lake Loop

This mostly pine and cedar–ringed human-made lake in an open granitic basin with a mountain backdrop is a Western Sierra summer recreation mecca. Although the southwest end of the lake's marinas, beaches, and rustic cabin resort services are the antithesis of a "wilderness" experience, the 4.0-mile National Recreation Trail stitching the lakeshore boasts a surprisingly stunning and ruggedly natural hiking experience. The trail crosses granite shelves and climbs up rock-terraced steps along the north and east stretch of the lake loop with refreshing dipping opportunities for you and Pooch.

**Start:** From Pinecrest Lake day-use parking lot on the left
**Distance:** 4.3-mile loop
**Approximate hiking time:** 2.5 hours
**Difficulty:** Easy
**Trailhead elevation:** 5,648 feet
**Highest point:** 5,720 feet
**Best season:** Late spring to late fall
**Trail surface:** Granite, pavement, and dirt
**Other trail users:** Hikers only
**Canine compatibility:** On leash
**Land status:** National Forest
**Fees and permits:** None
**Maps:** USGS Pinecrest; USGS Stanislaus National Forest
**Trail contacts:** Stanislaus National Forest, 19777 Greenley Rd., Sonora 95370; (209) 532-3671; www.fs.usda.gov/stanislaus; Summer Ranger District, 1 Pinecrest Lake Rd., Pinecrest 95364; (209) 965-3434; www.fs.usda.gov/stanislaus
**Nearest town:** Sonora
**Trail tips:** Dogs are not allowed on the public beaches between May 15 and September 15

**Finding the trailhead:** From Sonora at the intersection of CA 49 and CA 108, drive 28.0 miles east on CA 108/Sonora Pass. Turn right toward Pinecrest/Dodge Ridge. Drive 0.8 mile to the day-use parking lot on the left. The trailhead is on the far left of the parking lot. **GPS:** N38 11.58' / W119 59.61'

## The Hike

Members of the Sierra Me-Wuk tribe were the first to set up seasonal camps for trading in the Pinecrest area. The business of storing the "liquid gold" took root during the mining days of the Sierra Nevada and flourished in the logging era to supply the growing towns of the Sierra foothills. Strawberry Lake, named for the wild strawberries in the meadow, was created by a dam in 1856. In 1897 Stanislaus National Forest's almost 1 million acres, named after the Stanislaus River, became one of the first established national forests. The historic dam was improved with a rock and concrete dam in 1916, and the lake was subsequently renamed Pinecrest Lake in the 1960s for the colossal 8,445-foot Pinecrest Mountain embracing the alpine waters.

*Trail above Pinecrest Lake* ▶

*National Recreation Trail markers help define trail*

Pinecrest Lake is a joint management project between California's Pacific Gas and Electric Company and the Stanislaus National Forest. The dam generates electricity, while the lake provides water storage and recreation. Several tracts of private summer cabins built on leased Forest Service land overlook the lake's National Recreation Trail. These cabins were built between 1916 and 1940, when the newly formed Department of Agriculture and Forest Service adopted policies to promote the use of the national forests for public enjoyment.

The National Recreation Trail offers cultural history and an opportunity to bask in pockets of unexpectedly unspoiled wilderness with the nearby convenience of an easily accessed developed recreation area.

As you leash your dog and step onto the paved path at the trailhead, you will be greeted by several NO DOGS signs, which are designed to keep your pooch off public beaches during the peak of summer season, between May 15 and September 15. Initially you may be skeptical as to the quality of the nature experience ahead of you on the trail. But it quickly gets better as you leave the pavement behind and follow the dirt path between the private vacation cabins on the left and the lake on the right. Within 0.5 mile the trail becomes much more promising, crossing granite shelves between challenging root-laced sections requiring you to focus on some fancy footwork and your mountain goat skills. The bench at 0.6 mile is a preview of the treat ahead, as you look toward granite outcroppings across the dam and the hint of loose chain barriers tracing parts of the path. The metal catwalk and concrete pathway along the top of the dam where Pinecrest Lake pours into the North Fork Stanislaus River adds a unique dimension to the hike.

Ignore the unmarked spur trail on the other side of the dam and continue walking uphill as the trail wends up above the lake, rimmed by a beautiful granite escarpment on your left. The next mile of trail is a cross-country excursion over granite shelves and up terraced rock steps with open views to the lake's developed shore to the west.

You come to a trail junction for Catfish Lake to the left at 1.4 miles and one of several cabin tracts. Unlike a walk through suburbia, the rustic-themed cabins are architecturally pleasing, with the older historic cabins being the most interesting and romantic. Continue to follow the lakeshore, keeping an eye out for the metal National Recreation Trail markers hammered in the granite at foot level. The granite fingers reaching into the lake form idyllic coves dotted with pine and cedar trees. The next mile is the heart of the rugged beauty and your best bet for solitude and contemplation. This is a great stretch for finding a perch on a granite slab and enjoying a picnic lunch and water break with Pooch.

At 2.2 miles a wooden footbridge reaches over the boulder creek bed with a sheer granite face up the gorge.

Continue walking along the main trail past the trail junction for Cleo's Bath (seasonal pools) and Sunrise Point.

At 2.6 miles another tract of cabins on the left overlooks the trail and lake. The trail leaves the granite and passes through more riparian habitats closer to shore, where the trickle of streams feed the horsetail and travel into the fall. This section of the trail offers a more gentle shore access for Pooch to take a dip before reaching the public beach area less than 1.0 mile ahead. The trail will transition from dirt to a narrow concrete path shortly before emerging at the bottom of Lakeshore Drive and the lakefront lookout platform just short of 4.0 miles. You have reentered the recently improved developed area, past drinking fountains, flush toilets, and an amphitheater. Stay on the dog-friendly path back to the parking lot and the trailhead.

## Miles and Directions

**0.0** Start at the trailhead on the paved path left of the parking area.

**0.2** The paved trail transitions to dirt between cabins on your left and the lake on your right.

**0.6** Come to a bench on the granite shelf overlooking the dam and lake.

**0.8** Come to the metal catwalk that connects the trail to the path across the dam. Follow the catwalk and walk across the dam to the other side of the lake.

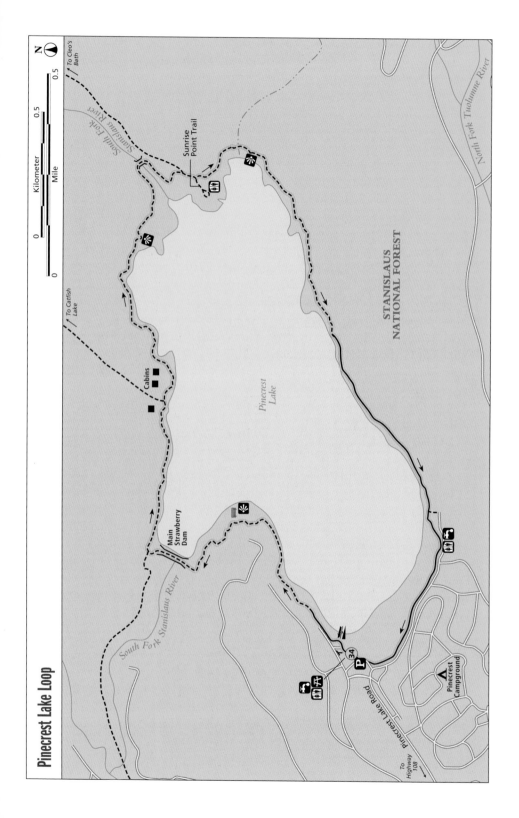

# Pinecrest Lake Loop

**N**

Kilometer
0          0.5

Mile
0          0.5

*To Cleo's Bath*

*South Fork*
*Stanislaus River*

*South Fork*

Sunrise
Point Trail

*To Catfish*
*Lake*

Cabins

Pinecrest
Lake

*South Fork Stanislaus River*

Main
Strawberry
Dam

STANISLAUS
NATIONAL FOREST

*North Fork Tuolumne River*

34

P

Pinecrest
Campground

Pinecrest Lake Road

*To*
*Highway*
*108*

**0.9** Come to an unmarked trail junction with a spur trail going down below the dam. Continue walking straight uphill.

**1.4** Come to a tract of cabins on your left and a trail junction to Catfish Lake.

**1.9** Come to a granite finger reaching into the lake. Keep an eye for the trail markers on the granite.

**2.2** Come to a wooden footbridge across the South Fork Stanislaus River. Walk across the bridge.

**2.3** Come to a trail junction for Cleo's Bath left. Continue walking straight.

**2.4** Come to a trail junction for the Sunrise Point Trail and a toilet to the right. Bear left and stay on the National Recreation Trail.

**2.6** Come to a tract of cabins on the left and views of the dam on the right.

**3.8** Arrive at the junction with Lakeshore Drive left. A lakeside viewing platform is on your right.

**3.85** Come to the flush toilets and water fountains.

**4.3** Arrive back at the parking area and trailhead.

## Creature Comforts

*Fueling Up*

**Pinecrest Lake General Store** (Summit Ave., Pinecrest 95364; 209-965-3661) is steps from the campground and lake.

*Resting Up*

**Pinecrest Campground,** 16 Pinecrest Ave., Pinecrest 95364; (877) 444-6777; reserve america.com. This campground has 200 tent and RV sites (no hookups).

**Meadowview Campground** in Pinecrest Recreation Area/Stanislaus National Forest off Dodge Ridge Road; (209) 586-3234; www.fs.usda.gov/recarea/stanislaus. This campground has one hundred tent and RV sites (no hookups) offered on a first-come, first-served basis.

Sonora has **dog-friendly motels.**

## Puppy Paws and Golden Years

**Pinecrest Lake Marina,** 31 Lakeshore Dr., Pinecrest 95364; (209) 965-3411; pinecrest lakeresort.com. The marina offers boat rentals (don't forget Pooch's life jacket).

# 35 Frog Lakes

Anytime you and your dog can drive up a paved road and set foot and paw on a trail that passes several lakes and streams with a backdrop of mountain peaks between patches of forest interrupted by wildflower meadows, that's a winning hike. The trail to the largest Frog Lake takes in four lakes, two streams, and a historic miner's cabin for scenic good measure, and it has more than a fair share of High Sierra scenery highlighted by evergreens and spring wildflower blooms.

**Start:** From Virginia Lakes Trail trailhead
**Distance:** 3.4 miles out and back
**Approximate hiking time:** 2 hours
**Difficulty:** Moderate
**Trailhead elevation:** 9,814 feet
**Highest point:** 10,360 feet
**Best season:** Summer to fall
**Trail surface:** Dirt trail with some rocky stretches
**Other trail users:** Horses
**Canine compatibility:** Voice control
**Land Status:** National Forest; Wilderness

**Fees and permits:** None
**Maps:** USGS Dunderberg Peak; USFS Humboldt-Toiyabe National Forest; Hoover Wilderness
**Trail contacts:** Humboldt-Toiyabe National Forest; www.fs.usda.gov/htnf
**Nearest town:** Lee Vining
**Trail tips:** The Big Virginia Lake shore closest to the parking lot is popular with families out for a day's fishing, and the wooden tables are a delightful setting to enjoy a picnic at the end of your hike.

**Finding the trailhead:** From Lee Vining on I-395, drive 12.0 miles north to the VIRGINIA LAKES sign at Conway Summit. Turn left toward Virginia Lakes and drive 6.0 miles to the Virginia Lakes Trail trailhead parking area. The pavement ends at 5.7 miles, and the last 0.3 mile to the parking area is gravel. The trailhead is at the information board left of Big Virginia Lake below the vault toilets. **GPS:** N38 02.88'/ W119 15.80'

## The Hike

The Hoover Wilderness's almost 125,000 acres borders the Yosemite Wilderness to the west. It was first established as a primitive area in 1931. In 1957 it became a "wild' area and in 1964 was designated a wilderness area within the Humboldt–Toiyabe National Forest. Beauty with accessibility attracts visitors. The Virginia Lakes trailhead portal to Frog Lakes has beauty and accessibility with the added convenience of Virginia Lakes Resort's twenty rustic housekeeping cabins and restaurant as a basecamp for fishers and hikers. Virginia Lakes Resort opened in the summer of 1924 as Virginia Lakes Camp with one house tent, five rowboats, twenty camp spaces, and four toilets. Coincidentally, a dog features in the long colorful history of the Virginia Lakes Resort. The Fosters of Los Angeles, original pioneers of Virginia Lakes Camp, had an Airedale terrier named Muggs. Walter Foster worked for a film studio at the end of

*Hiking past Blue Lake*

World War I, and just when Walter became unemployed and the Fosters' economic future looked its bleakest, a studio director spotted Muggs and offered the Fosters a contract to use the dog in a movie. Muggs the movie star helped the Fosters bank-roll Walter's dream to build a fishing camp on leased land from the Forest Service at Virginia Lakes.

Frog Lakes are three of at least eight lakes that comprise the Virginia Lakes cluster fed by perennial Virginia Creek. This hike begins at Big Virginia Lake, and within 0.5 mile you have entered the pristine wilderness area and spotted Blue Lake on the left shortly before a stream nourishes a meadow carpeted with spring and summer blue lupine opening views toward the backdrop of 8,000- to 12,000-foot peaks.

At 1.0 mile the historic miner's cabin built by J. P. Cooney, a local miner, is just a stone's throw from Cooney Lake, named after the local woodcutter/miner who helped the Fosters build the first vehicle road to Virginia Lakes.

The next 0.7 mile to Frog Lakes is in the open with patches of evergreens dotting the landscape and highlighting the starkly majestic backdrop.

# Frog Lakes

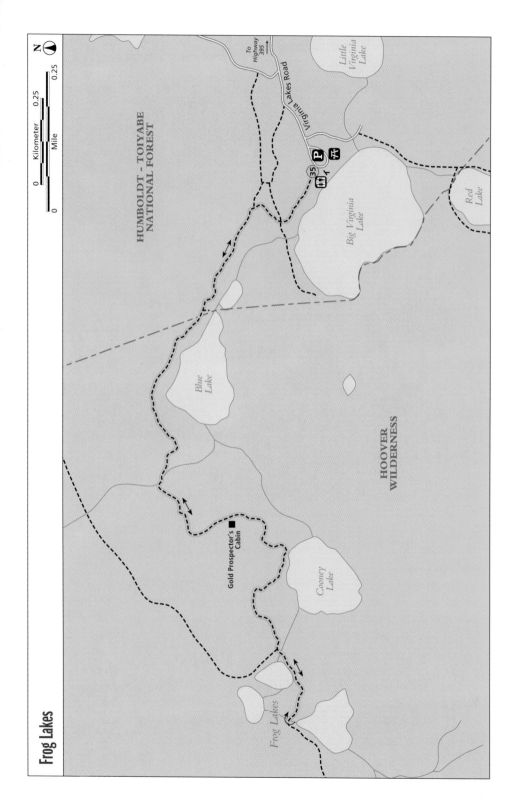

N

0        Kilometer        0.25

0                                    Mile                                    0.25

HUMBOLDT - TOIYABE
NATIONAL FOREST

To
Highway
395

Virginia Lakes Road

35

P

Little
Virginia
Lake

Big Virginia
Lake

Red
Lake

Blue
Lake

HOOVER
WILDERNESS

Gold Prospector's
Cabin

Cooney
Lake

Frog Lakes

Enjoy the stunning scenery and stake out a picnic site to share some snacks and a water break with Pooch before going back the way you came.

## Miles and Directions

**0.0** Start at the Virginia Lakes trailhead to the right of Big Virginia Lake.

**0.4** Enter the Hoover Wilderness at the fork. Continue uphill on the trail to the right.

**0.5** Come to Blue Lake on the left.

**0.8** Come to a stream crossing with a meadow on your right. The trail views open up.

**1.1** Arrive at an old miner's cabin on your left.

**1.2** Arrive at Cooney Lake on your left.

**1.5** Turn left and cross a stream. The trail continues across the stream.

**1.7** Arrive at the largest Frog Lake on your left. Elevation 10,360 feet. **GPS:** N38 02.93' / W119 16.91'

**3.4** Arrive back at the trailhead.

## Creature Comforts

### Fueling Up

**Virginia Lakes Resort** (760-647-6484; virginialakesresort.com) is on Virginia Lakes Road at Conway Summit off of US 395 between Lee Vining and Bridgeport. The resort is 6 miles west on the left side of Virginia Lakes Road. There is a general store and breakfast/lunch counter in the lodge.

### Resting Up

**Trumbull Lake Forest Service Campground** (760-932-7070 or 877-444-6777; www .recreation.gov; and 760-932-7092; www.fs.usda.gov/recarea/htnf) is on the north side of Virginia Lakes Road just before Virginia Lakes Resort. This campground offers forty-five tent and RV sites (no hookup).

**Virginia Lakes Resort** on Virginia Lakes Rd.; (760) 647-6484. This resort offers housekeeping cabins.

**Bridgeport** has a few dog-friendly motels.

## Puppy Paws and Golden Years:

**Virginia Lakes** (Big and Little Virginia Lakes) at Virginia Lakes Resort offer boat rentals. (Don't forget Pooch's life jacket.) Use the contact info that is above for Virginia Lakes Resort.

# 36 Gardisky Lake

This trail is short and steep and a stunning climb through pines along a creek that looks back westward toward Yosemite's kingdom. You crest onto a plateau with a picturesque sprawling shallow lake and panoramic views. Hikers with dogs lucked out here: Gardisky Lake is worthy of the Yosemite National Park embrace, but by some fluke of boundaries, it is in the national forest rather than within the national park and therefore dog compatible.

**Start:** Gardisky Lake trailhead
**Distance:** 1.7 miles out and back
**Approximate hiking time:** 1 hour
**Difficulty:** Strenuous, because of elevation and a steep grade
**Trailhead elevation:** 9,730 feet
**Highest point:** 10,460 feet
**Best season:** Summer and early fall
**Trail surface:** Dirt and some rock
**Other trail users:** Horses
**Canine compatibility:** Voice control

**Land status:** National Forest
**Fees and permits:** None
**Maps:** USGS Tioga Pass, Mount Dana; USFS Inyo National Forest
**Trail contacts:** Inyo National Forest, Mono Basin Scenic Area Visitors Center, I-395 at Lee Vining; (760) 647-3044; www.fs.usda.gov/gardiskylake
**Nearest town:** Lee Vining
**Trail tips:** The trail is steep, with sandy, slippery stretches coming downhill.

**Finding the trailhead:** From the intersection of I-395 and Tioga Pass Road/CA 120, drive 9.8 miles west on CA 120 toward Yosemite National Park. Turn right at the sign for Saddleback Lake. Follow the gravel road 1.0 mile to the trailhead parking lot on the left. The Gardisky Lake trailhead is across the road. **GPS:** N37 57.04' / W119 15.67'

## The Hike

Inyo National Forest is California's most visited national forest. Two million acres of raw beauty with a stupendous concentration of lakes and streams make it a recreation paradise. Inyo boasts the world's largest Jeffrey pine forest; the oldest tree (an ancient bristlecone named Methuselah); and the country's first national scenic area (Mono Basin).

Gardisky Lake and the shallow ponds that crown the high meadow epitomize "celestial" setting and do Inyo National Forest proud.

It is a pristine patch of hiking heaven and a privilege that it can be shared with your dog. There is something about staring across to Yosemite's majesty and being within a rock's throw of the park, where dogs are not welcomed on trails, that makes this hike extra special and calls on the best land-stewardship qualities you can muster. Being allowed to hike to Gardisky Lake with a dog makes one think that the person drawing the lines on the map for the park boundaries must have made a mistake in our favor as dog owner/hikers.

*Crossing a stream on the way to Gardisky Lake*

This trail is conveniently located off of Tioga Pass, and it is a stellar place to get acquainted with Inyo's dog-friendly playground on the way out of the park or to get one last fix of dog-friendly hiking on the way into the park.

The trail starts up a slope with a no-nonsense attitude the minute you cross the road from the parking lot to the trailhead. You soon emerge out of the forest and follow the creek tumbling downhill. At 0.4 mile you begin a couple of switchbacks for about 0.2 mile where the trail levels and opens up. The scenery opens up to the west almost immediately as you start up, and in less than 1.0 mile you are standing on an expansive plateau that feels like it is suspended at 10,000 feet. The shallow ponds and lake look like a mirage as you follow the plateau trail to the shoreline. Pooch will get the urge to spin out between darting at new invigorating smells. Find a nice boulder to soak up the solitude and beauty while enjoying a snack with your pal before heading back down.

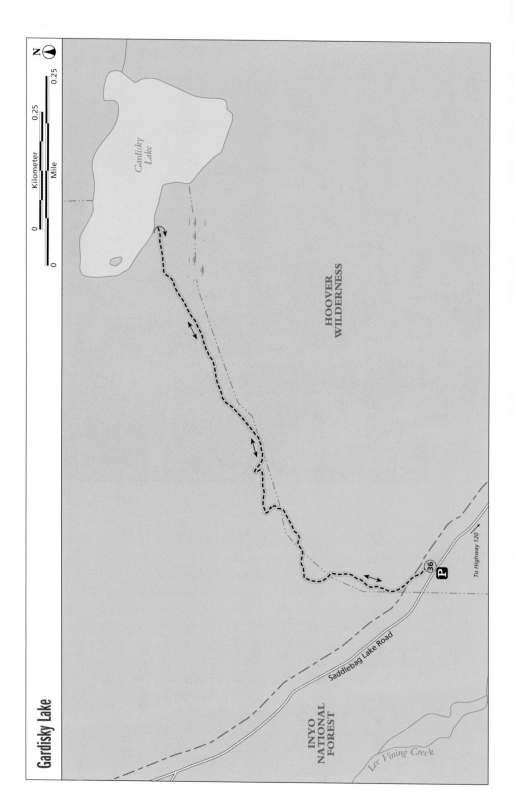

Gardisky Lake

## Miles and Directions

**0.0** Start at the Gardisky Lake trailhead across the road from the parking lot.

**0.2** Cross a stream.

**0.85** Arrive at Gardisky Lake. **GPS:** N37 57.36' / W119 15.18' Return the way you came.

**1.7** Arrive back at the trailhead.

## Creature Comforts

### *Fueling Up*

**Tioga Pass Resort Café,** 85 CA 120 West/Tioga Pass Road, Lee Vining 93541; no telephone; tiogapassresort.com. This cafe is a treat, but not a dog-friendly area. Get one of their sumptuous desserts to take back to your campsite.

**Whoa Nellie Deli** and **Tioga Gas Mart,** at the Mobil Station at the I-395 and CA 120/ Tioga Pass Road junction; (760) 647-1088; whoanellie deli.com. This is another good choice for takeout.

### *Resting Up*

**Inyo National Forest Junction Campground** at the Saddlebag Lake turnoff from CA 120/ Tioga Pass Rd.; (760) 647-3031; www.fs.usda.gov/inyo. This campground offers thirteen scenic tent and RV sites (no hookups) across from Ellery Lake and is just over 1.0 mile from the Gardisky Lake trailhead.

*Gardisky Lake*

**Murphey's Motel,** 51493 US-395, Lee Vining 93541; (760) 647-6316; murpheys yosemite.com.

## Puppy Paws and Golden Years

**Nunatak Nature Trail,** just west of Tioga Pass Resort, has a paved parking turnout on the north side of CA 120/Tioga Pass Road east of the Yosemite National Park entrance. The first 250 feet of this ADA-accessible interpretive trail are paved. The 0.5-mile loop with glacial tarns lets Pooch enjoy a micro-wilderness experience on or off leash—the latter is preferable as a safety precaution when you are farther away from the road. Visit www.fs.usda.gov/recarea/inyo.

# 37 Parker Lake

This accessible and easy hike starts in exposed high-desert sage country and quickly transitions to aspen and pines. The effort is minimal for maximum reward, as the trail traces cascading Parker Creek most of the way to lovely Parker Lake at the base of picturesque Parker Peak.

**Start:** Parker Lake trailhead
**Distance:** 3.8 miles out and back
**Approximate hiking time:** 2 hours
**Difficulty:** Easy
**Trailhead elevation:** 7,791 feet
**Highest point:** 8,320 feet
**Best season:** Early summer to late fall
**Trail surface:** Dirt trail with some rock
**Other trail users:** Horses
**Canine compatibility:** Voice control
**Land status:** National Forest; Wilderness Area
**Fees and permits:** None; no fires permitted

**Maps:** USGS Koip Peak; Inyo National Forest; Ansel Adams Wilderness
**Trail contacts:** Inyo National Forest, Mammoth Ranger Station and Welcome Center, 2510 Main St./CA 203 in the town of Mammoth Lakes; (760) 924-5500; www.fs.usda.gov/ inyo. Open year-round 7 days a week.
**Nearest town:** June Lake
**Trail tips:** Mosquitoes are especially voracious when passing through the aspen grove; bring repellent.

**Finding the trailhead:** From the intersection of US 395 and CA 158, take the June Lake Loop exit at the northern intersection of I-395 and CA 158 (CA 158 is the June Lake Loop that intersects with I-395 north and south). Head west on CA 158 and drive 1.2 miles to the PARKER LAKE ROAD sign. Turn right on Parker Lake Road (improved gravel road) and drive 2.5 miles to the parking lot and trailhead at the end of the road. **GPS:** N37 51.18' / W119 08.08'

## The Hike

Inyo National Forest is described as "where the desert meets mountains," and this trail to Parker Lake is one of the best examples. Your feet are ankle-deep in sagebrush at the trailhead, yet your eyes are feasting on mountain peaks straight ahead.

Maybe it's the sagebrush meadow guarding the Parker Lake trailhead at the end of the dusty albeit improved gravel road that misleads hikers into thinking Parker Lake is a dismissible destination. It could also be that with so many glorious hikes off of I-395 accessed along scenic paved roads, hikers have become jaded and spoiled. The fact that Parker Lake seems to be overlooked makes it doubly enjoyable for those lucky hikers with dogs who take a chance.

The hike begins in dry, high-desert, open sagebrush land uphill, but Parker Peak and mountains ahead in the distance hold promise for High Sierra scenery. You quickly trade sage for pines and the sound of Parker Creek as you enter the Ansel Adams Wilderness.

*Parker Lake*

At 1.7 miles you come to a trail junction for Silver Lake on your left, and Parker Creek invites your pooch for a dip on your right. Continue walking along Parker Creek under the shade of aspens and Jeffrey pines for another 0.2 mile to the shores of Parker Lake and the stunning backdrop of peaks. Take time to explore the shoreline and break for a snack with Pooch before going back the way you came to the trailhead.

## Miles and Directions

**0.0**  Start at the Parker Lake trailhead.

**0.2**  Enter Ansel Adams Wilderness.

# Parker Lake

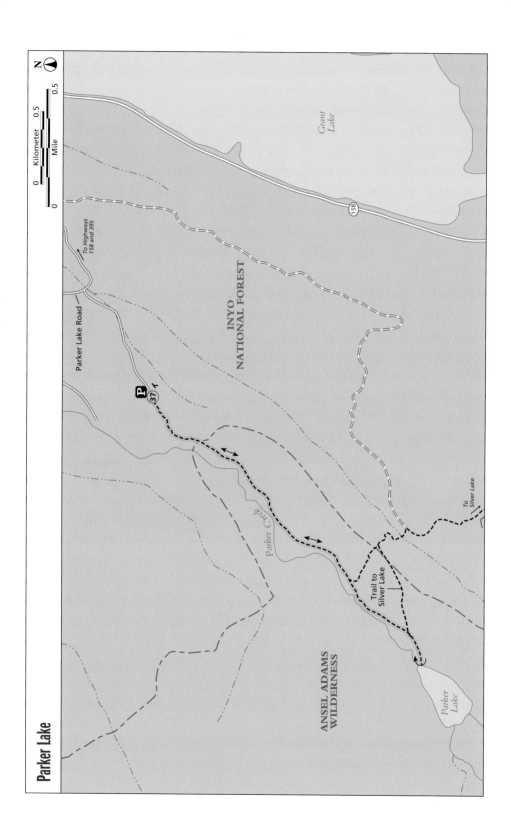

*Returning to the trailhead with Mono Lake in the distance*

**1.7** Come to the trail junction for Silver Lake on the left. Continue walking straight on the main trail through aspen and Jeffrey pine woodland with Parker Creek on your right.

**1.9** Arrive at Parker Lake. Enjoy a scenic snack before returning the way you came. Elevation 8,265 feet. **GPS:** N37 50.14' / W119 09.36'

**3.8** Arrive back at the trailhead.

## Creature Comforts

### *Fueling Up*

**June Lake General Store,** 2740 Boulder Dr., June Lake 93529; (760) 638-7771.
**Eagle's Landing Restaurant at Double Eagle Resort and Spa,** 5587 CA 158/June Lake Loop, June Lake 93529; (760) 648-7134; doubleeagle.com. Order food to go and share breakfast, lunch, or dinner at the outdoor picnic table. (No dogs allowed on the deck.)

### *Resting Up*

**Grant Lake Forest Service Campground,** CA 158, June Lake 93529; (760) 647-3044; www.fs.usda.gov/inyo. Of the six campgrounds in the June Lake area (Oh! Ridge, Pine Cliff Resort, Gull Lake, Reversed Creek, and June Lake), this is the closest to the Parker Lake trailhead.
**Double Eagle Resort and Spa,** 5587 CA 158/June Lake Loop, June Lake 93529; (760) 648-7134; doubleeagle.com. The resort offers cabins and rooms in a picturesque setting.

# 38 McLeod Lake

This hike defines "short and sweet." McLeod Lake is a true reward for beginner hikers or any hiker who seeks a quick fix of Eastern Sierra beauty. The wide dirt trail quickly leaves the fascinating, albeit unattractive area of pine trees killed by the release of CO2 in the soil. It is a moderate climb into the pine forest before reaching the lake tucked below the panoramic Mammoth Crest.

**Start:** From the Lakes Basin Path/Horseshoe Lake trailhead parking lot
**Distance:** 2.0-mile lollipop
**Approximate hiking time:** 1.5 hours
**Difficulty:** Easy
**Trailhead elevation:** 9,003 feet
**Highest point:** 9,317 feet
**Best season:** Summer to early fall
**Trail surface:** Dirt trail and pumice powder
**Other trail users:** Horses
**Canine compatibility:** Voice control
**Land status:** National Forest
**Fees and permits:** Campfire permits are always required where fires are permitted in undeveloped campgrounds. Although generally speaking fires are prohibited starting at 10,000 feet and above, it is important to check with the ranger station, as snow levels and weather conditions determine whether a blanket policy is in effect prohibiting all campfires outside of the developed campgrounds.
**Maps:** USGS Crystal Crag; USFS Inyo National Forest
**Trail contacts:** Inyo National Forest, Mammoth Ranger Station and Welcome Center, 2510 Main Street/CA 203 in the town of Mammoth Lakes 93546; (760) 924-5500; www.fs.usda .gov/inyo. Open year-round 7 days a week.
**Nearest town:** Mammoth Lakes
**Trail tips:** The trailhead parking lot has picnic tables, bear-proof waste containers, two flush toilets with water faucets, information board, interpretive signs, and a shuttle stop for the Lakes Basin. Dogs are allowed on shuttle (muzzle required). Shuttle has a bike rack. Heed the CO2 warning signs posted.

**Finding the trailhead:** From the Mammoth Lakes exit 263 at the intersection of US 395 and CA 203, drive west 3.7 miles to the intersection of CA 203/Minaret Road and Lake Mary Road. Continue straight uphill on Lake Mary Road for 4.9 miles to the Mammoth Lakes Basin and the Horseshoe Lake parking lot at the end of the road. The trailhead is to the right of the information board and map in the Horseshoe Lake parking lot. **GPS:** N37 36.78'/ W119 01.27'

## The Hike

Long before the Paiute People thought of California's most visited national forest as "Inyo" or the "dwelling place of a great spirit," volcanoes, ice, and earthquakes had been sculpting it into one of nature's most dramatic work of art for over four million years.

*Happy dogs at McLeod Lake*

Ironically the Inyo National Forest and the heart of its awesome landscape—which draws almost four million visitors each year to its seven wilderness areas brimming with lakes, streams, glades, and peaks to hike, bike, climb, fish, and kayak—would not exist in such pristine form were it not for one southern city's thirst. Inyo National Forest was first established as part of a strategy to secure riparian rights along the Owens River for Los Angeles expansion. The construction of an aqueduct in 1913 and diversion of creeks and streams contributed to the "water wars," which flared up again in the 1970s when the Mono Lake Basin ecosystem was threatened by excessive diversion of tributaries. By the 1990s grass roots efforts had succeeded in reversing the tide with litigation and public awareness campaigns to "Save Mono Lake."

The hike to McLeod Lake is one of many gems in Inyo National Forest's crown of destinations. Originally called Blue Lake, it was later renamed after Malcom McLeod, a Forest Service ranger at Red's Meadow below Blue Lake from 1921 to 1929.

The first thing you notice when you park at the Horseshoe Lake parking lot and look west is the ring of dead pine trees covering part of the slope. A recorded increase

# McLeod Lake

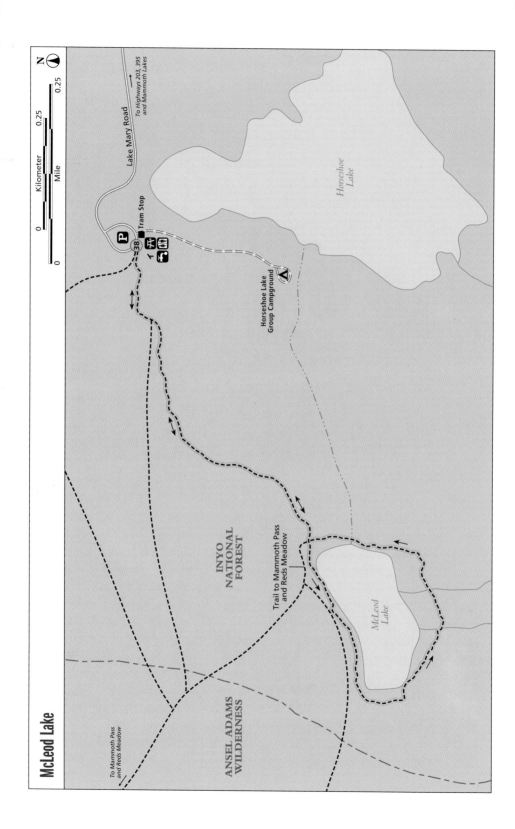

N

Kilometer
0      0.25

Mile
0      0.25

To Highways 203, 395
and Mammoth Lakes →

Lake Mary Road

Tram Stop

38

P

Horseshoe Lake
Group Campground

Horseshoe
Lake

INYO
NATIONAL
FOREST

Trail to Mammoth Pass
and Reds Meadow

McLeod
Lake

ANSEL ADAMS
WILDERNESS

To Mammoth Pass
and Reds Meadow

of small quakes from 1989 to 1990 is believed to have caused a pocket of magma to rise and cool below the surface, allowing a higher than normal concentration of $CO2$ to escape and settle in the soil, which killed the tree roots by depriving them of oxygen. It's a ghostly sight that also provides a unique opportunity to witness living geology.

Once you start uphill, the dusty trail leads you out of the gray tree cemetery very quickly as it wends and climbs into the healthy green pine forest and threads its way to the shores of lovely McLeod Lake.

## Miles and Directions

**0.0** Start at the Lakes Basin Path/Horseshoe trailhead. The trail sign for McLeod Lake is approximately 100 feet to the right.

**0.1** Come to a fork with a trail sign. Bear left to McLeod Lake.

**0.6** Come to a fork with a trail sign for Mammoth Pass and Reds Meadow to the right. Bear left and you will see McLeod Lake on your left. **GPS:** N37 36.39' / W119 01.85' Follow the path around McLeod Lake in a counterclockwise direction, taking time to snack, breathe in the views of the Mammoth Crest, and let Pooch soak her paws or paddle in the clear cool waters.

**1.5** Complete the lake loop and go back to the trailhead the way you came.

**2.0** Arrive back at the trailhead.

## Creature Comforts

### Fueling Up

The Village at Mammoth's pedestrian complex of condominiums, shops, and restaurants showcases several establishments with dog-friendly patios. **Gomez's Mexican Restaurant** (100 Canyon Blvd., Mammoth Lakes 93546; 760-924-2693; gomezs .com) is well-known for its margaritas and fresh guacamole. **The Smokeyard** (1111 Forest Trail Rd., #201, Mammoth Lakes 93546; 760-934-3300; smokeyard.com) offers burgers and beef ribs that will make Pooch drool. If gluten is an issue for you, the menu identifies its gluten-free (GF) and gluten-sensitive (GS) dishes. Also try **Schatz Bakery** (3305 Main St., Mammoth Lakes 93546; 760-935-6055; sheaschats bakery.com).

### Resting Up

There are three dog-friendly lodges with cabins in the Mammoth Lakes Basin. All have access to hiking trails, and each has its own appeal. The romantic **Tamarack Lodge** (163 Twin Lakes Rd., Mammoth Lakes 93546; 760-934-2442; tamaracklodge.com) in the Mammoth Lakes Basin offers well-appointed, updated, and new housekeeping cabins of various sizes. The three-bedroom "luxury" cabin is the first LEED-certified building (leading in energy and environmental design) in the Eastern Sierra. (Well-mannered dogs under one hundred pounds are welcome in the cabins.) If you want to treat yourself to a special dinner, without Bowser, the Lakefront Restaurant in the lodge is intimate and a palate pleaser. At **Crystal Crag Lodge** (40 Lake Mary

*McLeod Lake*

Rd., Mammoth Lakes 93546; 760-934-2436; crystalcraglodge.com) the comfortable housekeeping cabins across from Lake Mary are popular with families and fishing enthusiasts. The housekeeping cabins at **Woods Lodge** (800 Lake George Rd., Mammoth Lakes 93546; 760-934-2261; woodslodgemammoth.com) at the end of the paved road overlooking Lake George have the most stunning setting.

Located on Hillside Drive across from The Village, **Westin Monache Resort** (50 Hillside Dr., Mammoth Lakes 93546; 760-934-0400; westinmammoth.com/monache) is a treat for hikers and their dogs. All rooms have cooking facilities if you want to rustle up some chow for yourself and your canine. But no dog I ever traveled to Mammoth with has ever turned down room service at the end of a long trail. The staff is super friendly and welcomes their canine guests with "heavenly" dog beds, bowls, and poop bags. Dogs seem to like hanging around the concierge desk. Could it be there's a secret stash of biscuits in the area?

**Snowcreek Resort Condominiums,** 1254 Old Mammoth Rd., Mammoth Lakes 93546; (760) 934-3333; snowcreekresort.com. This is a dog's favorite setting of any condominium complex in Mammoth Lakes.

## WHEN POOCH NEEDS TO CLEAN UP HIS ACT

Tailwaggers Gourmet Dog Bakery and Boutique (437 Old Mammoth Rd., Mammoth Lakes 93546; 760-924-3400; mammothtailwaggers.com) in the Minaret Shopping Center on Old Mammoth Road has natural treats, toys, and accessories and a self-dog wash station for pooches who need to rinse off the trail dust.

There is also no shortage of **campgrounds** in town and in the Lakes Basin. There are at least seven Forest Service campgrounds for tents and self-contained trailers and RVs. They have toilets, water, picnic tables, and fire rings. There is one RV park on Main Street (**Mammoth Mountain RV,** 2667 Main St./CA 203, Mammoth Lakes 93546; 800-582-4603; mammothrv.com) that offers full hookups. Visit www.fs.usda .gov/recarea/inyo for other campgrounds in the town of Mammoth Lakes and in the Lakes Basin.

## Puppy Paws and Golden Years

Dogs are welcome on the **gondola** to the top of Mammoth Mountain, and it's a must-do for a unique bird's-eye view of the Sierra Nevada range. The **shuttle** that rides around town and in the Lakes Basin, moving people and bikes around, allows dogs, but they must wear a muzzle. It's a handy, comfortable way to circulate and size up the town while you and Pooch save feet and paws for the trail. If you happen to be in town on July 4 or Labor Day weekend, every hiker and his or her dog will be there socializing and at the **annual arts and craft fairs** between hikes. If your dog is due for a wardrobe makeover, some of the booths carry nifty dog gear. The dogs love to lap up or splash in the kiddie pools set up for their hydration and cooling pleasure. Check out visitmammoth.com for schedule of fairs.

The **downtown Mammoth** paved recreational path has several level stretches in the pines or along Mammoth Creek. The stretch behind **Shady Rest Campground** and the **visitor center on Main Street** and the stretch on the east side of **Old Mammoth Road** along Mammoth Creek are especially sweet. Have a picnic by the creek at the **Mammoth Museum** across the creek bridge off of Old Mammoth Road or at the **Vista Point picnic table** approximately 1.0 mile east of the gravel area off Old Mammoth Road. The latter is a dynamite moonrise-watching spot on a full moon night. **Snowcreek Meadow,** behind the Snowcreek condominium development off of Minaret Road, is laced with trails and streams with a Mammoth Mountain and Mammoth Rock backdrop that exudes a natural drug that makes dogs (on leash) of any age and energy go bonkers! The **Mammoth Ranger Station/Welcome Center** (2510 Main St., Mammoth Lakes 93546; 760-924-5500) can help you with maps and directions.

# 39 Crystal Lake

This hike is a "wow" at every bend. It ascends gradually on sweeping switchbacks in and out of the pine and fir forest, revealing stunning views of Lake George, Lake Mary, and the Mammoth Crest where the trail skirts the granitic perches.

**Start:** From Crystal Lake trailhead in the Lake George parking area
**Distance:** 3.0 miles out and back
**Approximate hiking time:** 2 hours
**Difficulty:** Strenuous because of elevation
**Trailhead elevation:** 9,055 feet
**Highest point:** 9,732 feet
**Best season:** Summer to early fall
**Trail surface:** Dirt and granite
**Other trail users:** Horses
**Canine compatibility:** Voice control
**Land status:** National Forest

**Fees and permits:** Campfire permits
**Maps:** USGS Crystal Crag; USFS Inyo National Forest
**Trail contacts:** Inyo National Forest, Mammoth Ranger Station and Welcome Center, 2510 Main Street, Mammoth Lakes 93546; (760) 924-5500; www.fs.usda.gov/inyo. Open year-round 7 days a week.
**Nearest town:** Mammoth Lakes
**Trail tips:** If your dog is the nosy type, leash him until you get past the back of the Woods Lodge cabins.

**Finding the trailhead:** From the Mammoth Lakes exit 263 at intersection of US 395 and CA 203, drive west 3.7 miles to the intersection of CA 203/Minaret Road and Lake Mary Road. Drive 3.8 miles up Lake Mary Road and turn left at the sign for Lake George and Woods Lodge. Follow the signs for Lake George. Drive 0.2 mile and turn right after the bridge at the sign for Lake George and Woods Lodge. Drive 0.2 mile up the road to the parking area for Lake George at the end of the paved road. A sign for the Crystal Lake trailhead is on your right as you reach the parking lot. **GPS:** N37 36.21' / W119 00.67'

## The Hike

This trail to Crystal Lake is not the Eastern Sierra's best-kept secret judging by the number of hikers and backpackers with dogs who travel to the lake and beyond. It is a very popular and easily accessible trail at the end of a paved road adjacent to a popular fishing lake, panoramic campground, and dog-friendly cabin resort. But then again, the popularity of some hikes is a reflection of how special or rewarding they are, and Crystal Lake fits that criteria.

The Mammoth Lakes Basin is a lake lover's pot of gold, and Crystal Lake boasts one of the most scenic settings beneath Crystal Crag's granite sentinel and jagged Mammoth Crest. That in itself would make Crystal Lake an idyllic destination, but the reel of views along the trail is one of three unique boons. The other two are your choice of overnight options: You can drive to the end of a paved road and camp in one of Inyo National Forest's best campgrounds overlooking beautiful Lake George,

*Panoramic views overlooking Lake George and Lake Mary*

or you can get cozy in a Woods Lodge dog-friendly cabin above Lake George. Few hikes as short and scenic as Crystal Lake and on the doorstep of a wilderness area allow this kind choice within steps of the trailhead.

The information board at the trailhead that welcomes you to the Ansel Adams Wilderness is the first clue that you are in for a treat. The well-worn and dusty trail begins with a gentle ascent and wends around behind the Woods Lodge cabins on the left above Lake George, passing through a stretch of manzanita, sage, and other High Sierra low brush that is lined with blue lupine through mid-summer. Approximately 0.5 mile up the trail you and Pooch enter the shade of pines and firs and begin the sweeping switchbacks and gradual ascent that allow your lungs to catch up with the elevation. The trail weaves to and from the open ridge over the next mile, revealing grandiose views of Lake George and Lake Mary in the background. These unmarked natural vista points are ideal for water breaks for your dog. The views are made more dramatic framed by Mammoth Crest and Crystal Crag to the southeast. At 1.0 mile Mammoth Mountain rises above Horseshoe Lake in the distance on your right. The trail levels just a short distance ahead, where you come to a fork for the Mammoth Crest Trail that goes up on your right. This is where Crystal Lake hikers generally part company with the backpackers who are heading up to Mammoth Crest and into the John Muir Wilderness or hard-core hikers who are climbing to Mammoth Crest toward Duck Pass for the grueling all-day loop back into the Lakes Basin at the southeast end of Mammoth Crest.

In less than a 0.5-mile gentle descent, you come to the shores of Crystal Lake on the right when you reach the lake's outflow. In good snowpack years, this outflow tumbles down a sheer face into Lake George, creating a waterfall visible from the trailhead through the summer and fall. Crystal Lake shimmers as it is cradled beneath Crystal Crag by a half-moon ring of evergreens on the east shore and the stark granite Mammoth Crest south. Depending on seasonal water conditions, it is possible to extend the hike by walking around the lake by crossing at the outflow and following a primitive trail that requires some scampering over granite slabs and crossing a marshy meadow at the head of the lake. Crystal Lake deserves that you and Pooch linger and enjoy a picnic lunch before you go back the way you came.

## Miles and Directions

**0.0** Start at the Crystal Lake trailhead.

**0.3** Come to cabins on the left with Lake George below.

**0.6** Come to a viewpoint overlooking Lake George below and Lake Mary in the background. Mammoth Crest rises with a towering Crystal Crag to the right of the lake.

**1.0** Come to a clearing and views of Mammoth Mountain and Horseshoe Lake to the northwest.

**1.2** Arrive at a trail junction for Mammoth Crest uphill to the right. Continue walking straight as the trail levels before descending gently toward Crystal Lake.

**1.5** Arrive at Crystal Lake on your right at the base of Crystal Crag and Mammoth Crest. Elevation 9,618 feet. **GPS:** N37 35.74' / W119 01.07' Stick around and soak in Mother Nature's work while sharing a snack and water break with your four-legged pal. Go back the way you came and enjoy a different perspective of this awesome panorama.

**3.0** Arrive back at the trailhead.

## Creature Comforts

### Fueling Up

The Village at Mammoth's pedestrian complex of condominiums, shops, and restaurants showcases several establishments with dog-friendly patios. **Gomez's Mexican Restaurant** (100 Canyon Blvd., Mammoth Lakes 93546; 760-924-2693; gomezs.com) is well-known for its margaritas and fresh guacamole. **The Smokeyard** (1111 Forest Trail Rd., #201, Mammoth Lakes 93546; 760-934-3300; smokeyard.com) offers burgers

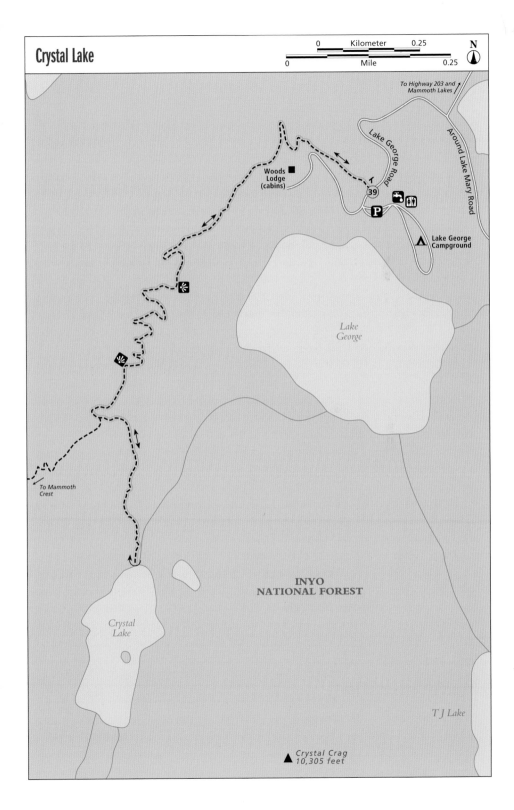

# Crystal Lake

0       Kilometer       0.25

0       Mile       0.25

N

To Highway 203 and
Mammoth Lakes

Lake George Road

Around Lake Mary Road

Woods
Lodge
(cabins)

39

P

Lake George
Campground

Lake
George

To Mammoth
Crest

INYO
NATIONAL FOREST

Crystal
Lake

T J Lake

▲ Crystal Crag
10,305 feet

and beef ribs that will make Pooch drool. If gluten is an issue for you, the menu identifies its gluten-free (GF) and gluten-sensitive (GS) dishes. Also try **Schatz Bakery** (3305 Main St., Mammoth Lakes 93546; 760-935-6055; sheaschatsbakery.com).

## Resting Up

There are three dog-friendly lodges with cabins in the Mammoth Lakes Basin. All have access to hiking trails, and each has its own appeal. The romantic **Tamarack Lodge** (163 Twin Lakes Rd., Mammoth Lakes 93546; 760-934-2442; tamaracklodge.com) in the Mammoth Lakes Basin offers well-appointed, updated, and new housekeeping cabins of various sizes. The three-bedroom "luxury" cabin is the first LEED-certified building (leading in energy and environmental design) in the Eastern Sierra. (Well-mannered dogs under one hundred pounds are welcome in the cabins.) If you want to treat yourself to a special dinner, without Bowser, the Lakefront Restaurant in the lodge is intimate and a palate pleaser. At **Crystal Crag Lodge** (40 Lake Mary Rd., Mammoth Lakes 93546; 760-934-2436; crystalcraglodge.com) the comfortable housekeeping cabins across from Lake Mary are popular with families and fishing enthusiasts. The housekeeping cabins at **Woods Lodge** (800 Lake George Rd., Mammoth Lakes 93546; 760-934-2261; woodslodgemammoth.com) at the end of the paved road overlooking Lake George have the most stunning setting.

Located on Hillside Drive across from The Village, **Westin Monache Resort** (50 Hillside Dr., Mammoth Lakes 93546; 760-934-0400; westinmammoth.com/monache) is a treat for hikers and their dogs. All rooms have cooking facilities if you want to rustle up some chow for yourself and your canine. But no dog I ever traveled to Mammoth with has ever turned down room service at the end of a long trail. The staff is super friendly and welcomes their canine guests with "heavenly" dog beds, bowls, and poop bags. Dogs seem to like hanging around the concierge desk. Could it be there's a secret stash of biscuits in the area?

**Snowcreek Resort Condominiums,** 1254 Old Mammoth Rd., Mammoth Lakes 93546; (760) 934-3333; snowcreekresort.com. This is a dog's favorite setting of any condominium complex in Mammoth Lakes.

There is also no shortage of **campgrounds** in town and in the Lakes Basin. There are at least seven Forest Service campgrounds for tents and self-contained trailers and RVs. They have toilets, water, picnic tables, and fire rings. There is one RV park on Main Street (**Mammoth Mountain RV,** 2667 Main St./CA 203, Mammoth Lakes 93546; 800-582-4603; mammothrv.com) that offers full hookups. Visit www.fs.usda .gov/recarea/inyo for other campgrounds in the town of Mammoth Lakes and in the Lakes Basin.

## Puppy Paws and Golden Years

Dogs are welcome on the **gondola** to the top of Mammoth Mountain, and it's a must-do for a unique bird's-eye view of the Sierra Nevada range. The **shuttle** that rides around town and in the Lakes Basin, moving people and bikes around, allows dogs,

*Crystal Lake*

but they must wear a muzzle. It's a handy, comfortable way to circulate and size up the town while you and Pooch save feet and paws for the trail. If you happen to be in town on July 4 or Labor Day weekend, every hiker and his or her dog will be there socializing and at the **annual arts and craft fairs** between hikes. If your dog is due for a wardrobe makeover, some of the booths carry nifty dog gear. The dogs love to lap up or splash in the kiddie pools set up for their hydration and cooling pleasure. Check out visitmammoth.com for schedule of fairs.

The **downtown Mammoth** paved recreational path has several level stretches in the pines or along Mammoth Creek. The stretch behind **Shady Rest Campground** and the **visitor center on Main Street** and the stretch on the east side of **Old Mammoth Road** along Mammoth Creek are especially sweet. Have a picnic by the creek at the **Mammoth Museum** across the creek bridge off of Old Mammoth Road or at the **Vista Point picnic table** approximately 1.0 mile east of the gravel area off Old Mammoth Road. The latter is a dynamite moonrise-watching spot on a full moon night. **Snowcreek Meadow,** behind the Snowcreek condominium development off of Minaret Road, is laced with trails and streams with a Mammoth Mountain and Mammoth Rock backdrop that exudes a natural drug that makes dogs (on leash) of any age and energy go bonkers! The **Mammoth Ranger Station/Welcome Center** (2510 Main St., Mammoth Lakes 93546; 760-924-5500) can help you with maps and directions.

# 40 Shadow of the Giants

There are no fancy signs or elaborate visitor centers at the trailhead for the Shadow of Giants National Recreation Trail, and at first glance it's easy to wonder why you bothered to drive the last dusty 0.5 mile for this. But it only takes stepping a few hundred yards along this self-guided trail with the lovely creek to spot the first of these magnificent giants and feel the reverence and the awe. This is a rare opportunity to hike in a Northern California sequoia grove in the company of your dog, since the next-closest groves are in Yosemite National Park.

**Start:** From the Sierra Beauty day-use turnout
**Distance:** 1.3-mile loop
**Approximate hiking time:** 1 hour
**Difficulty:** Easy
**Trailhead elevation:** 5,190 feet
**Highest point:** 5,343 feet
**Best season:** Spring to late fall
**Trail surface:** Dirt
**Other trail users:** Horses
**Canine compatibility:** Voice control

**Land status:** National Forest
**Fees and permits:** Campfire permit
**Maps:** USGS White Chief Mountain; USFS Sierra National Forest
**Trail contacts:** Sierra National Forest, Bass Lake Ranger Station, 57003 Road 225, North Fork 93643; (559) 877-2218; neldergrove.org
**Nearest town:** Oakhurst
**Trail tips:** The dirt road to the trailhead is extremely dusty.

**Finding the trailhead:** From Oakhurst at the intersection CA 49 and CA 41, drive 4.0 miles east on CA 41 to FR 632. Turn right onto FR 632, drive 6.5 miles, and turn left at the sign for Nelder Grove. This road is gravel and has some washboard sections. Drive 1.2 miles on the gravel road and turn left onto a dirt road at the fork toward Sugar Pine. Drive 0.5 mile on the narrower dirt road and park in the turnout at Sierra Beauty day-use area on the left. This day-use area, with a small wooden sign, is just short of the SHADOW OF THE GIANTS/NATIONAL RECREATION TRAIL sign 200 feet ahead on the left. The trailhead is on the right up a short, steep eroded dirt drive across from the road from the SHADOW OF THE GIANTS sign. The trailhead is to the left of the vault toilet. **GPS:** N37 25.58' / W119 35.76'

## The Hike

At the time the Sierra National Forest was created as a forest reserve, it was the second national forest established in California and covered 6 million acres of the Sierra Nevada. In 1907, reserves became national forests and parts of the Sierra National Forest eventually were absorbed to form four other national forests and three national parks—Yosemite, Sequoia, and Kings Canyon National Parks. Sierra National Forest is now 1,300,000 acres of beauty with five wilderness areas and a scenic byway that features several natural and historic attractions, including the 1,500-acre Nelder Grove area.

*Reading an interpretive sign along the trail*

The first inhabitants of Nelder Grove were Western Mono Native Americans, who revered the "big trees" they considered sacred and protected by the owl spirit. The Southern Sierra Miwok also found resources plentiful for thousands of years in the grove area. The grove is named after John Nelder, who came from New Orleans to find his gold fortune in California. A gold seeker turned nature worshipper, Nelder built among the sequoias in 1875. That same year John Muir, the passionate naturalist and founder of the Sierra Club, met Nelder at his cabin and found a kindred spirit in the man who "stroked the little snow bent sapling Sequoias" and hand-fed quail and squirrels.

Sequoia harvest reached its peak in the grove in the 1920s, and the one hundred or so remaining mature sequoias in the pine, fir, and cedar forest have been protected

# FIVE GIANT SEQUOIA FAST FACTS

- Giant Sequoias are the largest living things on Earth. (They are shorter than their coastal relatives, redwoods, but have wider trunks and branches, with up to a 35-foot base diameter.)
- The oldest known Sequoia is over 3,200 years old.
- They are the fastest growing trees in the world (an average of two feet a year to maturity).
- Sequoias grow at 6,500 foot elevation.
- Of the 60 million seeds produced by a Sequoia in its lifetime (a tree can be 800 to 3,000 years old) only 3 to 4 of those seeds will grow to be 100 years old.

for several decades. The Nelder Grove Historical Area, 0.5 mile up the road past the National Recreation Trail has a campground, two historical cabins, and an interpretive center with the remnants of the original logging camp's transport infrastructure.

The Shadow of the Giants Trail was constructed in 1965 and became a National Recreation Trail in 1978. Part of the charm of this trail is that it has convenient access from Oakhurst but it is just far enough from the beaten path that you and Pooch can have this intimate cathedral to yourselves even on a summer weekend. The trail is best walked clockwise, and the first interpretive sign about squirrels using the soft bark to make their nest is the first of ten such plaques that offer fascinating tidbits about the life of these titanic ancient beauties.

The trail threads to a lush woodland of black oak, pines, and firs, which makes the sudden appearance of the colossal towering sentinels startling and exciting. The grove setting is seductive and enchanting, where time seems to stand still as you find yourself wishing the 1.0-mile trail would never end.

At 0.7 mile you cross the first of two wooden footbridges over Nelder Creek. Hundred-year-old stumps dot the slopes embellished by floating dogwood blooms in the spring. The grove is both a graveyard and a nursery, where the towering mature giants stand as monuments in homage to their fallen ancestors—victims of a different era—while standing guard over the sapling giants of tomorrow.

At 1.2 miles the second bridge over Nelder Creek announces the inevitable end to your journey back in time in the Shadow of the Giants. Savor the last steps as you arrive back at the trailhead.

*Giant Sequoia Trees can grow 300 feet tall.* ▶

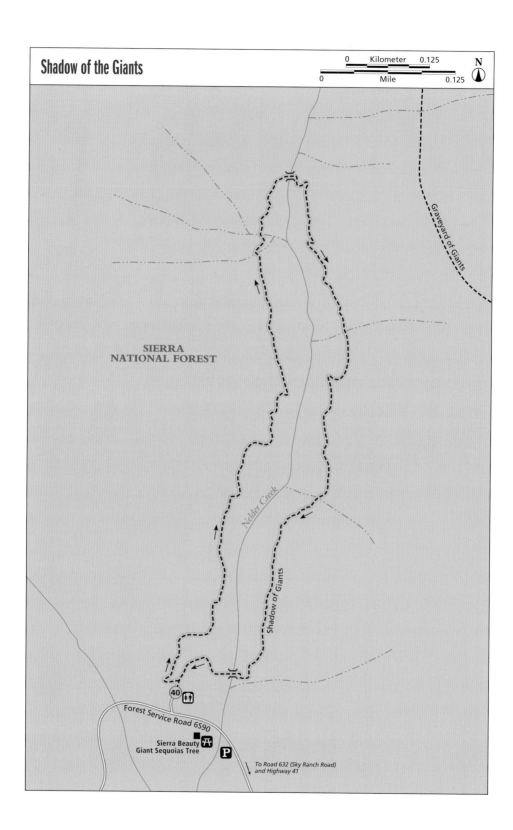

# Shadow of the Giants

Kilometer

0    0.125

Mile

0    0.125

N

SIERRA
NATIONAL FOREST

Graveyard of Giants

Nelder Creek

Shadow of Giants

40

Forest Service Road 6S90

Sierra Beauty
Giant Sequoias Tree

P

To Road 632 (Sky Ranch Road)
and Highway 41

## Miles and Directions

**0.0**  Start at the trailhead to the left of the vault toilet about 200 feet up the road from the Sierra Beauty day-use turnout. Begin the hike clockwise at the first interpretive sign.

**0.7**  Come to a log footbridge. Walk across Nelder Creek.

**1.2**  Come to a footbridge and walk back across Nelder Creek.

**1.3**  Arrive back at the trailhead and end of the loop.

## Creature Comforts

### Resting Up

**Sierra Sky Ranch,** 50552 Road 632, Oakhurst 93644; (559) 683-8040; sierraskyranch .com. This historic rustic ranch property was converted to accommodate guests with well-behaved canine guests in a cozy natural setting.

**Nelder Grove Sierra National Forest Service Campground** (www.fs.usda.gov/recarea/ sierra), approximately 0.5 mile across the turnoff for Shadow of the Giants, has seven tent and RV sites (no hookups). The primitive campground sits amid Nelder Grove giant sequoias on the site of a historic logging camp with two interpretive trails. You might be lucky and spot a Mountain Lady's Slipper, considered to be a rare orchid protected under Forest Service Sensitive Species.

# 41 Gem Lakes

This is one of the most popular summer hikes in the Eastern Sierra and for good reason. If you and your dog have dreamt of driving up a paved road to 10,000 feet, hopping out of the car, and following a gentle graded trail along streams linking lakes and meadows with a granite peak backdrop, this hike is your dream come true.

**Start:** Little Lakes Valley trailhead at Rock Creek
**Distance:** 7.6 miles out and back
**Approximate Hiking Time:** 4 hours
**Difficulty:** Easy
**Trailhead elevation:** 10,232 feet
**Highest point:** 10,910 feet
**Season:** Early summer to early fall
**Trail Surface:** Dirt trail
**Other Trail Users:** Horses
**Canine Compatibility:** Voice control
**Land Status:** National Forest; Wilderness
**Fees and permits:** None

**Maps:** USGS Mount Morgan and Mount Abbot; USFS Inyo National Forest; John Muir Wilderness
**Trail contacts:** Inyo National Forest, Mammoth Ranger Station and Welcome Center, 2510 Main St./CA 203, Mammoth Lakes 93546; (760) 924-5500; www.fs.usda.gov/inyo. Open year-round 7 days a week.
**Nearest town:** Mammoth Lakes
**Trail tips:** There are two vault toilets. Arrive at the trailhead in the morning so you can park in the main parking lot and avoid the frequent afternoon thunder showers that can bring hail at this altitude.

**Finding the trailhead:** From Mammoth Lakes at the intersection of CA 203 and US 395, drive 15.0 miles south to the Rock Creek Lake turnoff. Turn right at the Rock Creek Lake turnoff and drive 10.0 miles to the parking lot at end of the road. The trailhead is at the far end of the parking lot by the information board. **GPS:** N37 26.09' / W118 44.85'

## The Hike

Elevation and acclimatization aside (trailhead is at 10,000 feet), the Little Lakes Valley is the easiest hike to one, if not *the,* most breathtaking setting in the High Sierra. How often do you get to drive up a paved road on the doorstep of a wilderness area to witness and bask in the beauty that typically requires days of roughing it through the backcountry or miles of rocking and bouncing on a rutted, barely passable remote Forest Service road?

John Muir Wilderness established by the Wilderness Act of 1964, is named after the Sierra's most passionate advocate and covers over 100 miles of trails showcasing some of the High Sierra's most iconic landscape along the eastern escarpment.

On a summer weekend or holiday week, Little Lakes Valley parking lot at Mosquito Flats is full by noon and hikers must walk up to a mile from the overflow parking lot down the road. You drive up to the edge of the postcard, step out of the

*Overlooking Gem Lakes*

car, and are in the postcard. The information board at the far end of the parking lot has a very good map of the Little Lakes Valley identifying the various lakes and trail junctions to passes.

It's the type of location where you and Pooch can have a peak experience with an hour hike or a full day of exploring. Any streamside boulder or lakeside patch of grass just off the main trail is an idyllic snack stop or romp break for Pooch. The wildflowers of lupine bloom later at this elevation, which is an additional mid- to late summer treat.

From the trailhead at the map board, you will pass three lakes in the first mile with barely 500 feet in elevation gain. Any of those is worthy of a destination.

By mile 2.0, with several meadow-feeding ribbons of water and two more lakes, your camera-clicking finger will start to cramp from all the point-and-shoot exercise. Your dog will never have seemed so photogenic with this stunning snow-patched alpine backdrop

At 2.8 miles if you don't have time or energy for the last mile to gorgeous Gem Lakes, you can turn left at the Chickenfoot Lake trail junction. Chickenfoot is a hidden lake just over the rise and often unjustly overlooked.

The last mile to Gem Lakes brings you closer to the granite palisades that embrace the Little Lakes Valley. This stretch of trail is popular with rock climbers lured by the challenges of the granite spires above the basin and beyond Morgan Pass junction, where you turn right to Gem Lakes at 3.4 miles. Your destination is an easy scenic 0.4 mile ahead. This lake is the largest of the Gem Lakes and worthy of a leisurely picnic break. There is no specific trail connecting the string of smaller lakes in this basin, but you can explore part of the rim in a counterclockwise direction to view the other lakes before returning to the trailhead the way you came.

## Miles and Directions

**0.0**  Start at the trailhead at the right of the information board with the Little Lakes Valley map at the far end of the Mosquito Flats parking lot.

**0.2**  Enter the John Muir Wilderness.

**0.5**  Come to a fork for Morgan Pass to the left and Mono Pass to the right. Bear left toward Morgan Pass. The trail is terraced up with granite rock for the next 0.25 mile. Rock Creek is on your left.

**0.7**  Mack Lake appears on your left below the trail.

**0.9**  Come to a fork with an unmarked trail on your left leading to Marsh Lake, visible on your left. Continue straight on the trail.

**1.2**  Cross a stream on a footbridge overlooking Heart Lake. Cross a second footbridge just ahead.

**1.7**  Come to Box Lake on your left below the trail.

**2.1**  Reach Long Lake on your right.

**2.8**  Come to the trail junction for Chickenfoot Lake to the left. Continue walking uphill on the main trail.

**3.3**  Come to a stream crossing and a trail sign for Gem Lakes straight.

**3.4**  Come to a trail junction for Morgan Pass straight and Gem Lakes to the right. Turn right to Gem Lakes.

**3.8**  Arrive at the Gem Lakes. Pick a granite perch along the shore to enjoy a picnic with Pooch and savor the pristine beauty of this granite lake basin. Return the way you came.

**7.6**  Arrive back at the trailhead.

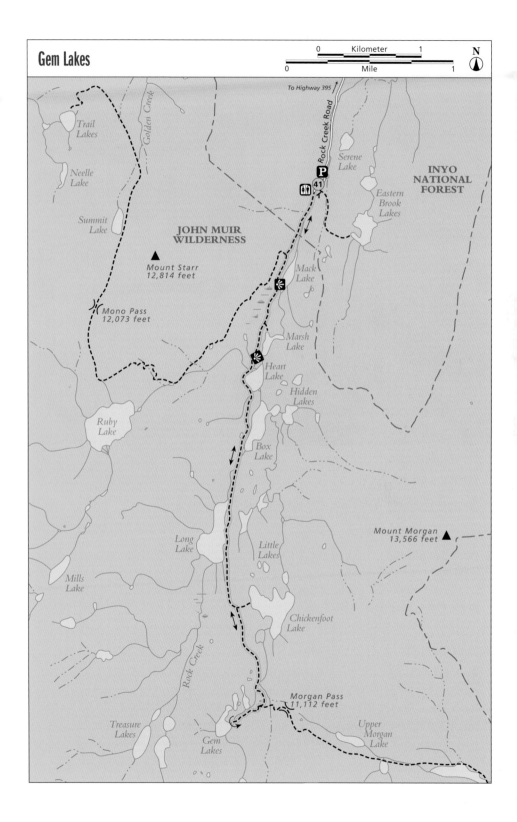

# Gem Lakes

0     Kilometer     1

0     Mile     1

N

To Highway 395

Rock Creek Road

P

41

Trail
Lakes

Golden Creek

Neelle
Lake

Serene
Lake

INYO
NATIONAL
FOREST

Eastern
Brook
Lakes

Summit
Lake

JOHN MUIR
WILDERNESS

Mount Starr
12,814 feet

Mack
Lake

Mono Pass
12,073 feet

Marsh
Lake

Heart
Lake

Hidden
Lakes

Ruby
Lake

Box
Lake

Mount Morgan
13,566 feet

Long
Lake

Little
Lakes

Mills
Lake

Chickenfoot
Lake

Rock Creek

Morgan Pass
11,112 feet

Treasure
Lakes

Upper
Morgan
Lake

Gem
Lakes

*Back to the trailhead*

## Creature Comforts

### Fueling Up

**Pie in the Sky Café,** 1 upper Rock Creek Rd., Bishop 93515; (760) 935-4311; rock
creeklake.com. The best posthike treat between June Lake and Bishop. Get your slice
on the way up to the trailhead. They sell out by noon in summer.

**Tom's Place Resort** (8180 Crowley Lake Dr., Crowley Lake 93546; 760-935-4239;
tomsplaceresort.com) has a cafe and a general store for supplies.

### Resting Up

**Rock Creek Lodge,** 88 Rock Creek Rd., Mammoth Lakes 93546; (877) 935-4170;
rockcreeklodge.com. The lodge offers housekeeping cabins and a campground.

**Tom's Place Resort,** 8180 Crowley Lake Dr., Crowley Lake 93546; (760) 935-4239;
tomsplaceresort.com. Located at the junction of I-395 and Rock Creek Road, rustic
housekeeping cabins 16, 17, and 18 are dog-friendly summer cabins.

# 42 Lamarck Lakes

You can drop your camera on the ground just about anywhere in the Eastern Sierra and snap a postcard shot. Lamarck Lakes is just one of many easily accessed trailheads that takes you on an I-can't-believe-how-beautiful-this-is hike. Just the fact that it is in the John Muir Wilderness guarantees heavenly meadows and streams or lakes cradled beneath granite peaks and crags. Lamarck delivers the idyllic streams and lakes with a granitic backdrop after a gradual ascent out of a lush aspen woodland.

**Start:** North Lake Campground
**Distance:** 5.0 miles out and back to Upper Lamarck Lake
**Approximate hiking time:** 3 hours
**Difficulty:** Strenuous, because of elevation and steep stretches
**Trailhead elevation:** 9,368 feet
**Highest point:** 10,950 feet
**Best season:** Summer to early fall
**Trail surface:** Dirt trail and rock
**Other trail users:** Horses
**Canine compatibility:** On leash through the campground; voice control on the trail
**Land status:** National Forest; Wilderness

**Fees and permits:** Permit for overnight camping in the wilderness; check with the ranger station about the status of campfire permits, which varies with the season, for individual trails at different elevations
**Maps:** USGS Mount Darwin and Mount Thompson; USFS Inyo National Forest; John Muir Wilderness
**Trail contacts:** Inyo National Forest, White Mountain Ranger Station, 798 North Main St., Bishop 93914; (760) 873-2500; www.fs.usda .gov/recarea/inyo
**Nearest town:** Bishop
**Trail tips:** Pooch needs to wear booties. Water sandals may be needed for stream crossings.

**Finding the trailhead:** From Bishop at the intersection of US 395 (Main Street) and CA 168 (West Line Road), drive west 17.5 miles up toward the Sierra mountain range. West Line Road becomes Sabrina Lake Road. Turn right to North Lake after the Sabrina Basin sign. Drive 1.5 miles uphill on the North Lake road, which alternates between pavement and improved gravel surface. Turn right at the Bishop Pack Outfitter sign on your right. The sign on the left side of the road directing hikers to the trailhead parking at the Bishop Pack Outfitter may be obscured by a bush. Drive 0.1 mile to the trailhead parking lot. The trailhead for Lamarck Lakes is in the North Lake Campground, but day-use parking is prohibited in the North Lake Campground. Hikers must park here, walk 0.1 mile to the main road, turn right, and walk 0.5 mile to the trailhead by the information board in the North Lake Campground. **GPS:** N37 13.64' / W118 37.66'

## The Hike

Once again, hiking trails on the east side of the Sierra is about stepping into the postcard after a relatively short drive on well-maintained roads regardless of whether they are paved or gravel. I have hiked ranges around the world, but none compares to Eastern Sierra for easy access to rugged jaw-dropping beauty. Add the fact that

*Lower Lamarck Lake*

Lamarck Lakes are in the John Muir Wilderness, and you are guaranteed to be awed. John Muir Wilderness, established by the Wilderness Act of 1964, is named after the Sierra's most passionate advocate. It covers over 100 miles of trails that showcase some of the High Sierra's most iconic landscape along the eastern escarpment. The hike to Lamarck Lakes does the wilderness's reputation justice every step of the way.

This hike progresses from a gentle climb with some seasonal stream crossings in aspen groves to switchbacks and a sweeping stairway to heaven against granite cliffs. Your eyes shift from red mountain heather to white ranger buttons to blushed-tipped alpine columbines tucked in granite crags as the trail unfurls boldly upward. Prepare to see flowers less-frequently seen on other high-country trails, like the purple western monkshood and pale purple pennyroyal.

At 0.8 mile the trail opens to a bench, and switchbacks are interrupted by another granite bench overlooking Grass Lake to the south and North Lake to the east at 1.2 miles. This calls for a rest and water break. Listen to the rushing waters out of Lower Lamarck Lake and soak up the views of Mount Emerson and rusty crags.

At 1.5 miles the trail reaches another promontory with panoramic views. The terrain becomes more arid with sagebrush as you ascend, trading the forests behind you for a mostly granite scape dotted with hardy pines.

At 1.8 miles don't miss the right turn to the banks of Lower Lamarck Lake, an excellent and worthy destination and turnaround point. Lower Lamarck deserves your and Pooch's time and makes a perfect rest and snack stop while you evaluate your energy reserves for the almost 1.0 mile left to climb to Upper Lamarck Lake. Something instinctive and obsessive drives some of us to shoot for the highest points, but in this instance, truly, Lower Lamarck Lake may well be the prettier and more visually nourishing destination.

The rest of the way to Upper Lamarck Lake includes a couple of stream crossings and some fancy footwork to keep your feet dry. Your dog will welcome the opportunity for another paw-cooling crossing. The granitic scenery is starkly stunning, highlighted by bright blooms of wildflowers clinging to the rocks.

At 2.4 miles don't be confused by the wooden unnamed trail sign with the very deliberately carved arrow directing you to turn left on the well-worn trail. It can easily distract you from the faint grassy trail heading straight, which is actually the correct way to Upper Lamarck Lake, which is barely 0.1 mile at the end of the grassy trail with a stream on the left of the trail.

*Upper Lamarck Lake*

The well-worn trail leads to the Lamarck col across and up along a dry, wind-swept, treeless, desolately beautiful rocky slope, which gets very precarious and is totally inappropriate and joyless for dogs.

Upper Lamarck Lake will reward you and Pooch with crystal-clear water and a feeling of accomplishment while you bask in the beauty and eat your trail treats.

## Miles and Directions

**0.0** Start at the Lamarck Lakes trailhead in the North Lake Campground, a 0.5-mile walk from the trailhead parking lot. Come to a fork 450 feet up the trail and bear left to Lamarck Lakes.

**0.1** Come to a stream and walk across the footbridge.

**0.2** Enter the John Muir Wilderness. The gradual climb out of the pine and aspen forest will steepen with switchbacks through a more exposed, stunning granite landscape.

**0.9** Come to a trail junction for Grass Lake on the left. Continue walking straight.

# Lamarck Lakes

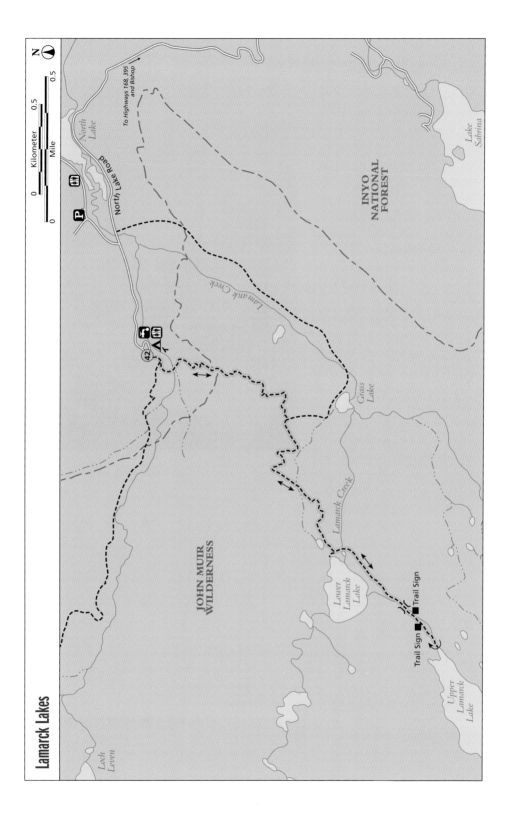

North Lake

North Lake Road

To Highways 168, 395
and Bishop

Lamarck Creek

INYO
NATIONAL
FOREST

Lake
Sabrina

42

Grass
Lake

Lamarck Creek

JOHN MUIR
WILDERNESS

Loch
Leven

Lower
Lamarck
Lake

Trail Sign

Trail Sign

Upper
Lamarck
Lake

**1.8** Arrive at an unmarked fork. Turn right and walk less than one hundred steps to Lower Lamarck Lake. This lake makes for a splendid stop for you and Pooch to have a snack while resting on a boulder. Pooch can cool off with a paddle in the lake, while you enjoy the lake's idyllic setting beneath the granite crag. If you both are up to it and want to continue to dramatic but slightly less user-friendly Upper Lamarck Lake, retrace your steps to the fork and turn right to continue to Upper Lamarck Lake.

**1.9** Come to the outflow of Lower Lamarck Lake and cross the stream. Continue walking uphill. Lower Lamarck Lake will become visible below on your right.

**2.3** Come to the outflow of Upper Lamarck Lake and cross the stream.

**2.4** Come to a fork and an unnamed trail sign with an arrow pointing left. Continue straight on the grassier trail with the stream on your left to Upper Lamarck Lake. It will be tempting to follow the arrow and bear left on the well-worn trail. Don't. This is the unmarked Lamarck Lakes col path to the steep, exposed, and precarious route for experienced hikers only and definitely unsafe for dogs.

**2.5** Arrive at Upper Lamarck Lake. This is your destination. Elevation 10,950 feet. **GPS:** N37 12.74'/ W118 38.77' You and your dog both deserve a boost with your favorite treats before going back the way you came.

**5.0** Arrive back at the trailhead. Walk the 0.5 mile back to the trailhead parking lot.

## Creature Comforts

### Fueling Up

**Cardinal Village Resort,** 321 Cardinal Rd., Bishop (in Aspendell community off CA 168/Sabrina Lake Road on the way to Lamarck Lakes); (760) 873-4789; cardinalvillage resort.com. The resort has a cafe that serves the best grilled cheese sandwich in addition to burgers and freshly baked apple pie. Your well-behaved pooch just might be allowed on the deck if you play it cool.

**Schatz Bakery,** 763 N. Main St., Bishop 93514; (760) 873-7156; erickschatsbakery .com. The bakery makes and bakes everything you would want for a trailside picnic. Turkey sandwiches are prepared with slices of fresh oven-roasted turkey. Your dog is sure to give you the stare down when you unwrap that sandwich. Schatz cookies and pastries take care of the sugar fix.

### Resting Up

There are several dog-friendly motels in Bishop, but if you and Fido want a "homier" experience, there is the **Chalfant House B&B** (213 Academy St., Bishop 93514; 760-872-1790; chalfanthouse.com).

**Joseph House Inn,** 376 W. Yaney St., Bishop 93514; (760) 872-3389; josephhouse inn.com.

**The North Lake Campground** in Inyo National Forest is located at the trailhead and has tent camping only. There are eleven sites with water, toilets, picnic tables, and fire rings. There are at least four other **Forest Service campgrounds** along CA 168 on the way to the Lamarck Lakes trailhead. Contact www.fs.usda.gov/recarea/inyo for information.

# South Coast Ranges

The South Coast Ranges run north and south, from San Francisco Bay to the north, the Central Valley to the east, the Transverse Ranges to the south, and the Pacific Ocean to the west. Junipero Serra Peak, at 5,862 feet, is the highest peak in the Santa Lucia Mountains. Mount Diablo, 3,849 feet and one of the northernmost peaks, is the second–most visible peak in the world. The Santa Lucia Range drops into the Pacific Ocean south of Monterey, creating the world-famous Big Sur Coast. The northern section of the Los Padres National Forest, which includes the Ventana Wilderness, lies above the Big Sur Coast.

The South Coast Ranges' climate is mild, with foggy summers and intermittent rain in winter along the coast, but hot dry summers and cold winters inland.

Spring following a reasonably wet winter brings an abundance of wildflowers. The vegetation is primarily chaparral and woodlands of oak, bay, cottonwood, pine, buckeye, and redwood canyons interrupted by steep to rolling grasslands.

Bears are rare, but mountain lions, bobcats, coyotes, deer, skunks, and ground squirrels find abundant habitat in these regions.

# 43 Mount Wanda

This is a short uphill sweep along a dirt fire road that shares the ridge with the East Bay Regional Park District network of trails. Hikers with dogs on leash get the privilege of hiking a national park trail that begins in an oak woodland and climbs to rolling grasslands, quickly revealing expansive views toward Mount Diablo and the Carquinez Strait shoreline. The oil refineries and storage tanks in the distance are the main detractors from an otherwise pristine horizon. But for any hiker and nature lover, the opportunity to literally walk in John Muir's footsteps on his land and to the top of a hill named after one of his daughters is a pilgrimage. Your pooch's phenomenal sense of smell may even pick up traces of Muir's own dog, Stickeen, from a past saunter up the hill.

**Start:** From the John Muir National Historic Site Mount Wanda trailhead
**Distance:** 2.2 miles out and back
**Approximate hiking time:** 1.5 hours
**Difficulty:** Easy
**Trailhead elevation:** 140 feet
**Highest point:** 675 feet
**Best season:** Year-round, but can be hot in summer
**Trail surface:** Dirt fire road with grassy single and double tracks
**Other trail users:** Horses and mountain bikes
**Canine compatibility:** On leash
**Land status:** National Park and Regional Park
**Fees and permits:** None
**Maps:** USGS Briones Valley; John Muir National Historic Site Mount Wanda map. On the USGS map, the labels for Mount Wanda and Mount Helen are opposite from what is shown on the National Park Service Mount Wanda map. The hike described here goes to the Mount Wanda shown on the National Park Service map.
**Trail contacts:** John Muir National Historic Site, 4202 Alhambra Ave., Martinez 94553; (925) 228-8860; www.nps.gov
**Nearest town:** Martinez
**Trail tips:** The hike trailhead parking lot is 0.1 mile from the John Muir Historical Site Visitor Center parking lot. Start at the visitor center for the twenty-minute film and self-guided tour of John Muir's house and property, then drive to the trailhead parking lot.

**Finding the trailhead:** From Walnut Creek, head on CA 680 North toward Sacramento and Concord and drive 7.0 miles to exit 53/West Martinez Hercules onto CA 4 west to Martinez and Hercules. Bear right onto CA 4 west and drive 3.5 miles to the Alhambra Avenue and John Muir National Historic Site exit 9. Turn right onto Alhambra Avenue, turn left at the signal, and make an immediate left into the visitor parking lot. Take time to view the twenty-minute film before strolling around the property and visiting John Muir's house.

From the visitor center parking lot, it's a short 0.1-mile drive to the trailhead parking area. Turn right onto Alhambra Avenue. Drive straight at the first signal and go under the freeway. Continue straight under the railroad trestle and straight at the second signal. Turn left at Franklin Canyon Road and make an immediate left into the parking lot on the corner of Franklin and Alhambra. There's a trail sign with an arrow pointing right on the hillside. Walk right to the John Muir National Historic Site sign. The trailhead is at the gate just left of the top of the wooden steps. **GPS:** N37 59.37' / W122 07.80'

*Trail to Mount Wanda with Mount Diablo in the distance*

## The Hike

What makes the Mount Wanda hike unusual also makes it special. It's a short stitch of national park trail at the edge of a populated area and in the heart of the East Bay Regional Park District's 112,000-plus-acre kingdom. Add the fact that it is part of the John Muir National Historic Site—*the* John Muir, the "father" of national parks and forest reserves we now know as national forests. He was America's loudest if not earliest voice for the conservation of wild spaces and the first president of the Sierra Club. It could be argued that without John Muir, there may not be much wild open space for you and your pooch to embrace and explore.

John Muir was born in Scotland in 1838 and grew up on a Wisconsin farm. He studied at the University of Wisconsin. Following a factory accident that almost cost him an eye at age 30, Muir turned to nature and fell in love at first sight with Yosemite. He married Louisa Strentzel in 1880 and spent several years devoted to fruit ranching on the Strentzel's 2,600 acres in Martinez. John Muir lived in the Strentzel's ranch house from 1890 until his death in 1914. The house and the remainder of the property that was not sold are open to visitors as the John Muir National Historic Site.

It is from the "scribble den" in the hilltop house that Muir wrote his books and conducted his campaign of awareness to create Yosemite National Park and save the Hetch Hetchy Valley from being flooded for a dam. Losing the Hetch Hetchy battle in 1913 is said to have been the second-biggest blow to Muir's spirit after the death of Louisa in 1905. There are several sanctuaries in California that pay homage to Muir's dedication to preserving "wildness," but the John Muir Historic Site in Martinez is the place where you will get most intimately acquainted with John Muir the man as well as the writer and conservation visionary.

The short scenic hike to the top of Mount Wanda is the perfect cap to a day in the life of John Muir after your visit to the visitor center. I was surprised that even our little dog Gypsy was allowed in the auditorium for the twenty-minute film about John Muir.

*Water break on top of Mount Wanda*

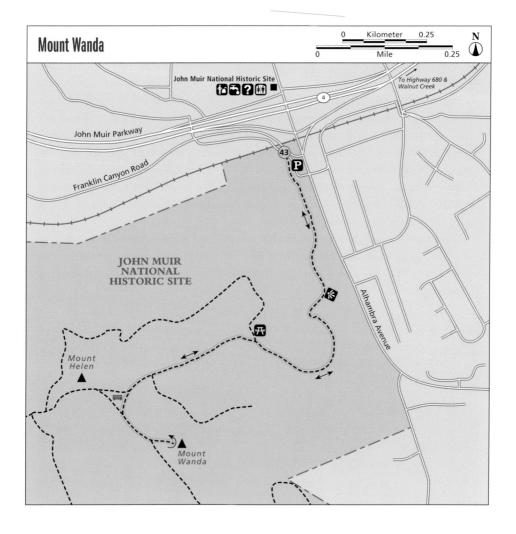

After leaving the visitor center for the 0.1-mile drive to the trailhead parking lot two blocks up Alhambra Avenue, you begin the hike at the John Muir Historic Site Mount Wanda trailhead. Muir had two daughters, Annie Wanda and Helen, both of whom have knoll tops named after them. Neither Mount Wanda nor Mount Helen has very specific marked trail directions, but Mount Wanda is the official hike within the historic site. The fire road behind the gate to the left of the JOHN MUIR NATIONAL HISTORIC SITE MOUNT WANDA sign is the trail. It begins by paralleling the parking lot and Alhambra Avenue below as you walk in the shade of an oak woodland just past the interpretive sign on the left. The sound of traffic is annoying at first but diminishes to a hum after about 0.3 mile, where the first open views southeast toward Mount Diablo's unmistakable twin peaks capture your attention. Your dog has been too busy sniffing in anticipation of his romp off the beaten pavement to be bothered by the urban drone.

The first trail junction on your right has another interpretive sign with a bench on the left and a picnic table on the right. Take advantage of junctions to admire the view and offer your dog a few laps of water. The dirt soon transitions to a shade-less rolling seasonal grassland landscape sprinkled with yellow buttercups, purple vetch, and wild hyacinth with occasional orange fiddleneck tracing the ridge of the over-grown ravine on the left. The refinery tanks on the northeast horizon are far away enough not to be too much of a scar on the view. After about 1.0 mile of walking, Mount Diablo gets more prominent to the southeast as the bridge appears across the Carquinez Strait northeast. You can see CA 4 worming with vehicles in the swale as you look northwest. As you continue uphill bearing left you come to a fork with a well-worn single-track path to a nob on the left. Mount Wanda and 360-degree views await up the gentle 0.1-mile slope. Although civilization has encroached on Muir's canvas since he walked this hill, it is a pleasant surprise to feast on an unexpectedly vast spread of unspoiled ridges to the south and west.

## Miles and Directions

**0.0** Start at the John Muir National Historic Site Mount Wanda trailhead up the wooden steps and to the left at the fire road gate. Trailhead elevation 140 feet. **GPS: N37 59.37' / W122 07.80'**

**0.3** Mount Diablo's twin peaks come into view southeast.

**0.7** Come to a trail junction for the Bay Area Ridge Trail and Nature Trail with an interpretive sign, bench, and picnic table on your right. Continue walking straight up on the Bay Area Ridge Trail.

**0.9** An unmarked trail comes in from the left. Continue straight uphill going west.

**1.0** Arrive at a fork with a bench. Bear left and continue walking uphill. Walk another 50 feet and you will see another unmarked trail coming in from the right. Continue straight, heading south.

**1.1** Come to another fork with a well-worn single-track path going left uphill. Bear left uphill to the knoll with the cement pad and metal post. This is the top of Mount Wanda. Elevation 675 feet. **GPS: N37 58.90' / W122 08.01'** Take in the 360-degree views and give your pup some water and a snack before going back the way you came.

**2.2** Arrive back at the trailhead.

## Creature Comforts

*Resting Up*

**Best Western Plus John Muir Inn,** 445 Muir Station Rd., Martinez 94553; (925) 229-1010; bestwestern.com.

# 44 Lands End

This is an easy and popular scenic coastal hike enjoyed by locals and tourists south of the Golden Gate Bridge. The hike is short and mostly shady and, on a sunny day, rewards with a stunning view of the Golden Gate Bridge from Eagles Point. Lands End is the link between San Francisco's urban heart and its naturally wild soul. The wooded trail of salt-tolerant vegetation passes scenic overlooks that highlight points of historic significance as well as natural landmarks. Whether you are hiking to the sound of the foghorn calling through the mist that gives the trail its air of mystery or on a sunny day when the Golden Gate shines like a rainbow bridging the headlands, this is a special taste of San Francisco's urban wilderness.

**Start:** From the Eagle Point trailhead
**Distance:** 3.3 miles out and back with a spur
**Approximate hiking time:** 1.5 hours
**Difficulty:** Easy, because of the short distance, but there is one stretch of over one hundred steps up
**Trailhead elevation:** 155 feet
**Highest point:** 292 feet
**Best season:** Year-round; sunnier and warmer in early fall
**Trail surface:** Dirt and some pavement
**Other trail users:** Horses and bikes allowed only along the first 0.7 mile
**Canine compatibility:** On leash
**Land status:** National Park

**Fees and permits:** None
**Maps:** USGS Point Bonita, San Francisco North; Golden Gate National Recreation Area; Golden Gate National Parks Conservancy
**Trail contacts:** Golden Gate National Recreation Area, Fort Mason Bldg. 201, San Francisco, 94123; (415) 561-4700; www.nps.gov/goga. Lands End Lookout, (415) 426-5240.
**Nearest town:** San Francisco
**Trail tips:** There are flush toilets and water at the visitor center. Summers can be foggy, cold, and windy in the San Francisco area. Carry fleece and/or a windbreaker. Mark Twain said that the coldest winter he ever spent was the summer he spent in San Francisco.

**Finding the trailhead:** From San Francisco at CA 1/Park Presidio and Geary Boulevard, drive 2.0 miles west on Geary Boulevard/Point Lobos Avenue. Turn right into the parking lot just below Point Lobos and Forty-Eighth Avenue next to the visitor center. If the parking lot is full, there is another across the street from the visitor center. **GPS:** N37 46.86' / W 122 30.70' The trailhead to Eagle Point is at the far end of the parking lot next to the Lands End Lookout Visitor Center.

## The Hike

This segment of California's Coastal Trail in the Golden Gate National Recreation area begins at the visitor center and lookout opened in 2004. On a clear day you will see at least four famous landmarks from the lookout. Seal Rock and Point Lobos (named by the Spanish for sea lions they called sea wolves) are natural landmarks. Just

*Eagle's Point turnaround with Golden Gate Bridge in the background*

below the visitor center are the ruins of the famous Sutro Baths, the world's largest indoor swimming complex built in 1892 by Adolph Sutro with his gold rush fortune as part of his vision for a lavish Victorian amusement park. To the left of the Sutro Baths is the iconic Cliff House. The current concrete building that houses a restaurant and gift shop is the third incarnation of the San Francisco tradition. The first building goes back to the Civil War era. Adolph Sutro resurrected the Cliff House after a fire destroyed it in 1894. Sutro's seven-story French Chateau–style dining venue survived the 1906 earthquake but burned in 1907. The Cliff House was rebuilt in 1909 and a century later still stands to the delight of San Franciscans and visitors alike.

It's always a thrill to hike any section of the dog-friendly California Coastal Trail, an ongoing project since 1972 for a hiking/biking/equestrian trail on or near the ocean the entire length of California. This scenic section has the added bonus of offering cultural history. The Ohlone Indians first lived here in seasonal villages, as shelter was easy and food was plentiful. Those were the days of grizzlies, elk, and sea lions. The Spanish conquerors and the mission system were the first of the drastic changes to the area. Mexican land grants marked another era of change for Lands

End. Adolph Sutro purchased the land around what is known as Lands End around 1879 to showcase his wealth with an oceanfront empire. Ferries, steam trains, mansions, gardens, an early version of a strip mall, and the Victorian amusement park followed.

The National Park Service began acquiring and managing the Sutro legacy of buildings and landmarks that surround Lands End in 1976. Since then the coastal habitat that consists of both native and nonnative plants and trees has been nurtured to provide hikers with an urban wilderness experience. California blackberry, poppies, bush lupine, and cypress trees share the setting with eucalyptus, pampas grass, and South African ice plant.

Marin County's rugged untamed shores are visible across the channel as you walk toward Eagles Point, and on exceptionally clear days you can spot the wave-battered Farrallon Islands, a National Wildlife Refuge 25.0 miles to the west.

Just short of 1.0 mile, there is a long, steep stretch of stairs to Mile Rock Beach on a spur trail to the left. You may want to continue along the trail to Eagles Point and consider doing the beach jaunt on the return. The stairs down really are long and steep, and the trek back up will really get your and your dog's heart beating.

The dirt trail to Eagles Point rolls gently until about the 1.0-mile point, where you come to a short but definite and inevitable huff and puff up one hundred steps. The trail cuts a natural corridor between the rugged Pacific's edge on your left and some of San Francisco's most exclusive neighborhoods above on your right. Eagles Point lookout is a short 0.5 mile ahead, always along the Coastal Trail.

## Miles and Directions

**0.0**   Start at the Coastal Trail marker and Eagles Point trailhead at the far end of the parking lot behind the Lands End Lookout Visitor Center. Walk 300 feet.

**0.2**   Come to a trail junction where the Coastal Trail merges in from the right. Continue walking toward Eagles Point.

**0.7**   Come to a trail junction. Continue walking along the Coastal Trail to Eagles Point. (No bicycles or horses beyond this point.)

**0.8**   Reach a spur trail on the right for Mile Rock Beach at Lands End. Continue walking straight along the Coastal Trail to Eagles Point. Take the spur trail and 266 steps down to Mile Rock Beach on the return.

**1.5**   Reach Eagles Point viewing deck. **GPS:** N37 47.21' / W122 29.68' Pooch will enjoy socializing on the deck while you snap scenic shots of the Golden Gate Bridge, which may peek through the fog or shine in all its glory on a clear day. Retrace your steps to the spur trail junction of Mile Rock Beach back at 0.8 mile and walk down the stairs to the beach.

**2.4**   Arrive at Mile Rock Beach. Go back up the stairs to the Coastal Trail.

**3.3**   Arrive back at the trailhead.

# Lands End

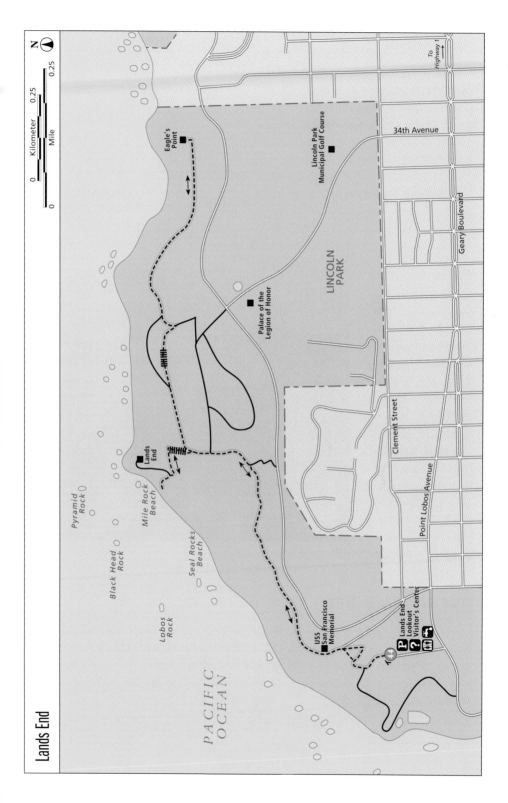

PACIFIC OCEAN

Pyramid Rock

Black Head Rock

Lobos Rock

Seal Rocks Beach

Mile Rock Beach

Lands End

Eagle's Point

Palace of the Legion of Honor

LINCOLN PARK

Lincoln Park Municipal Golf Course

34th Avenue

Geary Boulevard

Clement Street

Point Lobos Avenue

USS San Francisco Memorial

Lands End Lookout Visitor's Center

To Highway 1

N

Kilometer    0    0.25
Mile         0    0.25

*Fueling Up*

**Zazie,** 941 Cole St., San Francisco 94117; (415) 564-5332; zaziesf.com. Bring your pooch to dinner Monday night.

**Beach Chalet and Brewery Restaurant,** 1000 Great Hwy., San Francisco 94121; (415) 386-8439; beachchalet.com.

**Fisherman's Wharf Pier 39,** Beach Street and The Embarcadero, San Francisco 94133; (415) 981-7437. There are several outdoor eating areas here.

**Ferry Building Marketplace,** 1 Ferry Building, San Francisco 94111; (415) 983-8030; ferrybuildingmarketplace.com. The Marketplace offers a host of fresh food stalls to fill your picnic basket and munch with Pooch while sitting on the dock of the bay. It is also home to the **Ferry Plaza Farmers' Market** on Tuesday, Thursday, and Saturday.

*Resting Up*

San Francisco has a bounty of dog-friendly accommodations. **Inn at the Presidio,** 42 Moraga Ave., San Francisco 94129; (415) 800-7356; innatthepresidio .com. This army barracks turned boutique hotel on the National Register of Historic Places offers you and Pooch a unique lodging experience.

*Mile Rock Beach*

## Puppy Paws and Golden Years

Crissy Field's grassy spread on the former airfield and the beach area off Marina Boulevard south of the Golden Gate Bridge in the Golden Gate National Recreation Area (CCNR) has long been a favorite San Franciscan canine cut loose playground area for pooches at all stages of life. Contact GGNR Headquarters (415-561-4700) for current dog regulations.

# 45 Montara Mountain

The hike to the top of Montara Mountain is a climb above the Pacific Coast along a dirt fire road. The easy access off CA 1 and the privilege of hiking on state park land combined with spectacular coastal views on a clear day make this steady two-hour cardio workout an exhilarating excursion for fit dogs and humans.

**Start:** From the North Peak Access Road/ Pacifica and Top of Mountain trailhead
**Distance:** 7.8 miles out and back
**Approximate hiking time:** 3.5 hours
**Difficulty:** Strenuous
**Trailhead elevation:** 84 feet
**Highest point:** 1,898 feet
**Season:** Year-round
**Trail surface:** Dirt trail with decomposed granite and deteriorated asphalt
**Other trail users:** Horses and mountain bikes
**Canine compatibility:** On leash
**Land Status:** State Park
**Fees and permits:** None
**Maps:** USGS Montara Mountain; Montara State Beach
**Trail contacts:** California State Park Sector Office, 95 Kelly St., Half Moon Bay 94019; (650) 726-8819, (650) 726-8804; devils slidecoast.org, www.parks.ca.gov/montara mountain

**Nearest town:** Pacifica (north); Half Moon Bay (south); nearest services are south in Moss Beach
**Trail tips:** There is one portable toilet, no water, and no camping along this trail. Hikers with a strong interest in native plants can enjoy plant-identification walks with knowledgeable volunteers. Contact hmbplovers@hotmail .com for hike schedule, or call Angie Lovano, coordinator and interpreter at the Half Moon Bay Ranger Station (650-726-8819). The park visitor centers of the San Mateo area parks carry two excellent plant guides: *Plants and Plant Communities of the San Mateo Coast*, written by volunteers, and *Montara Mountain*, by Barbara Vanderwerf.

**Finding the trailhead:** From Half Moon Bay at CA 1 and CA 92, drive north 8.0 miles. Watch for the Montara State Beach/McNee Ranch sign on the east side of the highway. The sign is recessed from the small parking area off the shoulder. There is a larger parking area just short of 8.0 miles on the west side of the highway. The trailhead is at the fire lane gate in the parking area on the east side of the highway. You will see a sign on the right of the gate indicating that dogs need to be on leash. Walk around the gate and look to your left and you will see a trail marker post for the North Peak Access Road/Pacifica and Top of the Mountain trail. Proceed straight along the access road. **GPS:** N37 33.23' / W122 30.74'

## The Hike

A state park that allows dogs on trails or on the beach is a rare find in California. Montara State Beach/McNee Ranch is one of those exceptions. Duncan McNee, a Canadian who came to San Francisco in 1864, owned McNee Ranch as part of

*Top of Montara Mountain*

his 800,000-acre land baron empire. Cattle ranching and dairy farming are part of McNee Ranch's land-use history. The State of California purchased the 625-acre ranch on the west face of Montara Mountain in the 1970s, and it was opened as a state park in 1984.

Montara Mountain is at the northern end of the Santa Cruz Mountains. Looking at this rugged face of coastal shrub and chaparral with clumps of colorful spring wildflowers located less than an hour from San Francisco on one of the most traveled tourist byways, you would never guess that Montara Mountain is considered a unique "ecological island" of biological diversity with a variety of native plants. The San Bruno elfin butterfly flutters here, and the Hickman's potentilla's bright yellow blossoms grow happily on the mountain.

Begin your foray up Montara Mountain, keeping an eye out for Montara Mountain blue bush lupine, California poppy, wild strawberry, San Francisco wallflower, and the deep red–stemmed Montara manzanita. Walk around the fire lane gate in the trailhead parking lot with Martini Creek on your right and the canopy of cypress trees above. After a mile of occasional shady stands of pine, the road sweeps up the exposed southwest face. Be prepared with an extra layer, as cold waves of fog can blow in from the Pacific at any time and most commonly in summer. If you start in the fog, don't let the capricious coastal climate fool you, as you could just as easily break through the gray vapors and be stripping down under the scorching rays. Make sure you have plenty of water for Pooch.

The route is easy to follow, as all the trail junctions will be on your left once you pass the ranger's residence and your route is on the North Peak access road all the way to the communication towers. The trail climbs quickly, revealing coastline views that become more stunning at every turn. Approximately 2.0 miles up, the trail reaches more of a rolling ridgeline along a granite shelf. This is a popular hike and mountain bike ride on weekends, and your dog is sure to meet fellow canines taking their humans out for a workout.

At 3.7 miles you reach a trail junction between two sets of communication towers above your access road trail. Continue east, bearing right past the first set of towers and wend the slope for 0.2 mile to the second set of towers. Look for the round metal survey marker on the ground behind the towers. This is your highest point, at 1,898 feet. Mount Diablo rises on the eastern horizon, and Mount Tamalpais is visible to the north. If the skies are clear, you may even see San Francisco and Point Reyes. From the summit looking south you will get a unique view of the Santa Cruz Mountains' spine. Reward yourself and your dog with a snack and a cool drink of water before heading back down to the trailhead the way you came.

## Miles and Directions

**0.0** Start at the North Peak access road/Pacifica and Top of Mountain trailhead in the Montara State Beach/McNee Ranch parking area.

**0.2** Arrive at the trail junction for Old San Pedro Mountain Road and a restroom to the left. Continue on the North Peak access road.

**0.3** Come to an unnamed trail crossing a bridge on the right. Continue on the North Peak access road.

**0.8** Arrive at a trail junction where Old San Pedro Mountain Road merges in from the left. Continue on the North Peak access road.

**1.4** Come to a trail junction. Grey Whale Cove Trail drops off to the left. Continue on the North Peak access road.

**1.5** Come to a trail marker for Old Pedro Mountain Road to Pacifica going left. Bear right heading east to continue on the North Peak access road. Look north for a view of the new CA 1 tunnel to Pacifica.

**1.6** Come to a trail junction on the left for Pacifica/Linda Mar. Continue on the North Peak access road heading southeast.

**2.5** Trail reaches a ridgeline and granite shelf.

**2.7** Arrive at a trail junction for San Pedro Valley County Park to the left. Continue on the North Peak access road.

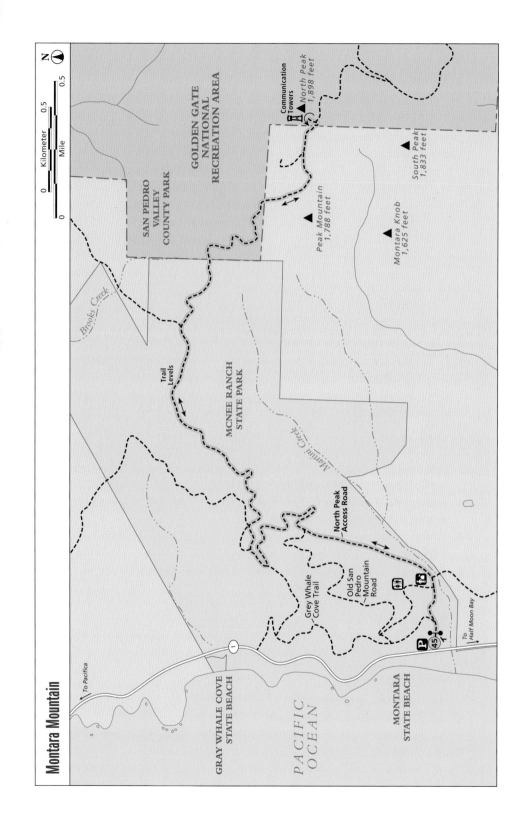

# Montara Mountain

**To Pacifica**

PACIFIC OCEAN

GRAY WHALE COVE STATE BEACH

MONTARA STATE BEACH

**To Half Moon Bay**

Grey Whale Cove Trail

Old San Pedro Mountain Road

North Peak Access Road

Trail Levels

Brooks Creek

Martini Creek

MCNEE RANCH STATE PARK

SAN PEDRO VALLEY COUNTY PARK

GOLDEN GATE NATIONAL RECREATION AREA

Peak Mountain
1,788 feet

Montara Knob
1,625 feet

South Peak
1,833 feet

Communication Towers

North Peak
1,898 feet

N

0    0.5    Kilometer
0    0.5    Mile

**3.7** Come to an unmarked trail junction between two sets of communication towers. The communication towers on the right are on the summit. Follow a wending trail uphill to the summit.

**3.9** Arrive at the summit. Elevation 1,898 feet. **GPS:** N37 33.69' / W122 28.66' You and your dog deserve a snack and a cool drink while you enjoy the spectacular view. Go back down to the trailhead the way you came.

**7.8** Arrive back at the trailhead.

## Creature Comforts

### Fueling Up

Moss Beach has several tasty seafood shacks with outdoor tables.

**The Moss Beach Distillery,** 140 Beach Way, Moss Beach 94038; (650) 728-5595; mossbeachdistillery.com. During Prohibition this isolated roadhouse at the head of a smuggling beach depot was a place for food, drink, and merriment. If you like ghost stories, ask about the "Blue Lady." Maybe your dog has a knack for sensing spirits? The Moss Beach Distillery serves a dog-food menu of mini–burger patties, kibble, scrambled eggs, or grilled chicken breast on the patio.

*Descending from Montara Mountain above the Pacific Coast*

**Miramar Beach Restaurant,** 131 Mirada Rd., Half Moon Bay 94019; (650) 726-9053; miramarbeachrestaurant.com. This spot is a relic from the colorful Prohibition era, with an enclosed patio to protect you and Pooch from the wind.

### Resting Up

**Comfort Inn,** 2930 Cabrillo Highway (CA 1), Half Moon Bay 94019; (650) 712-1999; choicehotels.com.

**Ritz Carlton Half Moon Bay,** Miramontes Point Rd., Half Moon Bay 94019; (650) 712-7000; ritzcarlton.com.

**The Inn at Mavericks,** 346 Princeton Ave., Half Moon Bay 94019; (650) 728-1572; innatMavericks.com.

**Seal Cove Inn,** 221 Cypress Ave., Moss Beach 94038; (800) 995-9987; sealcoveinn.com.

**Half Moon Bay State Beach Campground,** 95 Kelly Ave., Half Moon Bay 94019; (650) 726-8819, (650) 726-8820 (call for reservations and closure dates caused by campground improvements); www.parks.ca.gov/?page_id=531 (click on "Where can I take my dog.pdf" for more dog-friendly information).

# 46 Mission Peak Loop

This is a less-traveled loop version of an otherwise popular and crowded out-and-back summit hike. This route to the peak of a beautiful mountain is sculpted by oak woodland ravines, seasonal springs, and rock escarpments. The hike up is a cardiovascular workout and a scenic feast offering an unexpected accessible opportunity for you and your dog to enjoy a quick natural escape from urban and suburban distractions.

**Start:** From the Stanford Avenue Staging Area/Mission Regional Preserve and Ohlone Wilderness trailhead
**Distance:** 6.3-mile loop
**Approximate hiking time:** 3.5 hours
**Difficulty:** Strenuous, because of some very steep stretches
**Trailhead elevation:** 388 feet
**Highest point:** 2,530 feet
**Best season:** Year-round, but can be uncomfortably hot in the summer
**Trail surface:** Dirt trail with some rock and gravel
**Other trail users:** Horses and mountain bikes

**Canine compatibility:** Voice control
**Land Status:** Regional Park
**Fees and permits:** None
**Maps:** USGS Niles; Mission Peak Regional Preserve
**Trail contacts:** East Bay Regional Park District, 2950 Peralta Oaks Ct., Box 5381, Oakland 94605; (888) EBPARKS; www.ebparks.org/parks/mission
**Nearest town:** Fremont
**Trail tips:** There is a toilet, drinking water with a fountain and a faucet, picnic table, and dog-waste bag dispenser at the trailhead. Waste bags are available along the trail, too.

**Finding the trailhead:** From I-680 in Fremont, there are two exits for Mission Boulevard. If you are traveling north along I-680, the first Mission Boulevard exit is the shortest route to the trailhead. Take the first Mission Boulevard exit 12. Turn right onto Mission Boulevard and drive 0.5 mile to Stanford Avenue. Turn right onto Stanford Avenue and drive 0.5 mile to the Mission Peak Regional Preserve trailhead parking lot. The trailhead is at the east end of the parking lot.

If you are driving south on I-680, take the second Mission Boulevard exit 12 and turn left onto Mission Boulevard. Drive 0.5 mile on Mission Boulevard to Stanford Avenue. Turn right on Stanford Avenue and drive 0.5 mile to the Mission Peak Regional Preserve trailhead parking lot. **GPS:** N37 30.26' / W121 54.49'

## The Hike

Zipping along I-680's frenetic corridor that serves the bustling South Bay and East Bay bedroom communities between the metropolis of San Jose and San Francisco, it is difficult to imagine pristine open space and a gateway to wilderness in the heart of a suburban neighborhood. Fremont's Stanford Avenue Staging Area for the Mission Peak Regional Preserve, at the edge of the Sunol Regional Wilderness down the

*Taking a break on the way up to Mission Peak*

street from the Ohlone College campus, historic Mission San Jose de Guadalupe, and a spiffy commercial district, is exactly that.

Mission Peak Regional Preserve provides local residents, college students, and anyone lucky enough to take a five-minute side trip off the highway with almost 3,000 acres of scenic wandering on foot, horseback, or mountain bike. Both the Bay Area Ridge Trail and the Ohlone Wilderness Trail pass through the preserve. Although the Stanford Avenue Staging Area parking lot is overflowing into the side streets on weekends, you and Pooch can still climb to the peak in solitude along the southern edge of the preserve on the Horse Heaven Trail.

I had mixed feelings the first time I walked into the preserve on a holiday weekend and saw what felt like multitudes of people streaming up and down the wide gravel ranch road, which is like a "super highway" of trail surfaces. Then I adjusted my lens to see the positive. The crowd was evidence that even in the most gentrified of communities, people of all ages embrace the privilege of access to outdoor recreation, proving the need to provide and protect open space.

For dog owners, the presence of a dog-waste bag dispenser at the trailhead and then again in another 0.2 mile is a sure indicator that you are about to enter a

*Descending from the summit of Mission Peak*

dog-friendly realm conditional upon being a responsible dog owner. Then, as you read the dog rules posted on the gate, the dog perks just keep getting better, since well-trained dogs are allowed off leash under voice control.

In less than 0.3 mile of beginning the hike, you come to an unmarked fork and leave the swarms behind as you bear right along the eucalyptus trees on your right. Some of the trail markers have suffered abuse and neglect, and there are numerous unmarked forks and cattle paths crisscrossing the landscape. The good news is that there is a permanent trail map board in the parking area left of the single toilet building. Be sure to take one of the free maps at the trailhead.

You will be on Peak Meadow Road for the first 1.5 miles, until you branch right onto Horse Heaven Trail for most of the way up to the peak. The trail alternates between dirt single and double tracks, with occasional benches to savor the expansive vistas above the South Bay salt marshes reaching northwest toward Oakland's and San Francisco's skyline. Horse Heaven Trail is a delightful meander up and down swales, past oak woodland gullies, across seasonal streams, and along ridge traverses with switchbacks. Stay on the switchbacks even where the wooden barriers at the elbows have been taken down.

At approximately 2.0 miles be prepared for a 0.25-mile extra steep stitch. You will be rewarded with phenomenal views and an opportunity to stop and give your dog a rest with a drink of water. The exposed slopes can be cool and windy during the winter and early spring, but very hot and dry during the summer and early fall. Pace yourself and your dog accordingly and avoid this hike on summer afternoons.

By now you will have noticed the hilltop communication tower on your right, which should remain in plain view until you reach the summit, when most of the tower will be obstructed by a hill. At 2.4 miles the trail dips into a buckeye and bay tree canyon and crosses McClure Spring. The last 0.5 mile up to the peak has such an alpine feel that you almost expect to hear the echo of cowbells and spot a *horne hutte* (European alpine hut). In spring the hills are alive with yellow buttercups, black-eyed Susans, and golden California poppies.

At 3.1 miles continue up the rocky spine to the 2,530-foot summit rock outcrop. This is the place to be when the clouds break against the crisp blue sky in the wake of a Pacific storm. The lighting can make the view eastward over the Sunol Regional Wilderness and north to Mount Diablo especially breathtaking. You won't find warm apple strudel and hot chocolate Swiss Alp style here, but on a calm day, you and your dog should take time to enjoy your snacks on this majestic mountaintop greeted by orange fiddlenecks. The loop back to the trailhead is straightforward and faster. In spring the shoulders of the gravel-road superhighway are tumbling with lupine and buttercups and the plentiful viewpoint benches provide rest and photo stops.

As you leave the summit, continuing northwest along the rocky spine, bear left at the waste can site. A fence traces the slopes on your left as you walk downhill toward the restrooms. At 3.7 miles you come to a trail junction for Peak Meadow Trail and Hidden Valley Trail/Stanford Avenue Staging Area. Turn left onto the gravel road and continue to the trailhead along the sweeping gravel road, always following the signs for the Stanford Avenue Staging Area. The gravel road curves to the right at 4.0 miles. At 6.1 miles the gravel road merges with your original trail for 0.2 mile to complete your loop back to the trailhead.

## Miles and Directions

**0.0**   Start at the Stanford Avenue Staging Area Mission Regional Preserve/Ohlone Wilderness trailhead at the east end of the parking lot and walk through the gate.

**0.2**   Arrive at an unmarked fork with the left trail going uphill and the right going downhill east. Take the trail on the right going east that parallels the Eucalyptus trees. The trail on the left is the trail you will return on to complete your loop.

**0.25** Come to Agua Caliente seasonal creek. Walk across the creek.

**0.3**   Arrive at a gate and walk through the gate.

**0.9**   Arrive at a fork with a single-track trail rising steeply to the right. Bear left on the rolling ranch road. Views open to the west overlooking the salt marshes of the South Bay.

**1.3**   Arrive at a viewpoint with a bench and a boulder pile ahead east. The views west stretch toward San Francisco and Oakland.

**1.5**   Come to a fork for Peak Meadow Trail going left and Horse Heaven Trail going right. Continue uphill in a southeasterly direction on the single-track Horse Heaven Trail.

# Mission Peak Loop

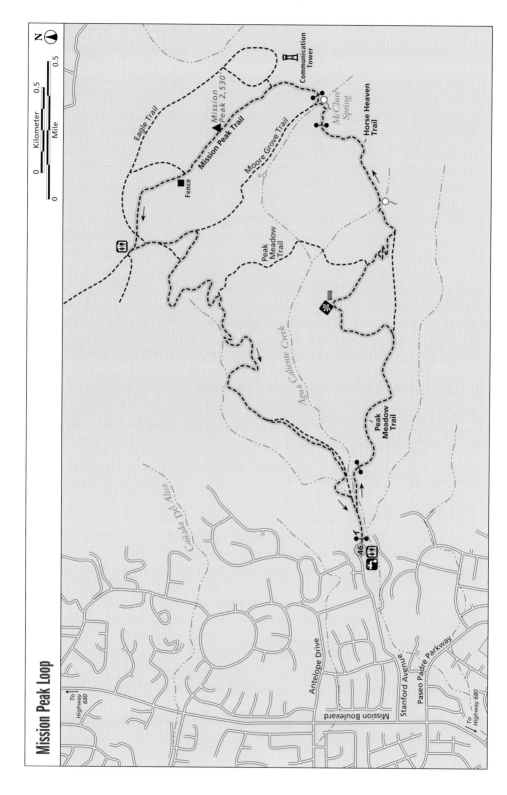

**1.6** Come to an unmarked fork. Bear right and follow the three trail switchbacks uphill heading southwest on the trail. You will see cutoffs in the switchbacks where the wooden barriers have been broken.

**1.8** Come to a trail marker for the Horse Heaven Trail. Continue uphill on the double track and bear left heading northeast.

**1.9** Come to a trail marker for the Horse Heaven Trail. Continue along the trail down into a gully and cross the seasonal spring before continuing uphill. The next 0.25 mile will be very steep.

**2.2** Arrive at trail marker for Horse Heaven and bear left on the lower trail as it sweeps up in a northwesterly direction revealing phenomenal views.

**2.3** Continue uphill at the trail marker.

**2.4** Arrive at a gate and wend through a buckeye and bay tree canyon.

**2.5** Come to McClure seasonal spring. Walk across the spring and stay on the Horse Heaven Trail up the switchback to a gate.

**2.6** Walk through the gate and up to the trail marker ahead.

**2.61** Arrive at a trail junction for the Moore Grove Trail and Mission Peak Trail going left. Continue walking on the Horse Heaven Trail uphill.

**2.8** Trail comes in from the communication tower on the right. The views open northeast across the valley and toward Mount Diablo. Continue walking uphill along the rocky spine.

**3.1** Arrive at the rock-outcrop summit of Mission Peak. Elevation 2,530 feet. **GPS:** N37 30.75' / W121 52.85' Begin your loop back to the trailhead.

**3.3** Arrive at a fork where you see two garbage-disposal barrels. Bear left on the spine of the trail and follow the fence line downhill toward the toilet building below. The fence will be on your left.

**3.7** Arrive at a trail junction and toilet. Turn left on the trail for Hidden Valley and the Stanford Avenue Staging Area.

**3.8** Come to trail marker 26 on your left. Continue on the Stanford Avenue Staging Area gravel road heading south downhill.

**4.0** Come to a trail junction. Continue on the Stanford Avenue Staging Area gravel road as it curves to the right.

**4.7** Come to a trail junction for the Peak Meadow Trail. Continue downhill to the right.

**5.6** Come to an unmarked fork. Bear right.

**6.1** Trail merges to complete your loop. Continue 0.2 mile back to the trailhead the way you came.

**6.3** Arrive back at the trailhead and the Stanford Avenue Staging Area.

## Creature Comforts

*Resting Up*

**Best Western Garden Court,** 5400 Mowry Ave., Fremont 94538; (510) 792-4300; garden courtinn.com.

**Residence Inn by Marriott,** 5400 Farwell Place, Fremont 94536; (510) 794-5900; marriottfremont.com.

# 47 H. Miller Site Loop

This is one of several pleasant trails crisscrossing Mount Madonna County Park. This easy wooded loop's appeal is its convenient access close to the entrance and the diversity of sights along the way, including the ranger visitor station, a white fallow deer enclosure, historic stone house ruins, and an archery course in a rich second-growth redwood grove with a seasonal spring.

**Start:** From the Blue Springs Trail and Rock Springs Trail junction
**Distance:** 2.5-mile loop
**Approximate hiking time:** 1.5 hours
**Difficulty:** Easy
**Trailhead elevation:** 1,562 feet
**Highest point:** 1,890 feet
**Best season:** Year-round with winter and spring seasonal streams; summers are warm
**Trail surface:** Dirt, redwood duff, and gravel
**Other trail users:** Horses
**Canine compatibility:** On leash
**Land status:** County Park
**Fees and permits:** None

**Maps:** USGS Mount Madonna; Mount Madonna County Park Trails
**Trail contacts:** Santa Clara County Parks and Recreation, (408) 355-2200; Mount Madonna County Park, 7850 Pole Line Rd., Watsonville 95076; (408) 842-2341; sccgov.org
**Nearest town:** Watsonville from the west side and Gilroy from the east side
**Trail tip:** Although water is available in campgrounds and the ranger station restrooms, there is no water along the trail. Carry water for your dog.

**Finding the trailhead:** From CA 1 take the Riverside Drive exit 425 for Watsonville to CA 152. Drive along Riverside Drive for 1.1 miles (you will go over train tracks). Turn left onto Main Street for CA 152. Notice the Victorian architecture as you drive through historic downtown. Drive 0.2 mile and turn right onto East Beach Street (notice the Martinelli apple juice plant on your left; in operation since 1868). Drive 0.3 mile and turn left onto Lincoln Street. Drive 0.1 mile and turn right onto East Lake Avenue (CA 152) and continue straight on CA 152 east. You are in berry- and apple-growing country. Drive 2.7 miles past the Santa Cruz County Fairgrounds. Drive 3.2 miles and past Carlton Road and a turnoff for Gizdich Farms (a succulent detour you will want to make on your return; see Creature Comforts section for details). CA 152 begins to climb and wend. Drive 5.1 miles and enter a redwood grove with views opening to the coast on your left. Drive 7.9 miles and arrive at the Hecker Pass summit (elevation 1,309 feet) and a sign for Santa Clara Madonna County Park. Drive 0.5 mile and stop at the pay station on your right. If the attendant is not on duty, use the self-pay envelopes at the station. The trailhead is 0.1 mile ahead. Turn left after the pay station, turn right toward Tan Oak Campground, and then turn right into the trailhead parking lot. **GPS:** N37 00.34' / W121 42.56'

*Up-close and personal with white deer*

## The Hike

Mount Madonna County Park's almost 4,000 acres straddle a ridge overlooking Santa Cruz County and the Monterey Bay to the west and Santa Clara County and its valley to the east, and the park is accessible from both sides via CA 152 at Hecker Pass from CA 1 from the west or CA 101 from the east. The park sits at the southern edge of the Santa Cruz Mountains.

The park stands on land that was once part of the vast expanse of hills rich in game and clear streams that supported hundreds or more Ohlone Indian tribes for over 3,000 years. Life changed irreversibly for the Ohlone in the 1800s with the arrival of the Spaniards. Like many other Native American tribes, the Ohlone's culture and way of life was in conflict with their European conquerors' religious, social, and commercial ideals. The native population was ultimately decimated by disease. Ohlone descendants continue to pay homage to their ancestors with an annual celebration on the summer solstice in Mount Madonna County Park.

The wealth of redwood timber in the Santa Cruz Mountains was a treasure trove for lumber companies' insatiable appetite, and old-growth groves were long gone by

*Along the trail*

the time cattle baron Henry Miller arrived here in 1859. Miller was born Heinrich Alfred Kreiser in Germany and immigrated to San Francisco in 1850. He was a skilled butcher who eventually formed a partnership with Charles Lux to lease and buy grazing land that would soon earn Miller the reputation of "Cattle King." Miller built an estate on the land that is now Mount Madonna County Park that he used as his family's vacation retreat from the late 1890s to 1916. Miller's heirs abandoned the property after his death, and in 1927 the State of California bought parts of the property to protect it. But it wasn't until 1952 that the land became a county park. More recently the Peninsula Open Space trust acquired the 260 Triple Buck Ranch, which will eventually be absorbed into Mount Madonna County Park.

This hike takes you through the park's display of biodiversity, from oak woodland and redwoods to manzanita scrub and meadows passing by the deer enclosure and the ruins of the Miller estate. The herd of white fallow deer are the descendants of a pair of deer gifted to the Miller family by newspaper magnate William Randolph Hearst in 1932.

If you like ghost stories, you will be happy to know that Mount Madonna County Park is believed to be haunted by the ghost of Sarah Miller, daughter of the rancher. Young Sarah is said to have died after her horse stumbled and fell on top of her while on a ride through the ranch, killing her. The ghost stories range from sightings of a woman riding on horseback at night to lights burning bright in buildings after they were turned off. By all accounts, they are people- and dog-friendly ghosts.

The hike begins in the parking lot for the Blue Springs and Rock Springs Trails and follows the Blue Springs Trail. The hike takes you to several junctions in mostly oak woodland until you cross the paved road at 0.6 mile and come to a meadow across the ranger station and along the deer enclosure. Follow the sign for the Miller Site and Upper Miller Trail for another .05 mile, where you will come to the Tan Oak Trail and stones steps going down to the ruins. Looking at the massive masonry remnants from fire and deterioration and the foundations smothered in vegetation it is easy to imagine the scope of this once grand estate sprawling with vineyards and orchards. The ruins are the heart of the park and this hike as you continue along the Lower Miller Trail to the Loop Trail before entering the camouflaged archery range at 1.6 miles. The redwood canyon is on your left with views of the valley east. The last mile of the hike back to the parking area and trailhead crosses several trail junctions before looping back up along the Rock Springs Trail.

## Miles and Directions

**0.0**  Start at the Blue Springs Trail and Rock Springs Trail trailhead junction. Turn left on the Blue Springs Trail. The sign for AMPHITHEATER H. MILLER SITE VISITOR CENTER will be on your right as you go up the trail.

**0.3**  Arrive at a four-way junction for the Blue Springs and Redwood Trails. Continue walking straight on the Blue Springs Trail. The trail levels off.

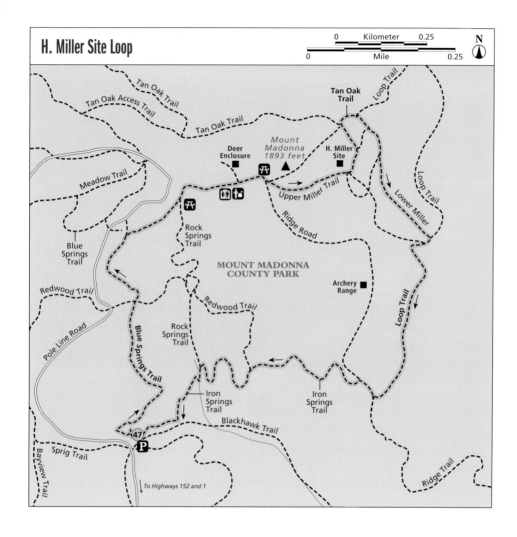

# H. Miller Site Loop

0       Kilometer     0.25     **N**

0           Mile           0.25

**MOUNT MADONNA COUNTY PARK**

**0.5**    Come to the junction for the Blue Springs and Upper Miller Trails. Turn right on the Upper Miller Trail. The trail narrows.

**0.6**    Come to the junction for the Upper Miller and Rock Springs Trails, where you see a staging area with picnic tables on the right and a paved road ahead. Continue walking on the Upper Miller Trail and cross the paved road to the signpost for Upper Miller Trail, where you will bear right.

**0.7**    Come to a ranger station with restrooms on your right and the white fallow deer enclosure on your left. Continue walking straight along the grassy meadow. The trail crosses the paved road on your right, just past the single picnic table under the redwood tree. This is the highest point on the trail—elevation 1,890 feet. **GPS:** N37 00.72' / W121 42.34'

**0.9**    You will see a sign for the Miller site and a trail signpost for the Upper Miller Trail. Continue on the Upper Miller Trail.

**1.0** Arrive at the junction for the Upper Miller and Tan Oak Trails. Turn left on the Tan Oak Trail.

**1.1** Notice the NATURE TRAIL sign pointing up a stone stairway to the Miller site on the left. This is your chance to explore the ruins at the Miller site. When you are done, return to the Tan Oak Trail to continue the hike.

**1.2** Arrive at the junction for the Tan Oak and Lower Miller Trails. Turn right and walk down the Lower Miller Trail.

**1.25** Come to the junction for the Lower Miller Trail and the Loop Trail Cut-Off. Continue right on the Lower Miller Trail.

**1.3** Arrive at the junction for the Lower Miller Trail and an unmarked trail on the right. Continue down on the Lower Miller Trail.

**1.5** Arrive at the junction for the Lower Miller and Loop Trails. Turn right on the Loop Trail and approximately 30 feet farther come to the junction for the Upper Miller and Loop Trails. Stay on the Loop Trail.

**1.6** Notice the sign for the archery range: STAY ON TRAILS. Good reason to have your dog on leash. There is a redwood grove on left and views overlooking Gilroy to the east.

**1.8** The trail appears to circle an island of vegetation. Bear right toward the signpost for junction of the Loop and Ridge Trails. Turn right on the Ridge Trail.

**1.85** Arrive at the junction for the Ridge and Iron Springs Trails. Turn left on the Iron Springs Trail. There will be archery stations on either side of the trail.

**2.1** Arrive at the junction for the Iron Springs and Redwood Trails. Continue on the Iron Springs Trail.

**2.3** Come to the junction for the Iron Springs Trail and a narrow unmarked trail to the right with a NO HORSES sign. Walk up the unmarked trail and you will see an AMPHITHEATER H. MILLER SITE sign. Just past this sign is a T junction for the Rock Springs Trail. Turn left on the Rock Springs Trail, a narrower hillside trail overlooking a redwood canyon on the left.

**2.5** Arrive back at the trailhead.

## Creature Comforts

*Fueling Up*

**Gizdich Ranch,** 55 Peckham Rd., Watsonville 95076; (831) 722-1056; www.gizdich-ranch.com. This has been a family-owned ranch since 1930s. Here you and Pooch can sit outside gorging on olallieberry pie and drinking fresh apple pie juice with a deli sandwich. You can pick your own seasonal berries and buy whole pies to go.

*Resting Up*

**Mount Madonna Campground,** Mount Madonna County Park, 7850 Pole Line Rd., Watsonville 95076; (408) 842-2341 or (408) 355-2201; gooutsideandplay.org. The camp has 118 tent and RV sites (17 partial hookups for electricity and water). There is a limit of two pets per site.

# 48 Juan Bautista De Anza National Historic Trail

This easily accessed, tucked-away historic gem is a multiuse trail situated in the Gavilan Range across from San Juan Bautista home, the fifteenth mission in the California mission system. The hike sweeps up a moderate, mostly exposed hillside to a crest before descending more steeply for the last 1.5 miles to the gate on the backside. The views stretch across the surrounding grazing land and a patchwork of farmsteads on the way to the crest. On a warm day you and Pooch will appreciate the corridor of oak and Monterey cypress trees for a shady break as you approach the crest. This trail is a rare opportunity to enjoy scenery and a slice of cultural history on rarely dog-compatible national park territory.

**Start:** From the gate just beyond the roadside parking area at the end of the unmarked Old Stage Coach Road
**Distance:** 8.0 miles out and back
**Approximate hiking time:** 3 to 4 hours
**Difficulty:** Moderate
**Trailhead elevation:** 246 feet
**Highest point:** 1,126 feet
**Best season:** Year-round
**Trail surface:** Compacted dirt trail along a historic stage coach road with sweeping switchbacks
**Other trail users:** Horse and mountain bikes
**Canine compatibility:** Voice control, but be aware there are cattle
**Land status:** National Park

**Fees and permits:** None
**Maps:** USGS San Juan Bautista
**Trail contact:** National Park Service; (415) 623-2344; nps.gov/juba
**Nearest town:** San Juan Bautista
**Trail tip:** There is a portable toilet at the trailhead. Bring water. There are some shady sections. Cattle will sometimes wander onto the trail. If in doubt of her good manners around cattle and to prevent harassment to the cattle, as well as potential injury to your dog, keep Pooch on a leash. If your dog is attracted to cow plop perfume, that's another good reason to keep her on leash before she decides to roll and lather herself with a fresh one.

**Finding the trailhead:** From Salinas, drive north on US 101 to San Juan Bautista. Take the San Juan Bautista exit 345 to CA 156 east San Juan Bautista/Hollister. Drive 3.0 miles to the signal at the Alameda Road intersection. The Alameda Road going to the left heads into San Juan Bautista. The slightly deteriorated road going right is actually Old Stagecoach Road, but it is unmarked. Turn at the Alameda Road signal onto the unmarked Old Stagecoach Road and go straight for approximately 0.33 mile. You will see a signpost for Fremont Peak and a large sign on the right for Juan Bautista De Anza National Historic Trail. Continue straight. There will be a three-way fork ahead. (San Juan Canyon Road to the left. Salinas Road to the right.) Stay on the middle road, which is still the unmarked Old Stagecoach Road Just ahead past the fork, the road will dead-end at a gate with a Juan Bautista De Anza National Historic Trail interpretive sign and a green portable toilet on the left behind the gate. Park on the right or left shoulder of the road and walk around the gate to the left to start the hike. **GPS:** N36 49.91' / W121 32.03'

*The trailhead for the historic Spanish explorers route*

## The Hike

The Anza was added to the National Trails System by Congress under George H. W. Bush in 1990. It is one of twenty-three trails in the system. California has a rich Spanish colonial past, and this is a stitch that travels along an old stagecoach road that was also the route first traveled by the local Native Americans before the 1776 Juan Bautista de Anza Expedition. The expedition passed through on their route from Sonora, Mexico to settle what is now San Francisco.

This out-and-back hike sweeps up gradually with views of the surrounding rolling hills dotted with cattle until you wend around through the grove shaded with oak and Monterey cypress. Fremont Peak's (elevation 3,170 feet) communication towers will become clearly visible to the southeast past the first bench and the second cattle guard.

At 2.5 miles the trail crests where it straddles views to the hills east and to the coast west. This is where the stagecoach used to rest the horses. Now there is a bench for you to rest and share water and a snack with your dog while you imagine this landscape relatively unchanged since Spanish explorers and stagecoach travelers experienced it. On a hot or less-energetic day, the crest makes an excellent turnaround point.

*Along the trail*

If you and Pooch still have an edge to burn, continue down the last 1.5-mile steeper stretch of trail to the backside. Remember the universal hiker's truth: "He who hikes down must come back up." The trail descends into a narrower canyon valley corralled between fenced pastures banked by grassy hills and California chaparral. Wild teasel, paintbrush, and Toyon berry bushes cling to the fence lines. You pass two exposed rock outcroppings on the hilltop to your right, indicating a change in geology and giving the scenery a more rugged feel. The trail flattens as you approach the gate and the 4.0-mile marker.

## Miles and Directions

- **0.0** Start at the interpretive sign at the end of Old Stagecoach Road.
- **0.2** Walk across a cattle guard.
- **0.7** Come to a bench on your left with views opening up to the north.
- **0.8** Walk across a cattle guard.
- **1.0** Come to a mile marker for the 1.0 mile on the right side of the trail.
- **1.1** Look left to see Fremont Peak (3,170 feet) to the southeast.
- **2.5** Arrive at the crest of the trail, elevation 1,126 feet. There is a bench on your right. **GPS:** N36 48.71' / W121 32.28'
- **3.0** Come to a mile marker for 3.0 miles on the right side of the trail.
- **4.0** Come to the end of trail at the gate. Elevation 543 feet. **GPS:** N36 48.34' / W121 33.68' There is a mile marker for 4.0 miles on the right and a shaded bench on the left. Return the way you came.
- **8.0** Arrive back at the trailhead.

## Creature Comforts

*Fueling Up*

**JJ's Burgers,** 100 The Alameda Rd., San Juan Bautista 95045; (831) 623-1748; jjshome madeburgers.com. There's nothing like a Harris Ranch beef patty for Bowser and a

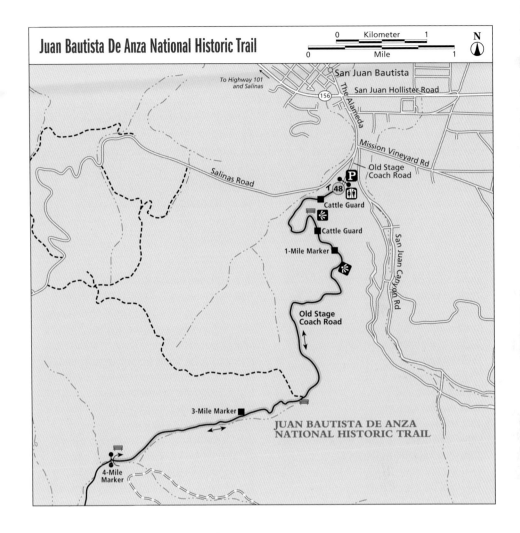

milkshake for you on the sunny patio. JJ's also makes a wicked-good chicken breast sandwich on a fresh bun with melted Monterey Jack cheese and guacamole.

## Resting Up

**San Juan Inn,** 410 The Alameda Rd., San Juan Bautista 95045; (831) 623-4380; san juaninnca.com.

**Fremont Peak State Park Campground,** 10700 San Juan Canyon Rd., San Juan Bautista 95045; (831) 623-4255; www.parks.ca.gov. This camp has twenty-five primitive tent and RV sites (no hookups) with expansive views of Monterey Bay.

# 49 Carmel Meadows

This trail is an opportunity for you and pooches of any fitness level to hike and picnic along one of the most beautiful oceanfront trails at the edge of one of the world's most famous seaside hamlets. Apart from a staircase up to the bluffs and a gentle hill for a double-lollipop hike, the hike is on mostly level ground. It is possible to hike the trail as a level out and back without sacrificing any of the scenic value for you and the natural enjoyment for your dog if for any reason stairs or an uphill climb proves to be too daunting for you, your dog, or other hiking companions. Wildflowers abound in the spring, and the year-round scenery is a treat of rolling hills, rock outcrops, and a blonde-sand beach separating the aquamarine Pacific surf from the lagoon patrolled by gulls, mallards, coots, and pelicans.

**Start:** From the parking lot at the end of the short unmarked paved road north of Monastery Beach

**Distance:** 1.9-mile double loop

**Approximate hiking time:** 1 hour

**Difficulty:** Easy

**Trailhead elevation:** 45 feet

**Highest point:** 103 feet

**Best season:** Year-round

**Trail surface:** Dirt

**Other trail users:** Mountain bikes and horses

**Canine compatibility:** On leash

**Land status:** State Park

**Fees and permits:** None

**Maps:** USGS Monterey

**Trail contacts:** California State Parks Monterey District, 2211 Garden Rd., Monterey 93940; (831) 649-2836; www.parks.ca.gov

**Nearest town:** Carmel-by-the-Sea

**Trail tips:** In winter the Carmel River slices through Carmel River State Beach at the north end when rains increase the river flow enough for it to reach the Pacific Ocean, making a river crossing on the beach precarious to impassable. But in summer, when the river recedes into a lagoon and the beach is uninterrupted, it is possible to hike along the Carmel Meadows Trail and continue your hike on the Carmel River State Beach north to the beach parking lot, where there are flush toilets and interpretive signs about the Carmel River Lagoon and Wetlands Natural Reserve. This seasonal change in the river also offers a pathway for you and your dog to continue your walk into Carmel along Scenic Avenue and dog-friendly (off leash) Carmel Beach.

**Finding the trailhead:** From Carmel at the intersection of CA 1 and Rio Road, drive 1.5 miles south on CA 1 and make a sharp right turn at the unmarked driveway in front of the little nursery school immediately north of the beach. There is room for about six vehicles on the right along the driveway near the state park boundary fence and pedestrian access. Note that the driveway on the left of the parking area is on private property. **GPS:** N36 31.56' / W121 55.39'

*Point Lobos in the distance*

## The Hike

The Carmel Meadows Trail above the Carmel River State Beach off CA 1 south of Carmel is a unique hike mostly known to locals. There are two accesses, and neither is publicized. One is in the cul-de-sac of an exclusive residential neighborhood, and the other is a sharp turn off CA 1 along an obscure unmarked paved road that is the driveway to a little red local preschool and a couple of privately owned and rented beach cottages. Not only do you and your dog get to hike on state park property, but you are hiking along one of the most expensive stretches of California real estate, boasting one of the most scenic stretches of coastline in the world at the edge of the Monterey Bay National Marine Sanctuary. In spring the meadows bloom gold with mustard splashed with violet bush lupine and poppies. Watch for the poison oak bushes hiding among the coffee berry, California blackberry, and wild rose bushes.

The narrow trail widens shortly after leaving the parking area. Point Lobos Reserve to the south across Monastery Beach Bay juts out into Pacific and will be a visible landmark along the entire hike. Point Lobos, off-limits to dogs even in a parked car, is said to have inspired Robert Louis Stevenson's *Treasure Island*.

At about 0.1 mile you come to a trail junction on your right coming down from the bluff. That is the trail you will return on to close the loop of your second lollipop. At 0.3 mile this trail junction allows you to access the beach on the left or walk up the wooden stairs to the bluff. About 0.1 mile ahead, you come to another trail junction for beach access on the left or one hundred wooden steps to the bluff. This is the staircase you will walk up on the return to trace the bluffs before reconnecting with the main trail at the end of the lollipop.

The level trail continues paralleling the beach, with several substantial homes with prime views standing guard above the trail. At 0.6 mile bear right to go uphill to the cross. Just ahead at the foot of the rise you see the historical inscription on a rock describing the place where the Spanish Portola-Crespi Expedition of 1769 erected a cross to signal the supply ship that never came.

The vantage point from the cross gives you a breathtaking panorama of hills, ocean, Point Lobos, lagoon, river valley, and the southern edge of the Carmel-by-the-Sea neighborhood at the north end of the lagoon. The trail traces the lagoon and contours the point at 1.0 mile where in winter the river would ripple into the ocean. This is one of many places where you can take time for a picnic on the beach. Follow the trail around and the ocean will be on your right. At 1.4 (same as 0.4 mile) turn left and walk up the stairs and turn right at the top of the stairs. Follow the bluff trail, which parallels the lower trail and the beach. On a clear day the views are even more stunning from above and you may be lucky enough to spot migrating whales in winter and early spring. Take advantage of the couple of benches to sit and snack while savoring the views.

It is not unusual for the fog to engulf the coast at the height of summer, but in spring and fall tails of drifting fog can really enhance the lighting and excite your inner photographer.

The trail will meander along the bluff with several trails crisscrossing. All eventually merge onto the main trail downhill to the lower trail. When in doubt, bear right. The trail on the downhill slope is eroded in some places. At 1.8 miles (same as 0.1 mile) you merge with the lower trail. Turn left and continue back to the trailhead.

## Miles and Directions

**0.0**  Start at the trailhead at the end of the paved road where there is pedestrian access to the right of the state park property line and Dogs On Leash sign.

**0.1**  Come to a trail junction with a trail going uphill. This is the trail you will return on to complete the second lollipop of the hike.

**0.3**  Come to a trail junction with trail access to the beach on the left and stairs to a bench and the bluff on the right.

**0.4**  Come to a trail junction with trail access to the beach on the left and one hundred steps to the bluff on the right. This is the set of stairs you will ascend on the return for the second loop.

**0.6**  Come to a fork and bear right toward the cross on the hill.

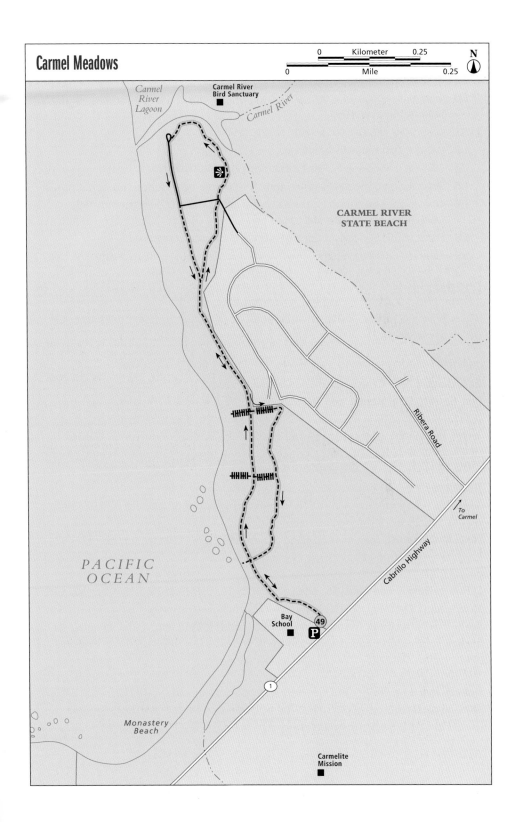

# Carmel Meadows

Kilometer
0    0.25

Mile
0    0.25

N

*Carmel River Lagoon*

Carmel River
Bird Sanctuary

*Carmel River*

**CARMEL RIVER
STATE BEACH**

Ribera Road

To Carmel

Cabrillo Highway

*PACIFIC
OCEAN*

Bay School

49

P

1

*Monastery
Beach*

Carmelite
Mission

**0.8** Come to an unmarked trail junction. Walk across the trail and bear right uphill to the cross, past the historical inscription on the stone at the foot of the hill.

**0.85** Arrive at the cross and turn left toward the lagoon.

**1.0** Arrive at the lagoon below the trail. Continue along the trail as it rounds the point. The ocean will be on your right.

**1.1** Come to an unmarked trail junction. Walk across the trail.

**1.2** (same as 0.6) Complete the first loop.

**1.4** (same as 0.4) Walk up the one hundred steps to the top of the bluff.

**1.5** Reach the top of the stairs and turn right.

**1.6** Come to stairs going down to lower trail on the right (top of stairs from bottom at 0.3). Continue walking along the bluff trail.

**1.8** (same as 0.1) Bluff trail merges with lower trail to complete second loop.

**1.9** Arrive back at the trailhead.

## Creature Comforts

There is such a variety of dog-friendly outdoor dining options and lodging in Carmel; where to begin?

### Fueling Up

**R. G. Burgers,** 201 Crossroads Blvd., Carmel 93923; (831) 626-8054; rgburgers.com.

**Sea Harvest Fish Market and Restaurant,** 100A Crossroads Blvd., Carmel 93923; (831) 626-3636. Enjoy fresh sustainable seafood on the dog-friendly patio.

**Terry's Restaurant,** in the Cypress Inn on Lincoln St. and Seventh Ave., Carmel-by-the-Sea 93921; (831) 624-3871; carmelterrys.com. Top dog hangout for dining in the lobby bar, living room, or patio.

**Treehouse Café,** San Carlos Ave. at Seventh St., Carmel-by-the-Sea 93921; (831) 626-1111; treehousecafecarmel.com. The Mediterranean dishes taste even better sitting on the rooftop deck caressed by trees.

**Forge in the Forest,** corner of Junipero St. and Fifth Ave., Carmel, 93921; (831) 624-2233; forgeintheforest.com. Brick, Ivy and an intimate V.I.P. (Very Important Pooch) courtyard.

**LaFayette Bakery and Café,** 3672 Barnyard, Carmel 93923; (831) 915-6286; lafayette bakery.com. Your dog doesn't have to be a French poodle called Fifi to be welcome in the cafe's courtyard. Even the most kibble-happy hiking dog will be begging for a flake of your *croissant au jambon et fromage.*

### Resting Up

**Cypress Inn,** Lincoln St. and Seventh Ave., Carmel-by-the-Sea 93921; (831) 624-3871; cypress-inn.com. Doris Day has made certain that all the canine guests are treated like V.I.P. (very important pooches).

**Tradewinds,** Carmel Hotel, Mission St. at Third Ave., Carmel-by-the-Sea 93921; (831) 624-2776; tradewindscarmel.com. Dogs find their Zen in this luxury boutique hotel with exotic Asian flair.

**Carmel River Inn,** 26600 Oliver Rd., Carmel 93923; (831) 624-1875; carmelriver inn.com.

**Carmel Mission Inn,** 3665 Rio Rd., Carmel 93923; (831) 624-1841; carmelmissioninn .com. This inn is next to the Barnyard Shopping Center and its line-up of dog-friendly dining.

**Big Sur Campground and Cabins,** 47000 CA 1, Big Sur 93920; (831) 667-2322; big surcamp.com.

**Pfeiffer Big Sur State Par,** 26.0 miles south of Carmel-by-the-Sea on CA 1; (800) 444-7275; reserveamerica.com; www.parks.ca.gov.

**Veterans Memorial Park Campground** at Skyline and Veterans Drive, Monterey 93940; (831) 646-3865. Campground offers tent and RV sites (no hookups) in a forested setting on a plateau at the edge of quiet residential neighborhoods within walking distance to historic downtown Monterey and iconic Fisherman's Wharf. Kick up your cardio and let Pooch enjoy a scamper up to Huckleberry Hill Nature Preserve at the far end of the campground. Contact Monterey Recreation Department, 546 Dutras Street, Monterey 93940; (831) 646-3866; monterey.org.

## Puppy Paws and Golden Years

**Carmel Beach,** at the bottom of Ocean Avenue in Carmel-by-the-Sea, is "dog fun central." It would be impossible to count the number of Carmel canines who took their first and last nature steps on Carmel Beach's 1.0-mile-long flat white sands. This beach is probably Northern California's most popular, scenic, and safe off-leash walk for puppies and seniors. Four-legged teens come here to chase balls and Frisbees and sprint in and out of the surf.

**Monterey Bay Coastal Recreational Trail** stretches 18.0 miles from Castroville north to Pacific Grove south, tracing the Monterey Marine Sanctuary. Park your vehicle by Fisherman's Wharf at the west end of the Monterey State Historic Park off of Del Monte Boulevard in Monterey. Walk down historic Fisherman's Wharf, keeping an ear and eye out for sea lions. You and Pooch can stroll north toward Del Monte Beach, stopping for fish-and-chips at the London Bridge Pub's waterfront patio, or you can head south along the marina past the coast guard pier toward Steinbeck's Cannery Row, the aquarium, and along the most panoramic mile to Pacific Grove's Lover's Point. The paved path ends, but a narrow dirt trail threads the scenic rugged coastline for several more miles past wave battered rocks and small sandy coves to dog-friendly Asilomar State Beach and the boardwalk at the edge of Spanish Bay Golf Resort. For more information contact Monterey Recreation, 546 Dutra St., Monterey 93940; (831) 646-3866; monterey.org.

# 50  Holt Road to Snivleys Ridge

Due to the fact that the Holt Road trailhead is in a residential gated neighborhood and has limited parking outside the walk-in gate, this westernmost access into popular Garland Ranch Regional Park is one of the least-used trails in the park. The lesser-known park access is via an easement through a walk-in gate in the Carmel Valley Ranch Estates gated community and along Carmel Valley Ranch Resort's golf course. This hike is a gradual sustained uphill with minimal shade along an old ranch road overlooking Carmel Valley Ranch Resort. The trail sweeps along the side of steep chamise-covered slopes and under oak canopies. On a clear day the views go from pleasant across the oak-studded hills to spectacularly panoramic, reaching to the edge of the Ventana Wilderness to the east and across Monterey Bay to the west. The ribbons of fog more typical of summer add an ethereal quality to this hike. Whether you hike 1.0 mile or 4.0 before turning around, this scenic, lightly used trail will exhilarate you and your four-legged pal.

**Start:** From the walk-in gate at the top of Holt Road

**Distance:** 8.2 miles out and back with mini loop

**Approximate hiking time:** 4 hours

**Difficulty:** Strenuous, because of length and some steep stretches

**Trailhead elevation:** 314 feet

**Highest point:** 2,029 feet

**Best season:** Year-round; winter rains make the hills turn a nourishing green into spring. This hike is a warm, sunny escape from the frequently foggier days of June, July, and August on the coast. Be aware that September and October afternoons can be hot.

**Trail surface:** Asphalt easement transitions to compacted dirt and decomposed granite on ranch roads, grassy double and single track trails

**Other trail users:** Horses

**Canine compatibility:** Leash and voice control

**Land status:** Regional Park District

**Fees and permits:** None

**Maps:** USGS Seaside and Mount Carmel; Garland Ranch Regional Park Trails

**Trail contact:** Monterey Peninsula Regional Park District, 600 Garden Ct. #325, Monterey 93940; (831) 372-3196; www.mprpd.org

**Nearest town:** Carmel-by-the-Sea

**Trail tips:** Keep your dog leashed from the parking lot until you pass the houses and golf course to avoid any disturbance to residents and to protect Fido from his impulse to run circles on the greens or chase the wild turkeys and herds of hoofed occupants that frequently graze on the course. What this hike lacks in shade and water, it makes up for in views. Wear sunscreen and bring extra water for Fido.

**Finding the trailhead:** From Carmel at CA 1 and Carmel Valley Road intersection, turn left at the signal onto Carmel Valley Road. Drive 6.0 miles and bear right just past Berwick Drive at the east end of the Mid-Valley Shopping Center, where there are two gas stations and a Safeway grocery store. Make a hard right onto Robinson Canyon Road and cross the Carmel River Bridge. Drive 0.01 mile and turn left onto Holt Road, which is the first street past the Carmel Valley Ranch Resort entrance. Drive 0.5 mile up Holt Road and park on the dirt shoulder on the left just short of the Carmel Valley Ranch Estates gate. Your trailhead is the walk-in gate to the right with the LEASH YOUR DOG sign. **GPS:** N36 30.88' / W121 48.16'

*Ascending along Snivleys Ridge*

## The Hike

Carmel Valley's sunshine-filled summers and rural character just down the road from foggier, albeit charming Carmel-by-the-Sea, with the more chichi lifestyle, is as wonderful a dog-friendly place to hike as it is to live. Carmel Valley and Garland Ranch's history weave Rumsen Indians, homesteads, hunting, logging, and Spanish ranchos.

Celebrities alongside movers and shakers have also found Carmel Valley to be the perfect retreat from paparazzi and the public-eye blitz. Fans and residents of Carmel Valley have included Charlie Chaplin, Merv Griffin, Clint Eastwood, dog-lover Doris Day, media mogul Rupert Murdoch, and public figures like Alan Greenspan and Leon Panetta.

*Water break at the turnaround point and fire tower in the distance*

The valley's glorious summer climate has always been a magnet for family cottages steps away from the Carmel River's refreshing swimming holes as an escape from the foggy coast. A Carmel River that flowed to the Pacific year-round with steelhead fishing as an annual event is under increased pressure to balance habitat with human thirst.

Although the valley has sprung three golf courses, a few resorts, and a village center breeding wine-tasting rooms, the character of the valley remains proudly rural, boasting Garland Ranch Regional Park's acres of dog-friendly playground as its centerpiece. Garland Ranch was the park's first acquisition and is known as the "granddaddy" of the Monterey Peninsula Regional Park District's (MPRPD) properties and the most popular. Since its creation in 1972, the MPRPD has protected over 12,500 acres of open space. The park covers 200 to 2,000 feet of elevation, with vegetation transitioning from riverbed willows and cottonwoods to oak woodlands and grasslands interrupted by dense patches of chaparral. Garland Park ridges are the northern crest of the Santa Lucias.

Coincidentally and fortuitously, John Pritzker, the current owner of the five-star Carmel Valley Ranch Resort and Golf Club on which the Holt Road easement gives hikers unique access to the west end of dog-friendly Garland Ranch Regional Park, believes "family friendly" includes the family's four-legged children. Roxy, a well-behaved miniature English bulldog, has been coming to work with her owner Gabrielle and greeting the resort's canine guests as they come and go from their hike ever since she was a puppy.

Non-resort guests begin the hike at the walk-in gate in Carmel Valley Ranch Estates residential neighborhood with a short walk on the paved road. Straight ahead you will see a bend in the road and a stone pillar for house number 9972 Holt Road on the right. The easement trail transitions to dirt on the left of the pillar at this unnamed trail junction identified by a regional park trailhead sign. Turn right on this narrow trail and follow it up between the golf course on the left and the concrete driveway traced by a low split-rail fence on the right. Notice the hillside Pinot grapes vineyard left of the golf course and the cluster of two-story hotel suites at the foot of the hillside ahead. The trail will curve right away from the golf course to another Monterey Peninsula Regional Park sign where the narrow path widens into a compacted dirt road under a moss-draped canopy of oaks. This stretch is one of the few shady corridors on the way to the top.

From here the trail sweeps up with occasional steeper stretches overlooking the resort's several golf holes and the valley, before grandeur views reveal unspoiled ridges between the Los Padres National Forest east and the Monterey Bay coastline northwest. Past the Horseshoe Trail and Mucklehead Trail junction, the taller stands of chamise close in your view for about 0.5 mile. Although commonly associated with dry arid terrain, chamise does put out clusters of delicate white flowers in spring. The white nob on a summit ahead and to the right is the abandoned Sid Ormsbee Lookout (elevation 2,249). It will come into view as the trail opens up and steepens and curves around to the north-facing slope. The lookout tower will reappear and remain a noticeable and consistent landmark on your right when you reach the grassy saddle at mile 3.0. The steep chaparral-coated hillside and poison-oak canyons bracing the trail for the first 3.0 miles serve as a natural "corral" that keep your dog on the trail and make this hike a safe off-leash excursion.

The deer, coyote, and bobcat scat on the trail is sure to give your dog's nose a workout. Don't be alarmed if Pooch bounces out of the chaparral with his teeth clamped on an old deer bone or two from a dried-out leftover carcass at a mountain lion buffet site. Sightings of these big cats are a very rare privilege and generally not a threat, but be aware that you are hiking in wildlife habitat.

On a clear day this hike is about views, solitude, and room for your dog to let his spirit soar. After about 3.5 miles of climbing, the 360-degree views on the 2,029-foot northern crest of the Santa Lucia Mountains are sure to give you a rush. Depending on your time and dog's energy, this is a natural turnaround point if you want to pass on the additional 0.5-mile downhill and back up to complete the mini loop.

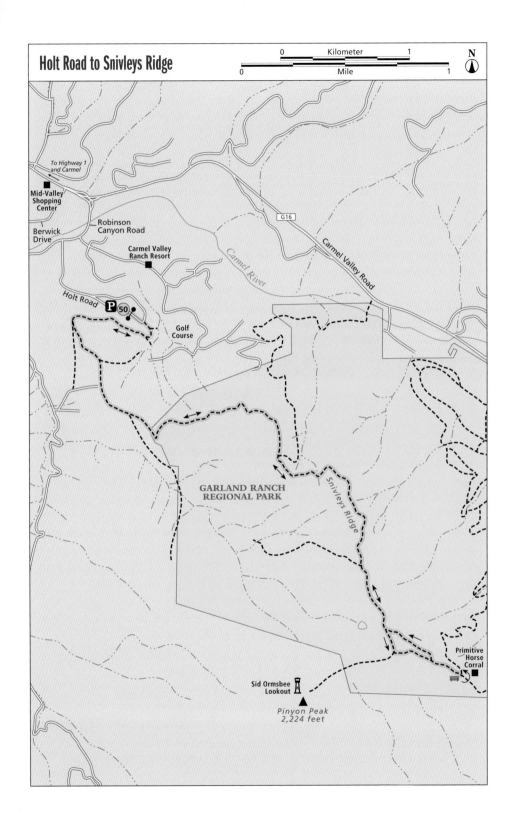

# Holt Road to Snivleys Ridge

Kilometer

0            1

Mile

0            1

N

To Highway 1
and Carmel

Mid-Valley
Shopping
Center

Berwick
Drive

Robinson
Canyon Road

Carmel Valley
Ranch Resort

G16

Carmel River

Carmel Valley Road

Holt Road

P 50

Golf
Course

GARLAND RANCH
REGIONAL PARK

Snivleys Ridge

Primitive
Horse
Corral

Sid Ormsbee
Lookout

Pinyon Peak
2,224 feet

## Miles and Directions

**0.0** Walk-in gate for Carmel Valley Ranch Estates at the top of Holt Road. Follow the paved street to the bend, elevation 310 feet.

**0.1** Come to a trail junction and trail marker post at the bend in the road on your right. Turn right onto the decomposed granite path just left of the stone pillar with house number 9972 Holt Road.

**0.2** Come to a trail junction with the golf course on your left and a ranch road on your right. There will be a sign on the left side of the road that reads CARMEL VALLEY RANCH TRAIL EASEMENT TO GARLAND RANCH REGIONAL PARK DISTRICT. Turn right and go up the road away from the golf course.

**0.6** Reach the trail junction for the Horseshoe Trail on the left and the Appaloosa Trail on the right. Bear left up the Horseshoe Trail.

**0.8** Reach the trail junction for the Horseshoe Trail on the left and the Mucklehead Trail on the right. Bear right and continue up Mucklehead Trail. The trail narrows under a canopy of oaks bordered by chaparral and some poison oak.

**1.2** The trail opens up, exposing a view of a cut in the hillside ahead. The cut is the trail to Snivleys Ridge.

**1.4** Trail junction with a closed trail to the right and Snivleys Ridge Trail post on your left. Bear left and follow the Snivleys Ridge Trail up. The white nob on the highest hill ahead in the distance is the abandoned Sid Ormsbee fire lookout on Pinyon Peak (2,224 feet) above Snivleys Ridge. the PALISADES TRAIL/SKY TRAIL arrow sign pointing up is just a few feet up from the junction. The trail gets steeper as it climbs in sweeping S curves with a view toward the coast on your left.

**2.3** Arrive at the trail junction for the Palisades Trail going down the slope on the left. Bear right and continue uphill. Mount Toro's cell towers are on the right and Fremont Peak is on the left with the backdrop of the Santa Cruz Mountains.

**2.8** The trail tapers off to a more gradual climb with first real dose of shade under oak and bay tree canopies on the north-facing slope.

**3.0** The trail emerges on an exposed saddle with a trail junction at TRAIL CLOSED sign on the right. Bear left on the main trail. The Los Padres National Forest and Ventana Wilderness ridge are in the distance.

**3.5** Reach the unmarked trail junction on your left where you will rejoin the trail after the mini loop. Sid Ormsbee fire lookout is on a hilltop to the right above the seasonal stock pond at the base of the slope. Continue straight up on the main trail.

**3.7** Reach an unmarked trail junction with a primitive trail to the fire lookout on the right (private property) and narrow primitive eroded trail going down on the left. Take in the panoramic views toward Carmel Bay and Monterey Bay across to Santa Cruz. This is the highest point on the hike. Elevation 2,029 feet. **GPS: N36 29.53' / W121 46.74'** Take the primitive trail on the left down toward the fenced paddock on Snivleys Ridge below.

**3.9** Reach an unmarked trail junction. Merge with the wider trail and turn right toward Snivleys Ridge.

**4.0** Reach the trail junction with the Sky Trail on your left and a bench on your right. This is your destination. Sit on the bench and breathe in the views with a snack and water break for you and Pooch. Elevation 1,740 feet. **GPS: N36 29.45' / W121 46.39'** Return the way you came for 0.1 mile. At the junction where the trail came down from the left, bear right to complete the mini loop back to the main trail.

**4.5** End of the mini loop. Bear right onto main trail and savor the views as you retrace your steps to the trailhead.

**8.2** Arrive back at the trailhead.

## Creature Comforts

*Fueling Up*

**Carmel Valley Ranch Resort,** 1 Old Ranch Rd. (off Robinson Canyon Road), Carmel 93923; (831) 625-9500; carmelvalleyranch.com. Serves breakfast, lunch, and dinner.
**Jeffrey's Grill and Catering,** 112 Mid-Valley Center, Carmel 93923; (831) 624-2029; jeffreysgrillandcaterng.com. Serves breakfast and lunch (closed on Monday)
**Edgar's at Quail Lodge,** Golf Clubhouse, 8205 Valley Greens Dr., Carmel 93923; (831) 620-8910; quaillodge.com. Hiking dogs get to socialize with resident golf course dogs on the patio.

*Resting Up*

**Carmel Valley Ranch Resort,** 1 Old Ranch Rd., Carmel 93923; (831) 625-9500; carmel valleyranch.com. Roxy the congenial bulldog concierge doesn't hike, but she loves the smell of adventure on the ranch's hiker guests.
**Quail Lodge Resort,** 8205 Valley Greens Dr., Carmel 93923; (888) 828-8787; quail lodge.com. The resort is newly renovated and reopened.

## Puppy Paws and Golden Years

**Garland Ranch Regional Park** (831-659-4488; www.mprpd.org) in Carmel Valley on Carmel Valley Road is approximately 7.0 miles east of Carmel-by-the-Sea. Turn east on Carmel Valley Road at the intersection of CA 1 and Carmel Valley Road. Garland Ranch Regional Park parking area is on the south side of Carmel Valley Road. For pooches who like to cool their paws and their bellies, the Carmel River runs through this park. The park has several wonderful hiking trails, but the Lupine and Cooper Ranch meadow loops are perfect romps for the very young and the very old. Late fall, winter, spring, and early summer are best to avoid foxtail time. Maps are available at the visitor center.

# 51 Sierra Hill in Brazil Ranch

Brazil Ranch's 1,255 acres at the north end of the Big Sur Coast are a fairly new addition to Los Padres National Forest network of trails. Given that the majority of the easily accessible trails along this coast are on state park land, where dogs are either unwelcome or restricted to a leash on some of the beaches, Brazil Ranch is a boon for dog owners with pooches responsive to voice commands. This 3.8-mile out-and-back hike combines asphalt and dirt ranch roads. The exposed slopes will deliver spectacular coastal views worth the steep incline before the terrain rolls over a series of knolls to the crest with a Ventana Wilderness backdrop.

**Start:** From the walk-in gate entrance to Brazil Ranch on the east side of CA 1, 0.5 mile south of Bixby Bridge

**Distance:** 3.8 miles out and back

**Approximate hiking time:** 2.5 hours

**Difficulty:** Strenuous, due to steep uphill stretches

**Trailhead elevation:** 429 feet

**Highest point:** 1,527 feet

**Best season:** Year-round; spring brings wild-flowers, summer can be hot

**Trail surface:** Asphalt road, grassy trail, and dirt ranch roads; some steep stretches

**Other trail users:** Horses

**Canine compatibility:** Voice control, but leashes recommended when cattle are grazing

**Land status:** National Forest

**Fees and permits:** None

**Maps:** USGS Point Sur; Los Padres National Forest Monterey and Santa Lucia Ranger District

**Trail contact:** Los Padres National Forest, Monterey Ranger District, 406 South Mildred, King City 93930; (831) 385-5434. Jeff Quansy, Resource Manager; (831) 667-1126. Big Sur Station, (831) 667-2315.

**Nearest town:** Carmel

**Trail tips:** Be prepared for exposed terrain, as there are no trees for shade. Temperatures can vary between windy and cool on the ridge on a foggy day or hot on sunny days. Bring extra water for Pooch.

**Finding the trailhead:** From Carmel at the intersection of CA 1 and Ocean Avenue, drive 14.0 miles south on CA 1 to the Bixby Bridge. Drive another 0.5 mile and park on the right shoulder (ocean side) of the road. The green metal gate with walk-in access on the left and a national forest sign are the only trailhead indicators. The coastal drive to the trailhead is a visual treat of its own. **GPS:** N36 21.80' / W121 53.99'

## The Hike

The El Sur Grande (The Big South), south of Monterey Peninsula, has always been a rugged and spectacular swath of wilderness described as "the Greatest Meeting of Land and Sea." Ohlone, Esselen, and Salinan Native American tribes were the first to make this coastline a seasonal home. In 1769 a Spanish expedition led by Gaspar de Portola set foot on the inhospitably steep shores before finally landing in Monterey in 1770. Monterey became the capital of Alta California, and the Spanish considered the

*View north along Big Sur Coast*

big country of the south "impenetrable." Mexico's independence from Spain in 1821
turned California into Mexican territory until the Mexican–American War of 1848.
The Homestead Act of 1862 lured hardy souls to settle in "Big Sur."

Many of the local sites retain the names of the early pioneers who persisted in
building a life and making a living on the rugged coast long before the two-lane
highway was opened in 1937 and would become the first State Scenic Highway in
1965. Gold mining, lumbering, dairy farming, and ranching all have had their day on
the Big Sur Coast. Artists, writers, movie stars, naturalists, and spiritualists have always
been inspired by Big Sur's wild solitary beauty, and many have made it home part of
the time, alongside the descendants of early pioneer families. The coast has remained
mostly unchanged, drawing tourists who enjoy the scenic drive and hikers who travel
the trails of the Los Padres National Forest and Ventana Wilderness, where streams,
hot springs, waterfalls, and redwood sanctuaries rule.

The Brazil Ranch was named after its original owners, the Brazil family. Over
the years the property operated as a farm, dairy, and ranch. In 1977 the ranch was
sold to Allen Funt, creator of the *Candid Camera* television show. Following his death,
the estate sold the land to a developer in 2000. In 2002 the Trust for Public Lands

acquired the 1,255 acres at the northern end of the Big Sur Coast, saving it from development and permanently protecting that stretch of California coastline. The land was transferred to the Los Padres National Forest, and a hiking trail was opened to the public. Currently a caretaker who was awarded a "stewardship contract" occupies the ranch buildings and is responsible for the care of the land in exchange for permission to graze cattle.

The trail leaves the winding panoramic paved road for the steeper double-track grassy path on your right marked by a wooden post with a double arrow sign that says TRAIL, indicating a trail to the right going up and a trail to the left across the paved road. Turn right on the grassy trail going up. The trail is hemmed in on both sides by chamise, with some poison oak weaved in with California blackberry on the steepest stretch. If you are prepared to bathe your dog to wash away any poison oak residue he may come into contact with, this is a great stretch of trail to have him off leash where he can safely get his edge off. If poison oak is a serious concern, keep him on leash.

There is no fresh water on this trail, and it can get hot in the summer. Make sure you bring plenty of water for hydration breaks for you and Pooch. The coastal views keep expanding northward, eventually taking in more of the mountain ranges to the east. The incline becomes more rolling. In the spring enjoy the crimson Indian paintbrush, white blooming wild onions, and bold California poppies. The saddle widens at about mile 1.0 after a cattle gate with a chained pedestrian access. From here upward the views just keep getting grander, reaching west to Hurricane Point, south to Point Sur Lighthouse, and east to the north face of Pico Blanco.

There will be a couple of intersections, mostly worn cattle trails. Bear right and stay on the main trail, which has only one other trail marker post. The trail and arrow sign at mile 1.6 at the foot of the last uphill stretch is sometimes on the ground rather than nailed to the post. The top of the crest referred to as "Sierra Hill" on some maps and "Cerro Hill" on other maps is the highest point for this hike and your turnaround destination.

According to Jeff Quansy, resource officer for the Monterey District of the Los Padres National Forest, the original name for the hill is *Cerro*, which is the Spanish translation for "hill" and probably has roots with the Cerra Creek that flows into the Little Sur River at the northern edge of the property under the Bixby Bridge. On a windless day this knoll makes a spectacular spot to have a picnic and take memorable photos of your pooch, as long as the cattle are grazing farther down the slope toward the fence line.

## Miles and Directions

**0.0**  Start at the trailhead at the walk-in gate. Be sure to relatch the gate. The first 0.5 mile of the trail is a paved service road. Elevation 429 feet.

**0.5**  Reach a trail sign on the right. Turn right and head south up the grassy trail. The first 50 yards are steep.

**0.7**  Continue past the fence posts on either side of the trail to the fork. Bear left and continue uphill on the trail.

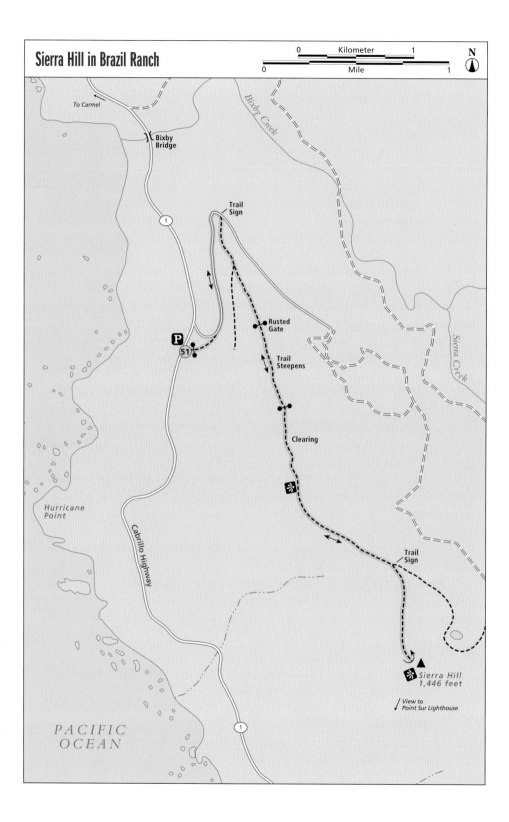

# Sierra Hill in Brazil Ranch

Kilometer
0                                                    1
Mile
0                                                    1

N

To Carmel

Bixby Bridge

Bixby Creek

1

Trail Sign

P

51

Rusted Gate

Trail Steepens

Clearing

Sierra Creek

Trail Sign

Hurricane Point

Cabrillo Highway

Sierra Hill
1,446 feet

View to
Point Sur Lighthouse

PACIFIC
OCEAN

1

**0.8** Continue past a rusted gate on right. The trail steepens over the next 0.2 mile.

**1.0** Arrive at a gate with walk-in access on the right. Be sure to relatch gate. This is a good spot for a water break for you and Pooch. The trail is gentler ahead.

**1.1** Come to a clearing on the left. Continue up the trail that becomes rougher from erosion.

**1.3** The trail emerges on the first of several grassy knolls with stunning coastal and mountain views.

**1.6** Trail forks with a signpost between the forks. Take the trail on the right uphill heading south.

**1.9** Arrive at Sierra Hill, elevation 1,527 feet. (**GPS:** N36 21.10' / W121 53.31') Revel in the 360-degree views. Pico Blanco, elevation 3,709 feet, is to the southeast. The Point Sur Lighthouse is to the southwest. The Ventana Wilderness is to the east. Retrace your steps to the trailhead.

**3.8** Arrive back at the trailhead.

## Creature Comforts

Carmel is a bonanza for hikers and their four-legged companions.

*Point Sur in the distance*

*Fueling Up*

**R. G. Burgers,** 201 Crossroads Blvd., Carmel 93923; (831) 626-8054; rgburgers.com.

**Sea Harvest Fish Market and Restaurant,** 100A Crossroads Blvd., Carmel 93923; (831) 626-3636. Enjoy fresh sustainable seafood on the dog-friendly patio.

**Terry's Restaurant,** in the Cypress Inn on Lincoln St. and Seventh Ave., Carmel-by-the-Sea 93921; (831) 624-3871; carmelterrys.com. Top dog hangout for dining in the lobby bar, living room, or patio.

**Treehouse Café,** San Carlos Ave. at Seventh St., Carmel-by-the-Sea 93921; (831) 626-1111; treehousecafecarmel.com. The Mediterranean dishes taste even better sitting on the rooftop deck caressed by trees.

**Forge in the Forest,** corner of Junipero St. and Fifth Ave., Carmel 93921; (831) 624-2233; forgeintheforest.com. Brick, Ivy and an intimate V.I.P. (Very Important Pooch) courtyard.

**LaFayette Bakery and Café,** 3672 Barnyard, Carmel 93923; (831) 915-6286; lafayette bakery.com. Your dog doesn't have to be a French poodle called Fifi to be welcome in the cafe's courtyard. Even the most kibble-happy hiking dog will be begging for a flake of your *croissant au jambon et fromage.*

*Resting Up*

**Cypress Inn,** Lincoln St. and Seventh Ave., Carmel-by-the-Sea 93921; (831) 624-3871; cypress-inn.com. Doris Day has made certain that all the canine guests are treated like V.I.P. (very important pooches).

**Tradewinds,** Carmel Hotel, Mission St. at Third Ave., Carmel-by-the-Sea 93921; (831) 624-2776; tradewindscarmel.com. Dogs find their Zen in this luxury boutique hotel with exotic Asian flair.

**Carmel River Inn,** 26600 Oliver Rd., Carmel 93923; (831) 624-1875; carmelriver inn.com.

**Carmel Mission Inn,** 3665 Rio Rd., Carmel 93923; (831) 624-1841; carmelmissioninn .com. This inn is next to the Barnyard Shopping Center and its line-up of dog-friendly dining.

**Big Sur Campground and Cabins,** 47000 CA 1, Big Sur 93920; (831) 667-2322; big surcamp.com.

**Pfeiffer Big Sur State Par,** 26.0 miles south of Carmel-by-the-Sea on CA 1; (800) 444-7275; reserveamerica.com; www.parks.ca.gov.

**Veterans Memorial Park Campground** at Skyline and Veterans Drive, Monterey 93940; (831) 646-3865. Campground offers tent and RV sites (no hookups) in a forested setting on a plateau at the edge of quiet residential neighborhoods within walking distance to historic downtown Monterey and iconic Fisherman's Wharf. Kick up your cardio and let Pooch enjoy a scamper up to Huckleberry Hill Nature Preserve at the far end of the campground. Contact Monterey Recreation Department, 546 Dutras Street, Monterey 93940; (831) 646-3866; monterey.org.

# Appendix A: Day Hike and Campout Checklist

## Day Hike Checklist

- ❑ Collar, harness, bandanna, leash, permanent ID tag with home/cell number, and temporary tag
- ❑ Health and vaccination certificate
- ❑ Collapsible water bowl and water supply in metal or plastic bottle (thirty-two-ounce bottle for half-day hikes (under four hours) and two-quart bottle for longer hikes). Eight ounces of water per dog per hour or 3.0 miles of hiking, in addition to water for you.
- ❑ Water purifier for full-day hike
- ❑ Kibbles for your dog and snacks for you at mealtimes on the trail and extra protein snacks for energy boost for both. Save the yummiest treats for "recalls."
- ❑ Plastic resealable bags for carrying food, treats, medication, and first-aid essentials. The bags can be converted into food and water bowls as well as poop-scoop bags to carry waste out if necessary.
- ❑ Biodegradable poop-scoop bags
- ❑ Booties for pup; sturdy waterproof hiking footwear for you
- ❑ Dog packs (optional)
- ❑ Reflective vest for both you and your pup (if hiking during hunting season)
- ❑ Life vest for both you and your pup (if planning to be on water)
- ❑ Flyers for a lost dog
- ❑ Flea and tick application prior to hike
- ❑ Bug repellent in sealed plastic bag
- ❑ Sunscreen for you and your dog (tips of dog's ears)
- ❑ Sunhat and glasses for you
- ❑ Wire grooming brush to help remove stickers and foxtails from your dog's coat
- ❑ Extra clothing: sweater or coat for a thin-coated dog; breathable long-sleeved sweater and rain-repelling windbreaker for you
- ❑ Extra large, heavy-duty plastic garbage bags (good to sit on or to make a handy poncho in case of rain or to line the inside of your backpack)
- ❑ Pocketknife (Swiss Army–type knife that includes additional tools)
- ❑ Flashlight
- ❑ Matches or cigarette lighter and emergency fire starter
- ❑ Space blanket
- ❑ Whistle

*Bring your dog's favorite toy on the hike.*

❑ USGS maps, compass, GPS
❑ Extra batteries for electronic devices and flashlight
❑ Camera
❑ First-aid kit (phone numbers for National Animal Poison Control Center and your veterinarian)

# Backpacking Checklist

## Dog Necessities

All items on day hike checklist, plus the following:

- ❏ Extra leash or rope
- ❏ Dog pack (optional)
- ❏ Doggie bedroll (foam sleeping pad)
- ❏ Dog's favorite chew toy
- ❏ Dog food (number of days on the trail x three meals a day)
- ❏ Additional water in a two-quart bottle
- ❏ Dog snacks (enough for six rest stops per hiking day)
- ❏ Nylon tie-out line in camp (expandable leash can be extra leash and tie-out rope)

## Human Necessities

- ❏ Tent with rain fly (large enough for you and your dog to sleep inside)
- ❏ Clothing (moisture-wicking socks, wind/raingear, gloves, fleece or knit hat, long pants, wicking top, fleece top)
- ❏ Camp stove and fuel bottle
- ❏ Iodine tablets (backup water purifier)
- ❏ Food: lightweight, nutritious carbs and proteins—instant oatmeal, energy bars, granola cereal, almond or peanut butter, dried fruits and nuts, dark chocolate for energy boosts, pasta, rice, canned tuna, dehydrated backpacking meals, tea bags or cocoa packets.
- ❏ Extra garbage bags (use one in your backpack as a liner to keep contents dry in case of rain)
- ❏ Bear-proof food canisters
- ❏ Pepper spray (if hiking in bear country)

★★★Always let someone at home know where you are going and when you plan to return.

*Sore paws means hitching a ride from Lock Leven Lakes*

# Appendix B: Trail Emergencies and First Aid

## Using a Leash

Planning, a common-sense approach, and a leash will help prevent most mishaps on the trail. Keep your dog on leash when:

- Hiking in territory known for its higher concentration of specific hazards (bears, mountain lions, snakes, skunks)
- Crossing fast-moving streams
- Negotiating narrow mountainside trails
- Hiking in wind and snow (dogs can become disoriented and lose their way)

## First Aid

If your dog gets into trouble, here are some basic first-aid treatments you can administer until you can get him to a vet.

### Bleeding from Cuts or Wounds

1. Remove any obvious foreign object.
2. Rinse the area with warm water or 3 percent hydrogen peroxide.
3. Cover the wound with clean gauze or cloth and apply firm, direct pressure over the wound for about ten minutes to allow clotting to occur and bleeding to stop.
4. Place a nonstick pad or gauze over the wound and bandage with gauze wraps (the stretchy, clingy type). For a paw wound, cover the bandaging with a bootie. (An old sock with duct tape on the bottom is a good bootie substitute. Use adhesive tape around the sock to prevent it from slipping off. Be careful not to strangle circulation.)

### Frostbite

Frostbite is the freezing of a body part exposed to extreme cold. Tips of ears and pads are the most vulnerable.

1. Remove your dog from the cold.
2. Apply a warm compress to the affected area without friction or pressure.

### Heatstroke

Heatstroke occurs when a dog's body temperature is rising rapidly above 104 degrees and panting is ineffective to regulate temperature.

1. Get your dog out of the sun and begin reducing body temperature (no lower than 103 degrees) by applying water-soaked towels on her head (to cool the brain), chest, abdomen, and feet.

2. Let your dog stand in a pond, lake, or stream while you gently pour water on her. Avoid icy water—it can chill her. Swabbing the footpads with alcohol will help.

## Hypothermia

Hypothermia occurs when a dog's body temperature drops below 95 degrees because of overexposure to cold weather.

1. Take the dog indoors or into a sheltered area where you can make a fire.

2. Wrap him in a blanket, towel, sleeping bag, your clothing, or whatever you have available.

3. Wrap him in warm towels or place warm water bottles in a towel next to him.

4. Hold him close to you for body heat.

## Insect Bites

Bee stings and spider bites may cause itching, swelling, and hives. If the stinger is still present, scrape it off with your nail or tweezers at the base away from the point of entry. (Pressing the stinger or trying to pick it from the top can release more toxin.) Apply a cold compress to the area and spray it with a topical analgesic like Benadryl spray to relieve the itch and pain. As a precaution, carry an over-the-counter antihistamine (such as Benadryl) and ask your vet about the appropriate dosage before you leave, in case your dog has an extreme allergic reaction with excessive swelling.

## Skunked

When your dog gets skunked, a potent, smelly cloud of spray burns his eyes and makes his mouth foam. The smell can make you gag, and contact with the spray on your dog's coat can give your skin a tingling, burning sensation. Apply de-skunking shampoo as soon as possible.

### De-Skunking Shampoo Mix

1 quart hydrogen peroxide
¼ cup baking soda
1 tablespoon dishwashing detergent

Put on rubber gloves and thoroughly wet your dog, apply mixture, and let stand for fifteen minutes; rinse and repeat as needed.

# FIRST-AID KIT CHECKLIST

☐ First-aid book, such as *Field Guide: Dog First Aid Emergency Care of the Outdoor Dog* by Randy Acker, DVM.

☐ Muzzle; most loving dogs can snap and bite when in pain. Muzzles come in different styles and sizes to fit all dog nose shapes.

☐ Ascriptin (buffered aspirin); older dogs in particular may be stiff and sore at the end of a hike or backpacking excursion. Consult your vet on the appropriate dosage.

☐ Antidiarrheal agents and gastrointestinal protectants; Pepto-Bismol—1 to 3ml/kg/day, Kaopectate—1 to 2 ml/kg every 2–6 hours

☐ Indigestion and stomach upset. Pepcid (famotidine) decreases gastric acid secretions. Try a dosage of 0.1 to 2 mg/kg every 12 to 24 hours.

☐ Scissors (with rounded tips) for trimming hair around a wound

☐ Hydrogen peroxide (3%) to disinfect surface abrasions and wounds

☐ Antiseptic ointment

☐ Gauze pads and gauze

☐ Clingy and elastic bandages

☐ Sock or bootie to protect a wounded foot

☐ Duct tape to wrap around the sole of a sock used as a bootie

☐ Tweezers to remove ticks, needles, or foreign objects in a wound

☐ Styptic powder for bleeding

☐ Rectal thermometer

☐ Hydrocortisone spray to relieve plant rashes and stings

☐ Lemon juice for quick rinse (recipe for de-skunking shampoo mix)

☐ Your veterinarian's telephone number and the ASPCA National Animal Poison Control Center, (888) 426- 4435, taped inside the kit

### Sore Muscles

1. Rest your dog.
2. Apply cold-water compresses to tight muscle areas to reduce inflammation.
3. Administer Ascriptin (buffered aspirin). Check with your vet on dosage for your dog's breed and weight.

### Venomous Bites

1. Keep your dog calm (activity stimulates the absorption of venom).
2. Rinse the area with water and transport your dog to the nearest vet.

### Cardiopulmonary Resuscitation

Check with your veterinarian or local humane society for pet CPR classes.

# Appendix C: Wildlife Conflicts

On the trail you and your dog are in someone else's home. Be the kind of guest you would want in your house. Be considerate of those who live there, disturb nothing as you pass through, and take only the memory of the experience and photographs of the beauty that moved you.

## Protecting Wildlife and Your Dog

The surest way to avoid wildlife conflicts is to keep your dog on a leash. Dogs chasing deer deplete the wild animal of its survival energy and can cause debilitating injury to both the pursued and the pursuer.

Curious dogs nosing around off leash risk incurring the pungent wrath of a skunk, the painful quills of a porcupine, or a bite from an ill-tempered rattlesnake. All are responding defensively to a perceived threat and are not lurking to attack you or your dog.

Birds nesting in meadows and low brush are vulnerable to roaming dogs in the spring and fawns can fall prey to your dog's primal instincts. These animals are not hosting you and your dog in their home by choice, so be respectful guests.

Some trails cross cattle- and sheep-grazing land. Keep in mind that a dog harassing stock can be shot.

Keep your dog on leash for the first thirty minutes of a hike to give her a chance to absorb some of the new sights, smells, and sounds that might make her go berserk with excitement fresh out of the starting gate and make her more likely to burn off excess energy chasing wildlife or trying to entice cattle in a game of tag.

*Even baby skunks can be a trail hazard*

## Preventing Encounters

With regard to predators, the potential for being attacked by a wild animal in Northern California is extremely low compared to many other natural hazards. Wildlife sightings are a privilege. Even if the young male wolf known as OR-7 that came south into Northern California from his Oregon pack in the fall of 2011 found the mate he came looking for to start his new life on the land his ancestors hunted almost one hundred years ago, he or any member of his pack would not be a threat to

*Seeing a bobcat adds a thrill to your hike.*

humans. I grew up in northern Quebec listening to their howls echo from a frozen river after a deer kill and watched a pack stealthily track a herd of deer across a trail on a misty autumn morning just yards in front of me. Wolves, bears, and mountain lions, when given the option, generally prefer avoidance over confrontation with humans unless you are a threat to them or their young.

Coyotes and bobcats are just as elusive and usually find rodents satisfying enough. But small dogs could be considered tender morsels and should be kept on leash especially at dawn and dusk, when predators are most likely to shop for food.

Development and human intrusion are at the core of encounter problems. Encroachment on habitat and more hikers in the backcountry have exposed bears and coyotes to human food and garbage. Animals accustomed to easy meals become brazen and can pose a threat to human safety. Sadly, humans create these "problem" animals. Destruction not relocation is their fate. There's a good reason for the "Don't feed wildlife" campaign.

It is not to say that a dog responsive to voice control should not enjoy tagging along and bounding with joy off leash, but be informed about the area where you plan to hike, and when in doubt make your presence known with a small bell attached to your pack, dog harness, or walking stick. Stay on the trail and talk or hum to avoid surprising a bear in the berry bushes or startling a big cat from his nap.

## Bear Safety

In bear country, when it comes to odor, the motto is "Less is safer." Pack all food items (human and dog) and any other odorous items in airtight resealable bags. Dispose of all items with food smells in airtight bags, in bear-proof storage containers. Clean your dishes and pet bowls as quickly as possible, so food smells do not float through the forest as a dinner invitation to the local bears. Some national forests and wilderness areas require that campers use plastic portable "bear-resistant food canisters." These canisters (some collapsible) are available for sale and rent at sporting goods stores and some ranger stations.

If you see a bear in the distance, stop, stay calm, and don't run. Keep your dog close to your side on leash. You should feel awe rather than panic. Walk a wide upwind detour so the animal can get your scent, and make loud banging or clanging noises as you leave the area. If the bear is at closer range, the same principles apply while you keep your eye on the bear and back down the trail slowly if the terrain doesn't allow you to negotiate a detour.

Avoid sudden movements that could spook or provoke the bear. Be cool, slow, but deliberate as you make your retreat.

## BEAR FACTS

- Bears can run, swim, and climb trees.
- Bears have good vision, excellent hearing, and a superior sense of smell.
- Bears are curious and attracted to food smells.
- Bears can be out at any time of day but are most active in the coolness of dawn and dusk and after dark.
- Bears and wild animals in general prefer anonymity. If they know you are out there, they will avoid your path.

## Mountain Lions

There are fewer mountain lions than bears in Northern California. Here are some tips.

- Keep your dog on leash on the trail.
- Keep your dog in the tent at night.
- Seeing doesn't mean attacking. If you come across a mountain lion, stay far enough away to give it the opportunity to avoid you. Do not approach or provoke the lion. Instead, walk away slowly and maintain eye contact. Running will stimulate the lion's predatory instinct to chase and hunt. Make yourself big by putting your arms above your head and waving them. Use your jacket or walking

## MOUNTAIN LION FACTS

Mountain lions are elusive, and preying on humans is uncharacteristic. Mountain lions are most active at dawn and dusk and usually hunt at night. They are solitary and secretive and require a vegetated habitat for camouflage while they stalk prey. Their meal of choice is big game (deer, bighorn sheep, and elk). In the absence of game, however, they can make a meal of domestic livestock and small mammals. They feed on what they kill. An unattended dog in camp is far more appetizing than his kibble.

stick above your head to appear bigger. Do not bend down or make any motion that will make you look or sound like easy prey. Shout and make noise. If necessary, walking sticks can be weapons, as can rocks or anything you can get your hands on to fight back with.

- For more information on hiking in mountain lion country, refer to *Mountain Lion Alert,* by Steven Torres (Falcon Publishing, 1997).

## Snakes

Most dogs have an instinctive aversion to anything that slithers and will jump away at first sight, sound, or touch. Snakebites are usually the result of stepping on a snake unknowingly rather than conscious provocation. Most snakebites occur on the nose or front legs and can be lethal to a small or young dog. If taken to the vet quickly, larger adult dogs will survive the majority of bites. Ask your veterinarian if the recently developed rattlesnake vaccine would benefit your dog. Ask your vet or local dog club about snake avoidance classes in your area. (See Appendix B for treatment of venomous bites.)

*Keep an eye out for snakes on the trail.*

# Appendix D: Sources for Pooch Gear, Useful Websites, and Books

## Websites

bringfido.com: to help locate dog-friendly lodging

natgeomaps.com: a source for trail maps

naturedogs.com: a source for dog-friendly hiking trails

petfoodexpress.com: to help you locate stores in Northern California to shop for quality food and treats, gear, accessories, and toys. Some locations also have vaccination clinics and affordable wellness centers.

rei.com: outdoor recreation gear cooperative with stores throughout California. You can shop for Fido's hiking gear, accessories, and dog-friendly hiking guide books.

recreation.gov: public land campground reservations

reserveamerica.com: online camping reservations

ruffwear.com: online source for outdoor gear and accessories for dogs.

store.usgs.gov: purchase of USGS maps

wilderness.net: online source for purchasing topographic maps and links to wilderness information.

wolfpacks.com: custom dog packs

## Helpful Reads

*Backpacker Trailside Navigation: Map & Compass* by *Backpacker* magazine, Guilford, CT: Globe Pequot Press, 2010.

*The Dog Lover's Companion to California* by Maria Goodavage, Berkeley, CA: Avalon Travel Publishing; 2011.

*Field Guide: Dog First Aid Emergency Care of the Outdoor Dog* by Randy Acker, DVM; Belgrade, MT: Wilderness Adventures Press; 2009. (Note: pocket size for your first-aid kit.)

*The Focused Puppy* by Deborah Jones and Judy Keller, South Hadley, MA: Clean Run Productions; 2010.

*Not Fit for a Dog* by Dr. Michael W. Fox, Fresno, CA: Quill Driver Books; 2009. (Note: dog nutrition.)

*Traveling with Your Pet: The AAA PetBook,* Heathrow, FL: AAA publishing; 2012. (Note: Membership in the American Automobile Association [AAA] gives you free access to US and Canada tour books and public land campground maps. The Northern California book includes a list and map of national, state, and other recreational areas, including a chart indicating which have hiking trails that allow pets on leash. Contact 800-JOIN-AAA; aaa.com/petbook.)

*Using a GPS* by *Backpacker* magazine, Guilford, CT: Globe Pequot Press, 2011.

*The Wolf Within* by David Alderton, Hoboken, NJ: Howell Book House, 1998.

# Hike Index

*Returning to the Bolinas Ridge Trail trailhead.*

# About the Authors

David S. Mullally, a native Californian, and Quebec-born Linda Mullally have been a husband-and-wife team adventuring around the globe and co-creating with her writing and his photography for thirty years. He an attorney/photographer and she a travel columnist/author and "Doggie-Nannie" share their passion for travel, hiking, and dogs through articles, books, and multi-media presentations. Her *Monterey Herald* travel column "Away We Go" inspires readers to go explore the world's bounty of natural and cultural treasures on bike and on foot. David and Linda share life at their California basecamps in Carmel on the Central Coast and Mammoth Lakes in the Eastern Sierra with the newest  member of their pack, Gypsy, a perky trail-happy 11-year-old Queensland/Chihuahua mix. *Best Dog Hikes Northern California* is their fifth book, and they have several other titles in progress.

*Returning to the Lake Aloha trailhead with Echo Lakes in the distance.*

Your next adventure begins here.

# falcon.com

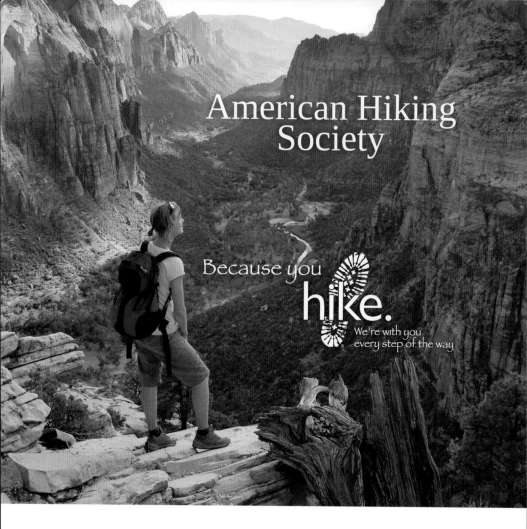

# American Hiking Society

**Because you hike.**
We're with you every step of the way

$A$s a national voice for hikers, **American Hiking Society** works every day:

- Building and maintaining hiking trails
- Educating and supporting hikers by providing information and resources
- Supporting hiking and trail organizations nationwide
- Speaking for hikers in the halls of Congress and with federal land managers

Whether you're a casual hiker or a seasoned backpacker, become a member of American Hiking Society and join the national hiking community! You'll enjoy great member benefits and help preserve the nation's hiking trails, so tomorrow's hike is even better than today's. We invite you to join us now!

American Hiking Society